Emotional Literacy in Criminal Justice

Emotional Literacy in Criminal Justice

Professional Practice with Offenders

Charlotte Knight
School of Applied Social Science, De Montfort University, UK

palgrave
macmillan

First published 2014 by
PALGRAVE MACMILLAN

Palgrave Macmillan in the UK is an imprint of Macmillan Publishers Limited, registered in England, company number 785998, of Houndmills, Basingstoke, Hampshire RG21 6XS.

Palgrave Macmillan in the US is a division of St Martin's Press LLC, 175 Fifth Avenue, New York, NY 10010.

Palgrave Macmillan is the global academic imprint of the above companies and has companies and representatives throughout the world.

Palgrave® and Macmillan® are registered trademarks in the United States, the United Kingdom, Europe and other countries.

ISBN 978–1–137–27320–8   hardback
ISBN 978–1–137–27319–2   paperback

This book is printed on paper suitable for recycling and made from fully managed and sustained forest sources. Logging, pulping and manufacturing processes are expected to conform to the environmental regulations of the country of origin.

A catalogue record for this book is available from the British Library.

A catalog record for this book is available from the Library of Congress.

Typeset by MPS Ltd, Chennai, India.

Contents

Acknowledgements

I would like to thank all the probation staff who, as research participants and seminar contributors, gave freely of their time, ideas and reflections. I would like to thank colleagues at De Montfort University for their support and their insights during the completion of my PhD and the subsequent writing of this book, in particular Brown, Dave Ward, Jean Hine, Rob Canton, Julie Fish, Jane Dominey and Sarah Hilder. Thanks to Derek Layder for the use of his models of social domains and of interpersonal emotional control, and his help in thinking through their application to the ideas in this book and to Denise Beardshaw for the opportunity to view emotional intelligence in action in her school. Particular thanks to my sister Val for her enduring love and support and to Fiona Purdie for her wisdom and kindness. Most of all my thanks to Sue for starting me on this road and being my main source of inspiration.

1
Introduction: The Challenge of Uncovering and Using Emotions in Criminal Justice

Introduction

We tend to see negative emotions and 'punitiveness' as understandable and appropriate responses to criminality. People who have transgressed the criminal law and caused harm to others are believed to be deserving of punishment for their offending regardless of whether this punishment makes any difference to their likelihood of reoffending in the future. Punishment conveys society's disapproval and condemnation of such behaviour. Both media and political discourse about criminal behaviour use punitive rhetoric and arguments for increasing levels of external control on offenders. However, the task of criminal justice practitioners is to manage, control and help offenders with fairness and decency; a challenging expectation in this culture of punitiveness. This book outlines the case for developing the skills of emotional literacy and the use of positive emotions in the criminal justice workforce. In interventions with offenders, such a skill can help offenders begin to take responsibility for their behaviour, to develop internal controls and seek to change those aspects of their behaviour that are the most damaging to society and to themselves. In all situations it can enable criminal justice practitioners to understand and regulate their own emotions and to make better informed judgements and decisions about their practice.

As adults, most of us manage our lives through our ability to think and respond rationally and logically to the social world in which we live. We are also emotional creatures who make many of the most important decisions in our lives, for example, concerning our long-term relationships, our work and our living arrangements, on the basis of 'feelings'. We are encouraged to understand the world in which we live through an accumulation of knowledge and the application of cognitive skills. However, we are also likely to deal better with our circumstances if we can think intelligently and reflectively about our feelings and their impact on, and interrelationship with, our cognitive skills (Howe 2008).

The criminal justice system is constituted to respond to, control and punish criminal behaviour in an objective, rational and just manner. As far as possible the system aims to exclude emotion on the basis that emotions are likely to interfere with and distort the process of justice (Karstedt et al. 2011). In a parallel process, criminology as the science and academic discipline that studies crime and criminal justice has been committed to the same ideals of reason and reasonable discourse in relation to modern penal law and the practice of criminal justice in its institutions (Karstedt et al. 2011). Karstedt argues that historically criminal justice and criminology have been suspicious of emotions and that criminology's approach to emotions has been cautious and circumspect (Karstedt et al. 2011). However, criminal justice is an emotional arena, a place where powerful emotions are experienced by, and impact on, offenders, victims and practitioners (Karstedt et al. 2011). Practitioners working in this system will encounter people who are often in highly emotional states associated with, or as a result of, their offending behaviour, and further aroused by being processed through a system that is designed to punish and control them, for this behaviour. Workers in the system have to manage and respond to these emotions, and the emotions engendered in themselves, on a daily basis. The dichotomy between the presentation of criminal justice as an emotion-free zone and the reality for practitioners, offenders, victims and witnesses within the system forms an important context for this book.

The book concerns itself with the 'feelings' and emotional skills of practitioners working within the criminal justice system. It is argued that in working with a transformative process, the managing of change in an offender population, practitioners need to be 'emotionally available' to the people they work with. Punishment can be a blunt instrument in enforcing change, often engendering resentment, shame, fear and powerlessness in its recipients. Whilst punishing and restricting the liberty of people who have committed very serious crimes is seen as an essential feature of criminal justice, as a blanket policy it does little to reach those offenders, the majority, who are capable of change and development. Emotional literacy, by contrast, is a communicative tool through which practitioners engage, understand and motivate the offenders they work with. Whilst punishing people for their criminal behaviour may make us, as a society, feel 'avenged' it has a limited role in affecting real or positive change in the offenders themselves. The skilfulness and emotional availability of practitioners can enable an offender to begin to undertake the hard work of recognising, and accepting responsibility for, the harm they have caused, and effecting change in their lives in order to reduce the risk of reoffending. Practitioners whose role may be more about managing and processing offenders through the system (e.g. police and prison officers) will be equally challenged by the emotional content of their work, and will benefit from having a greater understanding and 'literacy' in the manner in which they deploy their feelings in their work.

In any criminal justice practice, an understanding of the values and beliefs that underpin the work and how they impact on practice should be of central concern (Rutherford 1993). The participants in the research for this book identified the *active* use of their emotional skills, their ability to engage emotionally and their ability to be 'non-judgmental' towards offenders as crucial to the process of building relationships and enabling positive change in their lives (Knight 2012). Using the experiences of these probation practitioners who worked with humanitarian values, the book aims to offer some insights into the application of emotional literacy for all criminal justice workers.

Practice context

Whilst the modernisation of criminal justice during the 20th century may have placed 'reason' and 'rationality' at its core, and largely excluded 'emotion', there is a paradox in operation. Karstedt argues that after many decades of apparent 'objectivity', 'emotionality' has returned to the criminal justice arena (Karstedt et al. 2011). There has been a 're-emotionalisation of law' (De Haan and Loader 2002) with the return of 'shame' into criminal justice procedures, in particular through ideas of restorative justice (Braithwaite 1989) and with a stronger focus on victims and their emotional needs. The public are actively encouraged, through the media in particular, to express strong feelings in relation to crime and to expect that legislation will reflect these concerns (e.g. 'Sarah's Law' on the child sex offender disclosure scheme (Lipscombe 2012)).

The introduction of victim personal statements in which victims of particular crimes[1] are enabled to present to the court the impact that the crime has had on them and their families has also encouraged the view that sentencing can be influenced by powerful feelings generated by the harm caused by crime (Gelsthorpe 2009). This emotionality, identified in terms of 'the public demands this or that' (Gelsthorpe 2009: 191) is used to justify increasingly harsh punishments and the greater use of imprisonment. Sometimes courts are influenced directly by the emotions of the event; for example, the sentencing of people caught up in the riots of 2011 was seen to be responding very 'toughly' to an unusual set of circumstances and was commended by politicians at the time. The average prison sentence imposed for people convicted during the riots was 25% longer than normal, indicative of a more punitive response (Bottoms 1995, Travis and Simon 2011). Karstedt identifies this as the emergence of a highly emotional discourse on crime and justice (Karstedt et al. 2011), what Bottoms refers to as 'popular punitiveness' (Bottoms 1995). Increasingly, crime policies appear to be based on the expression of the collective emotions of anger and fear about crime, and politicians are seen to compete with each other to 'address the emotional needs of the public' (Karstedt 2002). The depth and impact of powerful emotions generated by the often traumatic terrain of crime and offending behaviour on practitioners working in the system, coupled with the 'emotionality' of the media and political discourse on crime and sentencing, confronts the workers in the system with particular dilemmas and tensions.

The concept of 'control' is a significant feature of the work of criminal justice and emotions are often closely linked to issues of control. Criminal justice practitioners are expected to control and limit the worst excesses of criminal conduct. To aid an understanding of how this control is exercised within different criminal justice settings, reference is made to Layder's theory of interpersonal emotional control (Layder 2004). Layder identifies a spectrum ranging from 'benign' control, exercised with a largely therapeutic and humanitarian aim, through to a more 'malign' or 'manipulative' form of emotional control, with a repressive aim all of which can be evidenced in criminal justice practice. The book presents an argument that the instrumental and administrative processes of criminal justice are the visible workings of the system, but of equal importance are these emotional processes, or 'underground emotion work' (Layder 2004) undertaken by practitioners which remains largely suppressed, invisible and unacknowledged.

Although there have been studies of the emotional *impact* of the work in terms of stress and burnout in relation to criminal justice practice (Tewksbury and Higgins 2006, Collins, Coffey et al. 2009, Griffin et al. 2009, Adams and Buck 2010, Schaible and Gecas 2010) there has been little written about how criminal justice practitioners actually manage and use their emotions in their work. Crawley has explored the emotional lives of prison officers (Crawley 2004, Crawley 2009). She identified that in the prison environment prison officers strive, with more or less success, to achieve a degree of emotional neutrality and detachment in their work. Van Stokkhom has reflected on the need for a better understanding of emotion management and emotional intelligence in policing, in the face of challenging and often negative emotional situations (Van Stokkom 2011). Other writers have examined soft power in prisons (Crewe 2011) and in relation to offenders (Puglia, Stough et al. 2005). There is literature that relates it to mental health (Akerjordet and Severinsson 2004), health care (Clarke 2006), and in a range of other settings (Salovey and Sluyter 1997, Bar-On and Parker 2000). The closest association for this book is the use of emotional intelligence in the field of social work, which is still in its infancy (Morrison 2007, Howe 2008), although there is a substantial body of literature on the importance of relationships within the social work context, for example, Thompson (2009) and Hennessey (2011).

Emotional intelligence

The more commonly used term in most writings on the subject is that of 'emotional intelligence'. Research and literature on emotional intelligence has, to date, been largely centred on the world of business, management and leadership (e.g. Goleman 1995, Bachmann, Stein et al. 2000). Until relatively recently a fairly narrow view of intelligence was promulgated – that it consisted of a narrow range of cognitive capacities (Barrett and Gross 2001). The idea that there might be more than one form of intelligence was first proposed by Howard Gardner in 1983 who has published since then on the theory of 'multiple intelligences' (Gardener 1984, Gardener 1993). Gardner argued that intelligence is not limited to the traditional view of IQ (intelligence quotient), but is in fact a collection of between seven and nine different intelligences. These include linguistic, logical–mathematical, musical, spatial, bodily/kinaesthetic, interpersonal and intrapersonal (Gardener 1984). The last two on this list are the most closely associated with the concept of emotional intelligence.

The first use of the term 'emotional intelligence' in psychology was by Payne who believed that emotional intelligence was stifled by a tendency to suppress emotions, leading to a range of mental health difficulties (Payne 1985 cited in Howe 2008: 11). Salovey and Mayer went on to define and develop this concept (Salovey and Mayer 1990):

> The capacity to reason about emotions, and of emotions to enhance thinking. It includes the abilities to accurately perceive emotions, to access and generate emotions to assist thought, to understand emotions and emotional knowledge, and to reflectively regulate emotions so as to promote emotional and intellectual growth. (Mayer and Salovey 1997: 197).

It spread fairly quickly to the media and popular science (Howe 2008). People with good emotional intelligence were seen to do well at school and at work, and in particular were good at social relationships. Goleman popularised the concept and extended it to business and leadership (Goleman 1995, Goleman 1996, Goleman 1998, Goleman et al. 2002). Goleman builds his ideas from a range of sources and identifies what he calls the 'great divide' in human abilities that lies between the mind and heart, or what he calls more technically between cognition and emotion (Cherniss and Goleman 2001). He argues that some abilities, such as IQ and technical expertise, are purely cognitive, and that other abilities integrate thought and feeling and fall within the domain of 'emotional intelligence'. However, other writers challenge the view that any abilities might be purely cognitive, and argue that all good decision-making is in fact 'embodied' or made with a combination of feelings, thoughts and reflections (LeDoux 2003, Lakoff 1987).

It is suggested that emotional intelligence is not just about managing or suppressing emotions but refers to the capacity to think and reflect on feelings rather than act impulsively, what Chamberlayne describes as 'experiential truth' or 'emotional thinking' (Chamberlayne 2004), and which is also referred to as 'emotion appraisal' (Gendron 2010). Attempts have been made to measure emotional intelligence and two tests have been developed; Situational Test of Emotion Management (STEM) and the Situational Test of Emotional Understanding (STEU) (Austin 2010). However, current definitions of emotional intelligence are inconsistent about what it measures; some indicate that it is dynamic and can be learned or increased (an intelligence that is malleable); and others that it is stable and cannot be increased (Mayer and Salovey 1997). One of the most recent training manuals on emotional intelligence uses the Emotional Quotient Inventories (EQ-1 and EQ3-60), which were developed from Bar-On's original EQ-1 model and recently updated. The significant difference in this most recent model is that it incorporates stress management as a component of emotional intelligence and includes flexibility, stress tolerance and optimism (Hughes and Bradford Terrell 2012).

However, as Fineman cautions, the movement to identify a measurement of emotional intelligence risks imposing a set of measurements and numbers on a quality that to some extent defies these parameters (Fineman 2004). Locke goes further and argues that emotional intelligence is an invalid concept both because it is not a form of intelligence and because it is defined so broadly and inclusively that it has no intelligible meaning (Locke 2005). He concludes that the only useful way to proceed is to focus on the skill of introspection, which he identifies as involving the identification of the contents and processes of one's own mind. Through introspection Locke argues it is possible to monitor such things as 'one's degree of focus, one's defensive reactions and one's emotional responses and their causes' (Locke 2005: 429), and that such monitoring has important implications for self-esteem and mental health.

Whilst some of the scepticism about emotional intelligence and its potential for measurement may be well founded, nevertheless, it will be argued that the concept of 'emotional literacy', as a skill, rather than emotional intelligence per se, offers a model for understanding how practitioners work with their own and other's emotions.

Emotional literacy

Emotional literacy as a concept in criminal justice defines the skills that criminal justice practitioners may use in understanding their own emotions and working effectively and appropriately with the emotions of offenders, victims and witnesses (Knight 2012). At its least complex, possessing a degree of emotional 'intelligence' provides a communicative tool that can enable a workforce to respond to its customer base with courtesy and respect, and to handle, albeit maybe only superficially, conflict situations that can arise. It can enable all workers to recognise that they will, on occasions, have strong feelings (reactions) to the situations confronting them. They may not always understand the cause of these feelings, but they can find ways of controlling and managing these feelings such that they do not compound any punishment already legitimately imposed on offenders, or 'corrupt' or 'interfere with' the due process of their work. At its best and most complex, emotional 'literacy' is about the worker being emotionally available to the service user. It can enable a worker to dig below the surface of the many defences, anxieties, fears and rages that can obscure a full understanding of why people commit crime, its impact on their lives and what might enable them to make changes in their lives. It can help people to tell their 'stories', often very painful stories, arising from traumatic events, or early childhood abuse or neglect, and perhaps never previously articulated. It can enable the worker to have the empathy, strength and resilience to 'hear' these stories, to be able to contain their own emotional distress in response to these stories and to help the storyteller to begin to make sense of their realities. It is argued that both the superficial and the more complex uses of emotional literacy are beneficial in the volatile and emotionally charged arena of criminal justice, although it is the latter that is the central theme of this book.

The knowledge base for emotional literacy builds on the concept of emotional intelligence. It has been defined as being about self-awareness:

> The capacity to register our emotional responses to the situations we are in and to acknowledge those responses to ourselves so that we recognize the ways in which they influence our thoughts and actions. (Orbach 2001: 2)

Orbach's work is less about profit and success within business and commerce (the focus of many writings on emotional intelligence) and more about people and their interrelationships. Orbach gives examples of what she means by emotional literacy and, in relation to the political realm, she recognises the emotional implications of political decision-making for people's lives. She argues that the engagement of their emotions and the use of emotional literacy by politicians could lead to deeper and better decision-making. She also understands that emotions can be used cynically by politicians to manipulate people (voters) and that the energy can go into the presentation of an issue rather than the formulation of the right policy (Orbach 2001). This has particular resonance in a criminal justice context where there is potential for emotions to be used to influence sentencing, and as a coercive or manipulative force for engaging compliance and/or change in offenders.

Spendlove identifies emotional literacy as an educational term, and a number of authors (Sharp 2001, Killick 2006, Park and Tew 2007, Spendlove 2008) have written manuals in which they set out a range of exercises and tests for teachers to use in developing an emotionally literate environment within their school. Killick also writing from an educational perspective, suggests that emotionally literate children will have greater resilience to emotional problems, thus implying that emotional literacy is something that children can exercise in the process of living, much like emotional intelligence (Killick 2006). Sharp suggests that emotional literacy is the process by which emotional intelligence is acquired. Other writers, however, use the term to refer to the application rather than the acquisition of emotional intelligence (Steiner 1997, Dayton 2000, Spendlove 2008). It seems that these terms are sometimes used interchangeably. The application of emotional intelligence in a 'literate' manner in work with people is the one that has been used in this book, as it seems to represent self-awareness, availability and sensitivity to others. It captures the phenomenon of 'emotion work' or the 'soft skills' that many practitioners use in pursuit of the 'hard work' of managing and enabling change in offenders.

Components of emotional literacy

Two writers on emotional literacy in schools, Sharp and Killick, have drawn together a range of perspectives in order to define the focus for teachers. Four of these perspectives – Salovey and Mayer (1990), Goleman (1996 and 1998), Steiner (1997) and Higgs and Dulewicz (1999) – are seen to share broad agreement about the main themes, with some semantic differences (Sharp 2001: 25). Killick summarises these themes in the following way:

Self-awareness
To know one's own emotional state, to be able to recognize what feelings are being experienced at any one time and being aware of the thoughts that are involved in this.
Self-regulation
To be able to manage one's emotions, to be able to respond and handle strong feelings such as fear or anger appropriately rather than act them out.
Motivation
The ability to motivate oneself to achieve one's goals.

Empathy
The ability to see how another person is feeling or seeing the world that is social perceptiveness.
Social competence
Interpersonal and social skills we need to get along with others and this involves being able to manage strong feelings in others and to manage relationships. (Killick 2006: 10–11)

Research context

The book uses data from research undertaken for a doctoral thesis (Knight 2012) with 28 experienced probation practitioners (the 'research participants') to illustrate some of these issues. The focus of the research was practitioners working with high-risk, predominately sex and domestic violence offenders. The research participants were asked about their understanding of emotions and their experiences of working with emotions; their own and those of the offenders for whom they were responsible. The research findings were tested in a focus group and through a number of seminars held with practitioners, academics and managers. The research participants are referred to by pseudonyms to protect their confidentiality.

The data was analysed with reference to Layder's social domain theory (Layder 2006). Layder identifies society as layered or 'stratified' and including both micro phenomena (people's individual lived experiences) and macro-phenomena (structural and institutional). He argues that social interaction is based upon and draws together psychological and social realities. This framework enabled an analysis of emotions and the skill of emotional literacy to reflect not just the individual experiences of probation practitioners but also the context in which they worked and the social structures that impacted on this work. Layder's social domain theory stresses that the creation of meaning by individuals is influenced by an amalgam of subjective, external and situated influences (Layder 2006). His theory maps the 'social' universe and considers four domains of social reality:

Contextual resources
Social Settings
Situated Activity
Psychobiography (Layder 2006: 273)

The four social domains on are represented as vertical layers of social reality

with the lower layers representing the more personalised and immediate elements of social reality while the higher ones are more remote and impersonal. (Layder 2006: 273)

All of them have a relationship with power and all are 'stretched across time and space'; Layder argues that this vertical dimension gives ontological depth.

The domain of psychobiography describes a person's existence and their career trajectory through time and space in the social world. It makes reference to the unique characteristics of that individual, their interactions with others, their experiences and how they have managed them. This is the domain within which the research for this thesis was originally conceptualised, taking a phenomenological perspective to interrogate the meanings that research participants to the study give to their emotional lives. However, Layder's domain theory identifies the individual as living both 'inside' and 'outside' society in that people can never escape social influences but are able to retain a significant degree of independence from them (Layder 2004).

The domain of situated activity, as the next layer, is 'an arena in which meaning is created' (Layder 2006: 277). Layder describes situated activity as

> a subtle and complex mix of the powers, emotions and mutual influences of multiple individuals that unfold in the real time of the encounter. (Layder 2006: 279)

Situated activity represents the practical focus of transactions between people in lived time and mediates between the subjective and objective elements of social reality. Layder highlights activities that go on under the surface, particularly emotions and feelings, some without the conscious awareness of the participants, and argues that all the individuals entering this encounter have emotional needs that they hope will be met. Such needs include approval and inclusion, so that the person's identity, security, self-esteem and self-value are affirmed and reaffirmed. He describes this as 'underground emotion work' (Layder 2006: 279), in which there is a constant shifting of feelings of alignment and attunement or estrangement and awkwardness, and suggests this is evidence of the highly skilled nature of being human.

The domain of social settings, sometimes referred to as the 'systems element' (Thompson 2006), provides the immediate environment of the situated activity. Layder suggests these settings can vary in their organisational form. In some the relationships are formal and structured, for example, schools, universities, hospitals, industrial/commercial firms and government bureaucracies, whilst others are based on informal, loosely patterned relationships such as friendships, partnerships and family networks. These settings constitute a collection or accumulation of reproduced social relations, positions and practices, the 'reproduced outcomes of past activities that influence behaviour in the present' (Layder 2006: 280). In more formal settings, such as an organisation like the probation service, social relationships are clearly defined and, according to Layder, usually hierarchical with a graded sequence of positions and statuses. Interaction within this setting is defined through these positions and commitment to them is through inducements such as career opportunities, pay.

The fourth domain of contextual resources is the outer layer of the four and represents the most encompassing feature of the social environment. Layder defines two key elements: how material resources are unevenly allocated and the historical accumulation of cultural resources such as 'stored knowledge' (cultural, ideological and institutional) through artefacts, media representations, fashion. The unequal distribution of resources he associates with groupings based on class, ethnicity, age, gender and status. These include resources that support the immediate socio-economic context of particular social settings, for example, education, occupation, family and neighbourhood, as well as the inner mental lives of individuals (Layder 2006: 281). These aspects of social reality – practical and cultural resources – have been reproduced in time and space through regular usage by successive generations of individuals. Layder suggests that historically they have become relatively independent of current activity and that this characteristic distinguishes them from the real, present time of unfolding situated activities. In this sense elements of agency and system interfuse and influence each other but without destroying their distinctive characteristics and generative power (Layder 2006). Although these four social domains are clearly distinguishable from each other Layder argues that it is important not to lose sight of the links and continuities between them.

Emotional intelligence has traditionally been understood within the domains of psychobiography (the individual) and situated activity (interactions between people). The research for this book identified that the social setting in which people interact, namely, the criminal justice organisation, and the contextual resources, such as the gendered nature of crime and how emotions are expressed and understood in our society, are of equal importance in understanding the meaning and development of emotional literacy.

Structure of the book

The first three chapters examine the literature and set out some of the parameters for understanding emotional literacy in criminal justice practice including issues of diversity, power, values and emotions. From Chapter 3 onwards the meaning of emotional literacy to practitioners and within practice is explored. Each chapter begins with a practice example to illustrate the different elements of emotional literacy and an identification of the key learning to be gained.

Emotions and criminal justice

Some of the connections between emotions and criminal justice are set out in Chapter 2 which examines a range of theories on emotion and emotion regulation and considers how criminology, with its history of being a scientific enterprise, has, until relatively recently, largely excluded the study of emotions within crime and criminality. This is now changing significantly through the work of feminist criminologists, but also increasingly through studies of neuroscience with a better understanding of how the brain and emotions are shaped and developed through external impacts from childhood onwards (Teicher 2000, Diamant 2001).

Diversity, power and emotions

Chapter 3 explores some of the ways in which the concept of diversity is understood within a criminal justice context and how the negative impact of individual and institutional discrimination can affect the rights and liberty of both victims and offenders. In particular this chapter begins to reflect on the ways in which power operates to reinforce feelings and attitudes that contribute to discrimination and disadvantage. The most significant diversity issue highlighted by the research in relation to both power and emotion was that of gender, and Chapter 3 explores the fact that men are over-represented in the offender population and also in management and leadership roles within criminal justice, and the implications of this for understanding emotional literacy. This chapter also considers some of the gender implications arising from the research and impacting on the work of practitioners who aspire to be emotionally literate. It examines the ways in which gender has an association with emotions and emotional literacy, the commonly held assumption that women are generally more emotionally aware than men and what this has meant for policy and management.

Values: positive and negative emotional control in work with offenders

Whilst it is acknowledged that not all workers in criminal justice organisations are necessarily concerned with 'enabling change' in offenders, it is argued that all workers should treat offenders (and victims and witnesses) with decency and respect (Rutherford 1993). Chapter 4 presents an argument that emotional literacy has a humanitarian value base of concern for the individual that business models of emotional intelligence may not always incorporate. For example, research on debt collectors discovered that those who were trained to be emotionally intelligent in the way that they approached debtors, that is, those who were considerate and sympathetic to their customers, were more likely to extract money from them (Bachmann et al. 2000). This could be viewed as a more manipulative use of emotional intelligence although it is acknowledged that a superficial expression of consideration or respect for the service user is rather better than an aggressive or bullying approach, particularly in the process of sanction enforcement. The expression of inauthentic emotions or feelings is clearly unlikely to lead to a genuine connection between worker and service user. However, as emotions portrayed or 'acted' in drama and television can draw the viewer into an emotional world, so too, the practitioner may begin to establish a more meaningful relationship if the emotional 'front' that they present to the service user is one of benign interest as opposed to hostility or manipulative control.

A humanitarian value base for emotional literacy promotes the capacity of people to change and adapt, and recognises that this change is most likely to happen through the medium of a positive relationship in which the worker is able to demonstrate empathy, kindness and a non-judgemental approach. It is associated with the concept of 'legitimacy', that is, people's perception as to whether law enforcement officials rightly have authority over them (Bottoms and Tankebe 2012). It is also associated increasingly with aspects of human rights, generally now built into statements of principle promoted by criminal justice agencies, identifying how workers in these settings should treat all people with proper respect as human beings, recognising issues such as their right to dignity and privacy. Tyler argues that such as approach is more likely to lead to an acceptance of the legitimacy of the agency and its workers (Tyler 2003).

Questions about the extent to which emotions govern and direct the practice of criminal justice workers remain largely unexplored. Chapter 4 examines one such question about the ways in which workers can express both positive and negative feelings towards service users. This can include compassion and concern, or, conversely, anger, resentment and punitiveness (in recognition of the fact that all workers are likely to feel a mixture of these emotions at different times). In a system established to control and punish criminal behaviour, some workers may legitimately believe that their own punitive attitudes and behaviour towards offenders will be condoned or supported by the wider public, particularly in the case of the most serious of crimes such as violent and sexual offending. Some of the political arguments for ratcheting up ever more controlling and punitive measures are based on a premise that 'prison works' (Howard 1993) and even when it does not it is still somehow 'deserved' and therefore legitimate. The arguments for a more sophisticated and humanistic approach to work with offending behaviour, including the promotion of the now well-researched accredited offending behaviour programmes such as the Community Sex Offender Groupwork Programme (C-SOGP) (Vanstone 2012), are much harder to make in a climate of popular punitiveness. So too are the arguments for a return to a 'welfare' ethos within the probation service, before it transmuted into 'punishment in the community' in the 1980s and 1990s (Whitehead 2010).

Exposure of some care staff operating in callous and brutal ways in institutions and hospitals with older service users and those with learning difficulties (e.g. Winterbourne View (Department of Health 2012)) has highlighted the risk of exploitation and abuse of vulnerable adults in institutional and domestic settings, with resulting public condemnation and calls for change. The care of offenders undergoing penal sanctions is of much less public concern; the belief that they are deserving of whatever punishment might be inflicted on them limits the level of public exposure of potential malpractice, or lack of care and respect, from staff. Only where very substantial harm or even death occurs (e.g. Keith 2006) is public outrage stirred.

The case, therefore, for examining and understanding how emotions can lead criminal justice practitioners to act out their controlling roles in either caring and compassionate ways, or with a more punitive and manipulative emphasis, is particularly powerful in a criminal justice context and within a culture of popular punitiveness (Bottoms 1995). Understanding how some criminal justice practitioners can act with a lack of care or respect for offenders is important in human rights terms and also because it is absolutely not their job to *add,* indiscriminately and inappropriately, to the punishment already legitimately imposed by the court system, be it community supervision, unpaid work or imprisonment. Understanding how other workers can use the skills of emotional literacy, the main theme for this book, as an active part of their practice repertoire, and to act with care and compassion towards offenders, is of equal importance. However, this approach is vulnerable to ridicule and dismissal in a popular and political culture that seeks for increasingly punitive responses to crime and criminality and claims the moral high ground in taking a 'tough' approach. How practitioners regulate and use these emotional forces should be of concern to all criminal justice organisations.

The ubiquity and invisibility of emotion

We tend to assume that we know what is meant by an 'emotion' or 'being emotional'. We are constantly confronted with emotions in ourselves and others; emotions are integral to our daily lives. However, although we may talk about how we feel in a given situation we do not routinely verbalise the meaning of these processes. Chapter 5 begins to explore what 'self-awareness' and 'self-regulation' meant to the research participants. Some of them, when asked what they considered these terms to mean, struggled to find words to explain or articulate them. For example, Aruna acknowledged that she routinely expected offenders to be able to articulate their feelings, without realising how difficult this could be until confronted with the question herself. Another participant, when asked what feelings she had, described incidents and events that *caused* positive and negative feelings rather than describing the actual feelings. Some participants were clearly unused to being asked about their 'feelings' and un-practiced at articulating in words and in a work context, how they *thought* about their feelings (Ansbro 2008, Oatley 2009, Izard 2010, Kagan 2010).

Goleman refers to the power of the 'emotional brain' to overpower or even paralyse the 'thinking brain' (Goleman 1996: 78). When powerful feelings are to the forefront the ability to *think* about them can be inhibited (Fargason 1995, Rogers 2004, Rogers 2004). By contrast, other research participants, particularly those who had worked for many years in the areas of sexual offending and domestic violence, seemed to have had more opportunity to process and then articulate their feelings, and were better able to explain them. For example, Indira, Sandy and Heather were all very articulate in this area and all had worked for ten or more years in the probation service, predominantly with high-risk offenders. Whilst we are creatures of emotion, the majority of us are not used to standing back from the feelings that we have and reflecting on why they have occurred or what they might mean for us. As children we are almost entirely driven by our feelings and it is only through a process of socialisation and education that we begin to learn to control some of our stronger emotions and temper them with reflection on what it is we might actually wish to achieve (Evans 2003). We may sometimes react in an unthinking way to feelings that are generated within us and later have cause to regret or reconsider our behaviour in the light of responses from others. We learn the importance of being able to postpone gratification in order to achieve a better or more fulfilling outcome in the longer term (Killick 2006). However, the opportunity to actively process, reflect on and modify our emotional reactions is not often easily available to us unless we choose to enter into counselling or other forms of therapeutic support. Most of the research participants had achieved this self-awareness and self-regulation through a process of on-the-job learning and life experience.

Building relationships to achieve change

Chapter 6 examines how the research participants considered that they used the skills of emotional literacy to build relationships with offenders. Howe argues that emotions define the character of the professional relationship that practitioners build with service users (Howe 2008). How such emotion is used but not exploited or allowed to dominate these relationships is explored including issues of building trust, getting emotionally close to offenders and negotiating the emotional boundaries to the relationship. It also reflects on the use of intuition and an awareness of the significance of offender motivation and offender readiness to change. Chapter 7 looks at the processes involved in managing community orders and working to achieve change in offenders. This includes how offenders are enabled and encouraged to disclose significant information about themselves that informs risk assessment and risk management. It also considers some of the ambivalence felt by the research participants in handling these disclosures, and how open and transparent they were able to be about enforcement procedures.

Emotions in organisations

Chapter 8 considers the role of emotions in organisational life – the extent to which organisations within the criminal justice system impose 'feeling rules' on their workers. It is suggested that in general workers are expected to operate in an emotionally neutral or 'objective' manner, regardless of the emotional challenges with which they are faced. It is argued that this managerial approach has had the effect of silencing the voices of practitioners as they have endeavoured to continue to work with the emotional lives of offenders within an organisation that largely denies the relevance of emotion. It examines how, in the face of the 'emotionality' of the criminal justice context, and the managerialism of their organisation, many of the research participants strived for professionalism and neutrality in their work. It explores how a combination of 'professional' rules and 'feeling rules' of the organisation (Hochschild 1983) impose a silence on the discourse of emotions and the endeavours of practitioners to surmount this in their daily working practices. Reference is made to Bolton's framework for the use of emotion in organisations, including emotion offered as a 'gift' by workers to service users. Concepts such as 'emotional labour' (Hochschild 1983), 'emotion work' (Bolton 2005) and 'emotional capital' (Reay 2004, Zembylas 2007) are examined. The term 'emotional labour' is generally used to define the commodification or exploitation of emotion in individual workers in the pursuit of organisational objectives (Hochschild 1983). Some writers also view this term as a gendered concept with women undertaking the majority of emotional labour both at home and at work (Smith 1992, Du Gay 2003, Bunting 2005, Garey and Hansen 2011).

Strategies for sustaining emotional literacy in the workplace

Chapter 9 reflects on some of the strategies that the research participants used to support themselves emotionally in the workplace. It offers recommendations for workplace policy in the building of emotional resources to support and develop emotional literacy in the workforce. The idea of building emotional resources evolves from ideas of 'emotional capital', with reference to Bourdieu's work on human capital (Reay 2004), and examines the accumulation of positive and enhancing emotional resources within a relationship, group or organisation.

Conclusion

This book explores the use of emotional literacy as a skill for practitioners working with offenders in the criminal justice system. Whilst its primary focus is work with a therapeutic or change-enhancing aim, it is also of relevance to all workers in the criminal justice system who strive to operate with decency and respect towards offenders, victims and witnesses. It reflects on some of the micro skills of emotional literacy including self-awareness, self-regulation, empathy and social competence. It places these skills in the wider organisational and social context and within a framework of human rights and a humanitarian approach to work with offenders.

2
Emotions and Criminal Justice

Practice example

Lisa has been asked to take up a secondment in a local probation hostel following her five years in an offender management team. Her line manager offers a number of reasons as to why this is a good career move for her including an opportunity to develop management skills through working with the staff in the hostel and group work skills through working with the residents. Lisa recognises the logic of this argument but feels very apprehensive about working in this environment. She decides to defer making a decision until she has had time to reflect on her feelings and talk with her partner. Later, when talking with her partner she becomes upset and recalls a time when she was set upon by a group of young men in a shopping centre and had her purse taken. She remembers the fear and powerlessness she felt at the time. She then reflects on whether she wants to put herself back in a potentially similar situation with a number of young offenders, although she recognises that she will be in a position of authority this time and will be able to seek help and support. After weighing the pros and cons, she decides to ask her line manager whether she could access either counselling or mentoring opportunities to help her work through her fear and learn skills and strategies to cope with potentially aggressive or threatening situations in the hostel were she to take up the post.

Key learning points
- Emotions are ubiquitous but not easily articulated.
- We may not always recognise the causes or triggers for our feelings unless we have an opportunity to feel them, reflect on them with support and then decide on a course of action.
- 'Rational' thinking may, on its own, be insufficient for important decision-making; feelings need to be integrated within the process.

Introduction

This chapter takes an overview of some theories of emotion and emotion regulation and locates them within the field of criminology and in a criminal justice setting. It considers the extent to which criminology and criminal justice have striven to operate within a paradigm of rationality, a scientific approach based on 'facts', 'evidence' and 'objectivity' to the exclusion of the subjective and of emotional processes that frequently define crime and criminality. There are, of course, good reasons for this. A criminal justice system based on the emotional responses of fear, revenge and anger, such as has existed historically in this country (Karstedt et al. 2011), is a system that functions with unfairness, discrimination and idiosyncrasy. The modern British criminal justice system has been held up as an exemplar of fairness, impartiality and rationality (Cavadino and Dignan 2006), with emotion largely excluded from its remit. In a parallel development criminology emerged as a separate social science discipline in the late 19th century and, whilst initially based on a classicist model of human behaviour,[1] soon evolved as a study of human behaviour based on a positivist paradigm, a focus on large-scale, quantitative surveys of criminal populations, rather than the smaller, qualitative examinations of processes and experiences (Newburn 2007). Research that takes a positivist approach is viewed as studying objective, observable evidence that is available for scrutiny by others and where the researcher is detached from the evidence (Bondi 2005). It is seen as grounded in rationality and logical argument and has explicit rules of engagement and interpretation.

Nevertheless, emotions do pervade the penal law and the criminal justice system (Scheff, Stanko et al. 2002). Significant numbers of crimes are committed when the perpetrator is in a highly emotional state or wanting to achieve an emotional 'buzz' (Katz 1999). Offenders, victims and witnesses bring their emotions to the court and the sentencing process, and judicial decisions can cause public outrage and anger. Offenders can feel shame and remorse; offences can provoke feelings of anger or disgust and victims as well as some offenders can evoke compassion and sympathy (Laster and O'Malley 1996, Karstedt 2002, Gelsthorpe 2009). There are significant areas of offending behaviour where rational thought and planning is essential. Much white-collar crime requires opportunity, premeditation and skill. Some high-level burglaries require detailed planning, surveillance, obtaining of specialist equipment and organising of other people as accomplices. Whilst emotions, for example, an adrenalin rush of fear and excitement, will undoubtedly be involved in the process of executing such crimes, nevertheless, these forms of offending behaviour are not primarily driven by the immediacy of powerful emotions. Other crimes, however, are more likely to be committed by people in the grip of strong emotions, particularly those of a violent or sexual nature. As well as the emotions engendered in offenders, Karstedt also highlights the return of a sense of 'emotionality' to the system, through increased media attention to the needs of victims and the 'drama' of particularly violent and salacious crime stories (Karstedt et al. 2011).

This chapter will reflect on some of the continuing influences of the positivist paradigm on the development of the 'What Works' movement within criminal justice. Notwithstanding the evolution of feminist and other radical thinking in criminology, which has challenged this focus on 'facts' and argued for a more nuanced and subjectivist approach to understanding criminality and criminal justice processes, it is suggested that, organisationally, the setting and monitoring of targets within a managerialist framework has been favoured over the more emotional processes of relationship building and responding to emotions in offenders. There is evidence of a renewed focus on the significance of relationships within work with offenders in a probation context (Dowden and Andrews 2004, Day, Casey et al. 2010, McNeill, Raynor et al. 2010) and in other associated areas of criminal justice work, such as drug and alcohol services (Mills et al. 2007, Roy, Fountain et al. 2007) and also through the literature on desistance (Maruna, Immarigeon 2004). This renewed focus has begun to challenge the managerialist and technocratic approach to work with offenders. An understanding of emotional literacy sits within this re-emergence of the 'relationship' in criminal justice practice.

Understanding the significance of emotional literacy within practice requires some knowledge and understanding of the concept of 'emotion', a seemingly ubiquitous term that even when unpacked proves to be complex, elusive and difficult to articulate. This chapter will reflect on some of this knowledge and on the gendered associations with emotions and emotionality, and the importance of developing emotion vocabularies.

Emotions

Emotion as a concept has been written and theorised about for thousands of years through philosophy, literature, drama, and spirituality. The Latin root of emotion is 'emovere' meaning to move out or away (Hughes and Bradford Terrell 2012), indicating a powerful association between emotion, movement and motivation – the desire to act. Philosophers including Descartes drew upon this Latin root of emotion to formulate their ideas on emotion (Harré and Parrott 1996). Aristotle emphasised that emotions serve to induce activity, have moral relevance and can affect our judgements. He provided a detailed discussion of emotions in his work *Rhetorica* (Harré and Parrott 1996). Emotion-arousal was viewed by Aristotle as essential in persuading people to form the right judgements, he believed that feelings can cause us to change and alter our judgements (Evans 2003).

Early theories of emotion

A 'scientific' approach to the understanding of emotions was initiated primarily by Darwin's 1872 publication *Expression of Emotions in Man and Animals* (Darwin 1998) in which he argued that emotions are the mental states that cause archetypical bodily expressions (Gendron 2010). Darwin identified the principal emotions in terms of how they are expressed and how the body behaves, and studied them in terms of their value for the survival of the species (Howe 2008). Darwin has largely been the source of what is commonly called the 'basic emotion' approach. Darwin had proposed a core or 'basic' set of human emotions (Ekman and Wallace 1975, Ekman and Wallace 2002). Ekman and colleagues also showed that there is an autonomic nervous system activity that corresponds to these basic emotions, namely, that these emotions are not learnt but are inherent in the human brain (Ekman and Wallace 1975). Building on Darwin's work and supported by subsequent research, humans are said to experience at least six 'primary' or 'basic' emotions, namely, anger, fear, sadness (or distress), happiness (or joy), surprise and disgust (Evans 2003, Turner 2009). By contrast, the 'cultural' theory of emotion, subsequently developed through the discipline of anthropology, argued that emotions are learned behaviours that are transmitted culturally in a way similar to language (Evans 2003). The cultural differences were seen as largely relating to rules of display – what was acceptable to present or hide (Evans 2003).

There are critics of the concept of basic emotions. It is argued that humans have the potential to experience a large number of different emotional states and the cultural and historical context in which we live selects the states that will possess particular relevance (Harré and Parrott 1996, Kagan 2010). Plutchik compared emotions to a colour wheel, with mixes of primary emotions at different points in the colour wheel generating varying secondary and tertiary emotions (Plutchik 1980). The analogy suggests that these primary colours contain a spectrum of hues and shades reflecting the strength of feeling and that they also mix with each other to produce more sophisticated and subtle emotions (Killick 2006:27). For example, some emotions such as 'jealousy' or 'shame' are described by a single word, when in fact they are likely to contain a complex mixture of other feelings including anger, fear and disappointment.

Descartes identified the hydraulic theory of emotion which viewed feelings as mental fluids that circulate in the mind, with 'the nerves as pneumatic pipes, transmitting the pressure of "animal spirits" from nerve endings to the brain, and thence to the muscles' (Evans 2003:55). Metaphors such as 'bottling up your feelings' and 'letting off steam' owe their origins to this 'humoural' theory which dominated medical thinking in the West until the 18th century (Lakoff 1987, Damasio 1996, Payne and Cooper 2001, Evans 2003). Freud drew on this theory in his explanation about the risks of inhibiting natural emotional expressions that could lead to dangerous consequences. The idea of catharsis, or 'cleansing', of being able to 'discharge' emotions and 'get them out of your system', has underpinned much psychotherapeutic thinking and practice. It has been argued that when the core emotions are suppressed and/or remain unexpressed it is likely that a more pervasive and unexamined 'mood' may take over and that mental ill-health can emerge (Freud and Freud 2005).

Contemporary theories of emotion

For the first part of the 20th century the disciplines of both psychology and sociology tended to dismiss the importance of emotions as relevant for scientific study or see them as contaminating the proper study of people and their behaviour (Howe 2008:3). The Behaviourists of the 1950s who began the ongoing developments around cognitive behavioural psychology that remain relevant to the work of the probation service today were suspicious of emotions (Howe 2008). It is only in the last 30 years or so that there has been a significant growth in theories of emotion through psychology, psychotherapy, sociology, and more recently neuroscience (Gendron 2010). There remain, however, substantial areas of disagreement including the nature of emotions, the degree to which emotions can be identified neurologically or are largely socially constructed, the number of distinctive emotional states produced by humans, the relationship between cognition and emotions, between behaviour and emotions and between emotions and rationality (Turner 2009). There is also a lack of agreement on definitions, the extent to which an emotion is understood as occurring in the brain or body, a verbal description, an interpretation or a behavioural response to a situation (Kagan 2010).

An early disagreement on definitions centred on whether emotion was the actual feeling or the process of evaluating that feeling; this is known as 'appraisal'. Within psychology there are a set of approaches emphasising that emotions are not formed until there is an appraisal of both objects and events; only after appraisal has occurred are the relevant emotions seen to be activated (Turner 2009). With the development of sophisticated technologies that enable imaging of brain states there are now claims that the brain state that mediates a feeling is the more accurate referent for an emotion (Damasio 1996).

Neuroscience has identified a section of our brain known as the amygdala that is implicated in evaluating stimuli as good or bad at a relatively early stage in the perceptual process (Franks 2010). Howe argues that emotions initially appear to operate outside of a person's immediate consciousness; their response to a stimulus in the environment comes via one or more of the senses (Howe 2008:30). Others have argued that there are 'higher cognitive emotions' which are not so automatic or fast as the basic ones and are not linked to a single facial expression, for example, love, guilt, pride, and that these involve greater levels of cortical processing in the brain (Evans 2003:20). LeDoux identifies a 'high' road and a 'low' road that he suggests is controlled by two separate pathways in the brain (LeDoux 2003). He argues that in the experience of fear the first pathway corresponds to the basic emotion; it is a rapid response to signs of potential danger and travels via the sensory thalamus to the amygdala. It can, however, often set off false alarms. The second pathway travels via the sensory cortex and LeDoux refers to this as the 'high road' which considers the situation more carefully and if it concludes that the danger is not real it cuts off the fear response initiated by the first pathway; these two pathways ideally operate together (LeDoux 2003).

Barbalet identifies emotion as an 'experience of involvement' (Barbalet 2002), either negatively or positively and either profoundly or slightly, or somewhere in between (Barbalet 2002). Similarly, Hochschild argues that emotion is a biologically given sense (and our most important one) and that, like other senses such as hearing and touch, it is a means by which we know about our relation to the world, and it is therefore crucial for the survival of human beings. She states that emotion is unique among the senses because it is related not only to an orientation towards action but also to an orientation towards cognition (Hochschild 1983:219). Most current emotion theorists now seem to suggest that emotion is simultaneously a physical, cognitive and social/cultural experience (Hubbard, Backett-Milburn et al. 2001); that emotions operate on many different levels of reality including biological, neurological, behavioural, cultural, structural and situational (Turner 2009:341). If the focus of study is neurological then the emphasis locates emotions in the arousal of bodily systems; if culture is seen as significant then ideologies, rules and emotional vocabularies are critical (Turner 2009). Oatley et al. identify the field of emotion theory as fast moving and caution against trying to establish too fixed or inflexible a definition (Oatley, Keltner et al. 2006).

Notwithstanding the complexity of finding a definition of 'emotion', the argument at the heart of most debates on emotion centres on whether emotions help or hurt our decision-making processes and whether they cause us to lose control (seen as a 'bad' thing) versus arguments that they provide important inputs to decision-making (Loewenstein 2010).

Emotion and reason

Plato saw emotions as obstacles to intelligent action; he is considered to have held a negative view of emotion (Evans 2003: 22). So too the stoics of ancient Greece believed that feelings undermined rational thought; that if we are to lead the good life we should not allow ourselves to be at the mercy of our passions (Howe 2008). At the core of much of the thinking on emotion is that of the potential for acting unreasonably as a result of our emotions (Frijda, Manstead et al. 2000). It is argued that we may not have a choice about what emotions we feel but we have a choice about what to do with that feeling

(Oatley 2010). The argument that has held powerful sway is one that states that if actions are to be considered rational it is necessary that we overcome our 'base' emotions. This has been promulgated by Western Philosophers such as Descartes and Kant who saw the emotions as basic, primitive and disruptive. They argued that human enlightenment required us to rid ourselves of our 'animal passions', to tame them and to rise above emotion (Bendelow and Williams 1998).

The 18th-century European Romantic Movement took a different perspective and saw emotions as central and life enhancing (Howe 2008:4). This movement considered that faced with a choice between emotion and reason the heart should predominate. The Enlightenment period, by contrast, placed emphasis on the power of reason and opposed superstition and intolerance. However, philosophers of the Enlightenment period such as David Hume, Adam Smith and Thomas Reid who wrote about 'sentiments' and passions' were also fascinated by emotion and considered that it was rational to be emotional and that no science of the mind could be complete without also addressing the 'heart' (Evans 2003:xiii). The emotions were considered to be an integral part of our individual and collective psychology and at the heart of what beliefs are about (Howe 2008). David Hume, an 18th-century empiricist, argued that the impulse for action comes not from reason, which is 'dispassionate', but from passion which provides the push and drive for action (Frijda et al. 2000).

Emotions can also lead us to make mistakes, to misjudge situations and to interpret present events through the lens of a memory distorted or clouded by feelings. Emotions can generate anxiety and disrupt our thinking (Howe 2008:16). They can also lead us to do things we might later regret (Evans 2003). However, an ability to respond rapidly to 'gut feelings' can be advantageous in certain circumstances, particularly in potentially risky situations (Gladwell 2005). Experiencing a range of emotions is now generally seen as an important aspect of living a rich and fulfilling life. Whilst certain 'negative' emotions can be a major source of misery they also have their place in, for example, highlighting injustice and motivating action. People crave emotions, and spend time seeking out certain emotions, for example, fear on roller coasters, sadness from tragic films and disgust at Halloween. In addressing this paradox it is proposed that negative emotions are often sought in situations in which the outcomes that the emotions typically signal are absent (Andrade and Cohen 2007). This vicarious activity divorces fear from any actual danger and provides a sensation with no consequences.

Western philosophical thought has tended to juxtapose emotionality and rationality at opposite ends of a continuum. Traditionally, reason was equated with objectivism. The mind was seen as an abstract machine and thought was abstract and disembodied, independent of the limitations of the physical body (Lakoff 1987). More recent studies, especially within anthropology, linguistics, neuroscience and psychology, have produced evidence which has challenged this objectivist view of the mind. Freshwater sees the endeavour to separate out emotion from reason as a:

> dangerous polarisation of will and desire with the aim to conquer unruly nature so indicative of the scientific community. (Freshwater and Robertson 2002:216)

The more common argument now is that thought is in fact 'embodied', that the structures used to form our conceptual processes grow out of our bodily experiences and make sense in terms of them (Lakoff 1987). Lakoff argues that if we understand reason as mechanical then we devalue human intelligence, particularly as computers become ever more efficient. This is not, however, to deny the potentially harmful influence of emotional bias and that emotions can cause difficulties in the reasoning process (Damasio 1996), but rather that the denial of emotion is equally damaging and just as capable of compromising rationality (Loewenstein 2010).

Emotion regulation

The idea of being able to control or regulate emotions has a long history, for example, Plato's concerns about the dangers of 'emotional incontinence' (Barbalet 2011). Many of the earlier writings on theories of emotion endeavoured to find ways in which emotion could be categorised in order to control it. A more functional approach (Harré and Parrott 1996, Tamir 2011) suggests that regulating emotions is important in terms of achieving instrumental goals rather than necessarily making the recipient feel good (Tamir 2011). Goleman argues that accomplishment of every sort is based on emotional self-control, whereby gratification is delayed and impulsiveness stifled (Goleman 1996). He describes the feeling of being 'flooded' or overwhelmed by feelings and refers to this as 'emotional hijacking'. When emotions are running high there is a tendency to talk and act more; the person may be in the grip of many different and conflicting emotions that can make rational behaviour and decision-making problematic (Howe 2008). This suggests a negative view of an individual being governed by their emotions, lacking self-regulation and the need to regulate these emotions in order to obtain sought-after goals (Tamir 2011). It is this approach that is largely taken in the work on emotional intelligence, in particular with reference to successful management and leadership (Cherniss and Goleman 2001). Whilst there is evidence that the 'regulation' of emotions as opposed to their 'suppression' can have important consequences for physical and psychological health and for operating with flexibility and adaptability in a range of situations (Tamir 2011), such writers also argue that too much constraint risks losing something essential about our humanity and agency.

Supporting Freud's view of the importance of catharsis, research has identified the suppression of emotions leading to an increase in blood pressure, an increased risk of cancer and a decrease in rapport with others (Ciarrochi, Forgas et al. 2001). However, assuming that a degree of emotional regulation is necessary in day-to-day social life, the issue of which emotions should be the most controlled is another key question. Some researchers on emotion regulation assume that individuals see unpleasant emotions as undesirable and pleasant emotions as desirable (Campos, Walle et al. 2011, Charland 2011), but people may seek instrumental goals rather than hedonistic ones; emotions such as anger can generate the motivation to act, for example, against perceived injustices (Tamir 2011). Feeling 'better' may not be the desired end-state of the transaction. People may renounce short-term pleasure if it can lead to greater benefits defined as 'long-term pleasure' (Izard 2010); the decisions about what and how to regulate are made continuously.

Emotion vocabularies

Wierzbicka argues that it is the combination of being able to 'feel' and 'think' which distinguishes emotions from 'sensations', that the ability to talk about feelings is a central concept in the understanding of what emotion means and is central to research into emotion (Wierzbicka 2010). It is suggested that appraisal of feelings can be combined in many different ways to produce finely nuanced and differently experienced feeling states although, in reality, we only use a comparatively small number of verbal labels to actually communicate them (Kuppens 2010). People asked to describe how they feel after a very traumatic event will often say that they have no words to express their feelings (Cameron 2011). The metaphor 'lost for words' stands in for these unutterable feelings.

Although we may not use a wide emotional vocabulary, a research project led by Simon Baron-Cohen at Cambridge University found that the English language has at least 1,512 emotion words (Baron-Cohen 2003). He identified that emotional vocabularies developed with age and his taxonomy sought to establish different levels of sophistication of emotional expression (Baron-Cohen 2003). The majority of children gradually learn a degree of control in their emotional self-expression and by adulthood the average person has increased their cognitive abilities to the extent that they can identify and locate the source of their emotions and, at least in their working lives, generally maintain control on their more overt expression (Fischer 2000).

In the field of psychotherapy the lack of a significant vocabulary to describe feelings is called 'alexithymia', a condition in which a person, particularly male, has difficulty in articulating emotion (Bar-On and Parker 2000). It was first introduced by Sifnoes in 1972, and means 'having no words for emotions' (Muller 2000). Muller suggests that people who are unable to verbally express emotions will have trouble discharging and neutralising their emotions physiologically as well as psychically. Alexithymia is sometimes also referred to as 'mind-blindness' (Baron-Cohen 2003), which includes being uninterested in the emotional states of others, and is apparently common in autistic children. There are links here with violence perpetrated by men within a domestic and/or sexual context who may struggle to identify a range of emotions, and respond instead from the position of being aroused but unaware. This may be accompanied by demonstrations of aggressive, controlling or violent behaviour (Lane and Nadel 2000, Romito 2008). However, it is also acknowledged that for some men not articulating feelings may be an active or strategic choice in holding on to power. In a more therapeutic context, the gradual expansion of emotional vocabularies is seen to help develop the process of clarifying and understanding what another person feels (Ekman 2008), and a developing emotional vocabulary is seen as one of the key building blocks of emotional literacy (Sharp 2001).

Use of metaphor

A 'metaphor' is defined as a 'figure of speech', talking about something in terms of something else (Cameron 2011), of contrasting something else into ongoing talk (Cameron and Low 1999) or substituting the name of an attribute for that of the thing meant (e.g. '"turf" for horse-racing' (Lakoff 1987:xi)). Metaphors are ubiquitous in everyday speech and writing but often unacknowledged. It is suggested that everyday language is not adequate for capturing the experience of emotions, especially intense ones, and that metaphorical language makes it possible for people to convey what would otherwise be difficult or impossible to express (Coupland, Brown et al. 2009, Crawford 2009), for example, 'swept off her feet'. People unsure of the safety of the emotional climate of their workplace, for example, or indeed the research interview, may use metaphor as a safe device to explain feelings. It can be a way of uncovering or revealing what is going on under the surface of a discourse (Cameron et al. 2009). Metaphors are an agreed way of sharing our views of the world; they also challenge the 'traditional' view that argues that reason is abstract, disembodied and transcendental by building connections between ideas and feelings (Lakoff 1987). Hochschild argues that metaphors that suggest 'agency', 'residence' and 'continuity through time' often convey with 'uncanny precision' just what it feels like to experience an emotion (Hochschild 1983:204).

This difficulty in expressing how we feel in literal language may reflect the difficulties in conceptualising it. Crawford argues that emotions are abstract and not clearly defined in their own terms. Whilst emotions are the foundations of social life she suggests it is nearly impossible to communicate them, and instead we refer to physical dimensions such as brightness, auditory pitch and size, for example, 'light and dark', to represent happiness and sadness, respectively, and positive feelings as 'up' and negative feelings as 'down' (Crawford 2009:138). The idea of emotion as part of a hydraulic system (Descartes' theory) continues to be represented in such metaphors as 'she was filled with sadness', 'he was overflowing with joy', 'she was swept off her feet', 'he was engulfed by anger', 'letting off steam' and 'blood boiling' (Crawford 2009:130). Similarly, fine art, music, poetry and novels are often viewed as better vehicles for the expression and conveyance of feelings than prosaic language.

Emotion and gender

A number of writers have identified a process of gender socialisation through which they argue women are more likely than men to see the significance of emotional connections with others (Miller and Stiver 1997, Kram and McCullom 1998, Cherniss and Goleman 2001). Baron-Cohen identified that girls learn expressive language including more extensive and earlier vocabularies, reading abilities and word fluency than boys (Baron-Cohen 2003). Girls as young as one year have been found to react with more empathy and distress than their same-age male counterparts (Fischer 2000:30), which suggests a mutual dynamic between the ability to articulate feelings and empathy. Other research has found that women are generally perceived to have a greater emotional vocabulary than men and to have greater facility in using it (Langford 1997, Bunting 2005, De Coster and Zito 2010). Research by Glenberg et al. found that women understand sentences about sad events with greater facility than men and men understand sentences about angry events with greater facility than women (Glenberg, Webster et al. 2009). Collaborative and nurturing behaviour is also more often reinforced by women (Cherniss and Goleman 2001), with the suggestion that women have a greater tendency than men to have the personal and interpersonal skills to engage in relational learning. However, Cherniss and Goleman devote only two pages to the implications of gender in developing emotional competence and emotional intelligence through relationships at work.

Fischer argues that men are, in fact, just as emotional as women, citing examples of male behaviour when watching sport, when angry, when trying to avoid embarrassment and so on, and instead challenges the persistence of the dichotomy between the stereotype of emotional women and unemotional men (Fischer 2000). However, some emotional expressions are associated negatively with women (e.g. crying, being anxious, being fearful (Katz 1999, Fischer 2000)) whilst other emotions such as anger, more commonly associated with men, are seen as instrumental in achieving a goal rather than as 'being emotional'. It is argued that women may cry rather than externalise the anger they are actually feeling and men may get angry rather than get in touch with feelings of vulnerability, humiliation or fear (Katz 1999). It is also suggested that it is often these emotional qualities that make women very effective managers, although other attributes such as assertiveness and self-confidence, more generally associated with men, are the ones most likely to lead to promotion in the workplace (Ryam and Haslam 2005). This may be one of the reasons why, despite the majority of the workforce being female, the management of the probation service is still unrepresentatively male compared to the probation workforce as a whole (see Chapter three).

Emotion and criminal justice

It is argued that:

> it is hard to see how the analysis of crime and justice can adequately proceed without some serious attention being paid to the place of emotions in social life. (deHaan and Loader 2002:243)

Emotions are deeply implicated within criminal justice, whether through the dynamics of domestic violence within a family, victims of hate crime, the policing of mass protest, the anger, guilt and shame of offenders or the fear and humiliation of victims. However, the study of emotions has generally remained peripheral to the criminological enterprise. Whilst many theoretical perspectives, for example, rational choice theory, routine activities theory, control theory, have pondered over the motivation for crime, there has been less curiosity about the underlying emotional processes and influences on offending (deHaan and Loader 2002), given the development in other disciplines within the humanities and social sciences as outlined earlier.

There are relatively few studies that refer specifically to the link between emotions and crime although Karstedt et al.'s recent book makes a substantive contribution in this area (Karstedt, Loader et al. 2011), as do Scheff, Stanko et al. (2002) and Gelsthorpe (2009). The evolving literature on desistance, for example Farrall and Calverley (2006), makes some links. Crawley has identified the largely negative emotions apparent in prisons when things go wrong including the anger of the prisoners concerning the conditions of their confinement, the disgust of prison officers at the damage to the prison and the confusion and fear generated by disturbances (Crawley 2009). However, the emotional life of prisons when things are routine has attracted much less interest. Crawley argues that the day-to-day emotional life of prisons is in fact highly significant because:

> it is through the day-to-day performance and management of emotion that the prison itself is 'accomplished'. (Crawley 2009:412)

King suggests that strong feelings are often engendered in the public when concern is expressed about criminal sanctions, but that much less is known about

empathy, forgiveness, mercy and the sanctions that align with these sentiments than about the punitive orientations (King 2008). The media powerfully
manipulates the negative emotions in its choice of graphic crime stories to grip
the attention of readers and viewers. Issues of power, manipulation, coercion,
and shame can be very significant in the processing of offenders through the
system (Karstedt, Loader et al. 2011), and yet it seems that theorising and
policymaking in relation to crime and punishment has sought to set aside
the question of emotions in the pursuit of a 'rational' and 'objective' system
(Loader 2005).

As an example of emotions going to the heart of the sentencing process,
three studies identified how people perceive crime as being more serious when
fewer people are affected. Nordgren and McDonnell undertook a test using
students and also examined cases between 2000 and 2010 in which individuals from corporations had been found guilty by juries of negligently exposing
members of the public to substances such as asbestos, lead paint or toxic mould
and their victims had suffered significantly (Nordgren and McDonell 2010).
These studies confirmed the researchers' hypothesis that people who harm
large numbers of people get significantly lower punitive damages than people
who harm a smaller number.

Goldacre argues that although there may be factors such as large companies
being able to employ competent lawyers, it is hard to discount the contribu-
tory effect of empathy (Goldacre 2010). In other words, in cases where there
are large numbers of victims this has the effect of reducing the sense of griev-
ance and understanding of culpability; the smaller the number of victims the
more 'sentencers' can feel aggrieved on their behalf and seek to impose greater
sanctions on their perpetrators. This offers one example of the power of emotions to influence the apparent objectivity of sentencing; others, for example
Fitzmaurice and Pease (1986), have written about this phenomenon. The
research reaffirms that it is the personal and individual narratives about crime
that impact emotionally and it is, of course, the personal crime stories that sell
newspapers and bring in audiences for TV crime dramas. Individual victims of
terrible crimes are used by the media to campaign for more punitive sanctions –
what has been referred to as a 'moral panic' (e.g. the killings of James Bulger
and Sarah Payne) – even when there is little statistical or 'scientific' evidence
to indicate that the risk of further such serious events occurring is anything
other than small or would be made smaller by the use of more punitive sanctions (Cohen 1972).

Emotion and criminology

The drive towards modernity with its emphasis on science and scientific explanations for all phenomena which began in the late 19th century and continued into the 20th century has had the effect of devaluing and suppressing the

role of emotion in criminology. Criminology as a discipline had its beginnings in the 18th and early 19th centuries with Beccaria and the establishment of the classical school of criminology (Taylor, Walton et al. 1973). Garland identifies the Enlightenment writers such as Beccaria, Bentham and Howard as writing

> secular, materialist analyses, emphasising the importance of reason and experience and denigrating theological forms of reasoning. (Garland 2002:20)

This saw the beginnings of criminology as a scientific enterprise and by the middle of the 19th century Garland argues that this 'scientific' style of reasoning about crime had become a distinctive feature of the emerging culture of amateur social science (Garland 2002). The tendency to look to 'scientific' knowledge as a source of solutions to social and personal problems was becoming apparent not just within political thinking but also within the wider society. As the influence of religious and moral discourse began to wane the idea of the expert practitioner began to emerge (Garland 2002).

The evolution of positivist criminology and increasingly large-scale quantitative studies of criminal behaviour was almost exclusively led by male academics and with male offenders as the subjects of research. Feminist criminologists, beginning in the 1970s with the work of Carol Smart (Smart 1977), struggled to assert a different approach in the context of the history of criminology as a male preserve based on a scientific enterprise. Smart argued that the experiences of women as victims and as offenders were fundamentally different from those of men. She also claimed that the position of 'malestream' criminology – the belief that their scientific studies had universal application – was mistaken. Smart, and the feminist criminologists who followed her, for example, Heidensohn (1985), Morris (1987) and Gelsthorpe (1989), began to reclaim the emotional territory in criminology by identifying the validity and relevance of women's (and men's) subjective experiences. It was this understanding of a feminist 'standpoint' (Smart 1995) that validated the experiences of women as offenders and victims of crime and identified previously largely invisible areas of crime against women and children. This emergence of feminist perspectives, with an explicit attention to conscious partiality and experience, has contributed to this re-enchantment of the social and of emotion in the criminological field (Gelsthorpe 2009:183), particularly in relation to expressive justice and restorative justice. Work on restorative justice in particular has highlighted the use of 'shame' in achieving compliance with the law, and a focus on offender empathy for victims as well as victim empathy for offenders (Gelsthorpe 2009). The emotional power of the bringing together of victims and offenders can be significant in promoting empathy and change in attitude (Van Stokkom 2002). However, this understanding of the significance of the subjective, emotional experience of women offenders and victims has been slow to translate itself within criminology, and still occupies a somewhat marginal place in the discipline, although work on 'masculinities' has begun to challenge this (Silvestri and Crowther-Dowey 2008).

The significance of the 'relationship' within criminal justice practice

The significance of the relationship between probation officer and offender has a strong historical base, beginning with the role of the early police court missionary, using a religious imperative of redemption and repentance to encourage offenders to change their ways (McWilliams 1983). Probation subsequently became a branch of social work from the 1960s until the 1990s and many of the skills of assessment, relationship building and referral to a range of resources for help with personal and family problems were viewed as core to both professions. Through its connection with social work, the association with psychotherapy was a significant influence in probation training and practice from the early 1950s through to the 1970s (Smith 2006). Probation training at that time included models of counselling informed by psychotherapeutic principles, in particular, person-centred counselling which originated with Carl Rogers (Rogers 1943).

The forming of a strong relationship based on a person-centred model of therapy was seen as key to aiding the process of change in offenders and, where the offender might show some resistance, the worker was offered strategies and techniques to overcome these based on the use of the relationship (Jordan 1970, Monger 1972). One of the useful insights arising from a psychotherapeutic approach was an understanding of the potential for transference and counter-transference of feelings between therapist and client, between probation officer and offender. Transference refers to a client (offender), transferring feelings onto the therapist (probation officer), for example, seeing them as a 'parent' figure. Counter-transference refers to the therapist having attitudes towards the client resulting from the therapist's unconscious or unexamined feelings related to earlier events or relationships (Truax and Carkhuff 1967, Herman 1997, Rogers 2004, Schaverien 2006, Murdin 2010). It can include the invoking of past trauma experienced by the therapist on hearing the painful narratives of the client (Herman 1997).

The psychotherapeutic approach promoted the view that the quality of the therapeutic relationship and the personal qualities of the therapist were more important influences on outcomes than the theory and methods that the counsellor employed (Truax and Carkhuff 1967). Truax and Carkhuff identified these qualitative factors as 'acceptance', 'accurate empathy' and 'non-possessive warmth' (Truax and Carkhuff 1967:1). However, there were limits to the understandings offered by this approach, shaped by the culture and norms of the time (Nellis 2007). As indicated in Chapter four, the article 'Sentenced to Social Work' challenged probation officers of the time to reflect on the risk of imposing more coercive and manipulative elements of social work interventions within probation supervision (Bryant, Coker et al. 1978), through a form of paternalism and 'enforced help'.

The revival of 'rehabilitation'

The 'What Works' movement placed a strong emphasis on the use of accredited programmes aimed at tackling offending behaviour based on a cognitive behavioural approach. The adherence to a prescriptive programme manual for a time shifted the emphasis away from the significance of the relationship in promoting engagement and change. More recently, Andrews and Bonta have argued that the 'get tough' approach to offenders and increasingly punitive measures have failed to reduce criminal recidivism and that a better option for dealing with crime is to place more emphasis on rehabilitation and on approaches that adhere to the Offender Management model (OMM) (Andrews and Bonta 2010). Something of a revival in the principles of rehabilitation and the recognition of the importance of staff practices in achieving this had in fact begun towards the end of the 1990s. Rex and others have argued that people on probation are prepared to accept and even to welcome a firmly directive style on the part of supervisors, a sense of 'legitimacy' (Chapman and Hough 1998, Rex 2005), as long as it is accompanied by a demonstration of concern and respect for the person, a return perhaps to the use of 'authority' and the balancing of 'care' and 'control' (Foren and Bailey 1968, Rex 1999, Marshall and Serran 2004). Like earlier writers, Rex too believed that there was every reason to think that the quality of the relationship mattered as much in group work programmes as in one-to-one supervision.

The gradual rehabilitative 'revival' was further encouraged by a paper that emphasised the importance of staff practice and the ability to demonstrate warmth, enthusiasm, respect and likeability in work with offenders (Dowden and Andrews 2004). The term 'therapeutic alliance' used by Dowden and Andrews (2004) realigned the idea of therapy with 'treatment' in a probation context. Marshall et al. (Marshall and Serran 2004), undertook research that examined the characteristics of therapists in the treatment of sex offenders. Empathy, as a quality shown by a practitioner, appeared across all the institutions in which the research was carried out and was seen as statistically significant. The researchers indicated that this was contrary to previous claims that if a programme is consistently delivered to the same standard the therapist characteristics should not be relevant, and they recommended that therapists should pay attention to the influence of their behaviour and attempt to adopt a more empathic, warm and rewarding style (Marshall and Serran 2004). Andrews and Bonta have subsequently recommended that:

> staff should be selected partly on their ability and potential to build high quality relationships with a difficult clientele, and then be given training that further enhances these skills. (Andrews and Bonta 2010:50)

Dowden and Andrews introduced the model of 'Core Correctional Practice Skills' (CCPS), which continued to be informed by the risk, need and general responsivity principles, but reviewed the evidence from meta-analysis that identified staff characteristics and training in core skills as essential in order to ensure the maximum therapeutic impact of programmes of intervention (Dowden and Andrews 2004). Building on the CCPS model the OMM includes a staff characteristic of 'Forming and working through warm, open and enthusiastic relationships' (NOMS 2006). All of these features were examined in the Jersey study (Raynor, Ugwudike et al. 2010), which, interestingly, showed that the Jersey officers, trained in a social work model, concentrated more on the skills needed to establish and maintain relationships. However, no specific reference is made in the CCPS model or in the Jersey study to the significance of self-awareness of emotions, or of the effective management and regulation of emotion in workers

Theories of desistance

Alongside these developments in the late 1990s and early 2000s was an emergence of the criminal careers literature which discussed the wider social processes that cause people to stop offending (Rex 1999). From this has evolved models of desistance from offending as offering a more positive and maturational model of change in offenders, with desistance from crime understood not as a single event but as a process of maturation and change (Rex 1999, Farrall 2002, Maruna, Immarigeon et al. 2004, McNeill 2004, Burnett and McNeill 2005, McNeill 2006, Maruna and LeBel 2010). The general maturation of the offender is seen, in this literature, as more important than any single programme of intervention. The model takes the individual narrative of the offenders as its focus (McNeill 2009, McNeill, Raynor et al. 2010), in some contrast to the rehabilitative model which borrows from the medical model in being a top-down imposed set of ideas and constructs that are imposed on the individual in order to change and correct them. Associated with the desistance movement has been the development of strengths-based models of rehabilitation (Ward, Polaschek et al. 2006), including the 'Good Lives Model' (GLM) and the 'Better Lives Model' particularly in relation to sex offenders (Day, Casey et al. 2010). The GLM considers offender supervision from the perspective of the offender and identifies the resources and capital in their lives that can be harnessed to enable them to move away from offending (Ward, Polaschek et al. 2006, McNeill, Raynor et al. 2010, Raynor, Ugwudike et al. 2010). This model also makes connections with the significance of relationships and stresses that individuals should be understood in a holistic, integrated manner.

A recognition of the importance of the relationship was supported by the Offender Engagement Programme (OEP) (Ministry of Justice 2010, Rex 2012), established within the NOMS, which undertook research on the nature of the offender/worker relationship and reinforced the idea that one of the central components of offender management is the relationship between the offender and their offender manager. One of the pilot initiatives, entitled the Reflective Supervision Model (RSM), is looking at how middle managers and trust leaders can support practitioners in building effective relationships with service users (Ministry of Justice 2010).

Revisiting attachment theory

The desistance literature in particular highlights the importance of understanding the perspectives and feelings of the client group – the offenders. Whilst there has been research examining potential causes of crime ranging from individual pathology to environmental and social causes, the studies that focus more specifically on childhood trauma, abuse and disadvantage are less substantial. Research undertaken by Boswell on young offenders in secure institutions has highlighted how childhood trauma can be linked to later violence (Boswell 1996, Boswell 2000). Bowlby, in his work on attachment, speculated that potentially a lengthy period of maternal deprivation could be a significant cause of subsequent delinquency (Bowlby 1969, Bowlby 1978, Bowlby 1980). Attachment theory identifies that children who experience sensitive and responsive caregivers (i.e. is able to form a secure attachment to his or her caregivers) have been found to be more cooperative, cry less, explore more and be more comfortable with less familiar adults. In contrast, those who suffered sexual, emotional or physical abuse, rejection, lack of support, emotional coldness or disruptive experiences with their parents in childhood are much more likely to be insecurely attached, to have problems relating to others in adolescence and adulthood and to be more likely to suffer from emotional loneliness (Moriarty, Stough et al. 2001, Rich 2006).

One area in which contemporary probation workers have retained aspects of this approach in both assessment and intervention is in sexual offending. Recent work that uses attachment theory in the understanding of some sexual and violent offenders (Renn 2000, Rich 2006, Ansbro 2008) has highlighted the significance of early damage causing later criminality. Marshall and Barbaree's model (Marshall and Barbaree 1990) refers to attachment theory, and Pat

Crittenden has led the field in making the links between early childhood abuse and deprivation and later sexual offending in adolescence and adulthood (Crittenden and Claussen 2000). There is a growing body of research evidence that suggests that significant areas of impulsive (generally male) offending behaviour such as violence and more controlling forms of sexual and domestic violence can be traced to the process of the 'acting out' of unprocessed and unresolved feelings from childhood and a failure of attachment to the original caregiver(s) (Seidler 1998, Dayton 2000, Dobash, Dobash et al. 2000). There is evidence that male child sex offenders experience high levels of emotional loneliness, fear of intimacy and isolation (Ward, Polaschek et al. 2006) (Ward, Polaschek et al. 2006:194), and Marshall was the first to make links between intimacy deficits and sexual offending (Marshall 1989). Ansbro makes a plea for the return of the use of attachment theory in work with offenders and suggests it has congruence with theories of desistance in which offenders are encouraged to 'rewrite' the narrative scripts of their lives away from offending; she too claims that the relationship between worker and offender is pivotal in this (Ansbro 2008). Renn also provides a powerful example of the effectiveness of attachment theory used in the case of a man with a history of violence and alcohol abuse (Renn 2000).

Conclusion

This chapter has offered a brief overview of some of the historical and contemporary understandings of emotion and its connection with reason and decision-making. Links have been built with an understanding of gender and crime and the ways in which criminology, as a science, has tended to minimise or devalue the significance of an understanding of emotions within crime and criminality. This approach has neglected the importance of emotions in practice and generally favoured large-scale quantitative criminological studies over small-scale qualitative processes, in furthering an understanding of causes and examples of criminality. The renewed interest in relationships and methods of offender engagement within the National Offender Management Service offers a platform for a study of these emotional skills.

3
Diversity, Power and Emotion

Practice example

Malcolm is a 22-year-old white male convicted of indecent exposure to women in the park near to his home, and of being verbally threatening and abusive to one young woman. He lives with his parents and one older sibling. Malcolm has mild learning difficulties, suffers with a skin disorder and has not worked since leaving school. He has been sentenced to a community order with a requirement to attend the Community Sex Offending Groupwork Programme (C-SOGP). The female group work facilitator on the C-SOGP programme undertook the initial assessment of Malcolm and is aware of his anxiety about talking in the group in front of other people and of his fear of ridicule because of his skin disorder and his lack of confidence. She recognises that he has offended against women, and that she could be, or become, a target of his behaviour. As a male Malcolm is abusing his power in relation to women. However, as someone with diversity issues relating to his health and learning difficulties, which affect his confidence, his employment opportunities and render him at a disadvantage in the eyes of his peers, he is also quite vulnerable. Malcolm needs to be encouraged to feel safe enough to begin to talk about his feelings, his behaviour and his attitudes towards women. The worker(s) need to handle both of these positions and maintain a balance that meets the learning needs of Malcolm and other group members whilst also protecting the integrity and authority of the group facilitators. The female worker in particular needs to feel supported by her male co-worker and able to assert her authority in the group work setting with an all-male offending group. The facilitators ultimately have the power to determine whether Malcolm can continue in the group although he has some power to potentially undermine and destabilise the female group worker.

Key learning points

- Criminal justice practitioners benefit from having the emotional literacy to understand both the potential and the actual workings of diversity, power and emotion in situations such as this
- It is more common for female practitioners to value and practice with emotional literacy than their male colleagues and managers although both genders have the capacity to develop this skill
- Female practitioners have authority as workers but may feel powerless when working in a predominately male-dominated hierarchical organisation and with male offenders who may exhibit misogyny
- Offenders can be vulnerable as well as abusive

Introduction

Diversity is addressed as a principle within statements of objectives for criminal justice organisations, with targets set for policy and practice initiatives. This chapter examines some of the evidence for linking the concept of 'diversity' to the continuing discrimination and disadvantage of certain groups in society and how these processes are held in place by issues of power and emotion. Although 'race' remains a very important diversity issue in terms of the continuing disadvantage of black and minority ethnic people as victims, offenders and staff, it was gender that emerged from the research for this book as being of particular significance in relation to emotions and emotional literacy. There is evidence that gender effects who holds power in terms of legislation, policy and management, and in terms of who are the people most likely to offend in society. There are also gendered implications for the operation of emotional literacy. This chapter reflects on some of the ways in which emotional literacy is understood and practiced in a criminal justice system organised and managed predominately by men, for a predominately male offender group, but with female staff in a majority at grass-roots practice in the probation service and in voluntary sector organisations.

Diversity

Since the mid-1970s, debates on ethics and values in the criminal justice system have incorporated an increasingly complex agenda of diversity, initially framed as 'equality of opportunity' and 'anti-oppressive practice' (Thompson 2006), then as 'valuing difference' (Knight, Dominey et al. 2008) and more recently through the lens of human rights (Gelsthorpe and McIvor 2007, Canton 2009). These debates identify an understanding of the issues of diversity and discrimination as of fundamental importance to the values underpinning criminal justice practice, given that the negative impact of individual and institutional discrimination on the rights and liberty of both offenders and victims can be profound, as evidenced from research and inquiries (Knight, Dominey et al. 2008). Unexamined and prejudicial feelings towards any particular group within society different from themselves is likely to limit the capacity of the worker to value these differences, express empathy and demonstrate the skills of emotional literacy with individuals from these groups.

The evidence for continuing discrimination and disadvantage in contemporary British society is considerable. Statistical evidence is available through a range of sources, in particular the first Triennial Review by the Equality and Human Rights Commission (EHRC), 'How Fair is Britain' (Equality and Human Rights Commission 2010), the Marmot Review (Marmot 2010) and the 'The Spirit Level', which pulls together a wide range of research from many different sources to identify the differences in, for example, health inequalities and career opportunities between people (Wilkinson and Pickett 2010). The Spirit Level highlights how rates of imprisonment and of mental illness can be five times higher in the most unequal compared to the most equal societies (Wilkinson and Pickett 2010:176). Murder rates are also likely to be higher. These reports and other recent literature identify ways in which British society has been changing since the introduction of legislation to outlaw discrimination over the last 30 years (Bagihole 2009). The most recent piece of anti-discrimination legislation is the Equality Act (2010) which brings together all of the different areas of legislation in what are now referred to as the 'protected characteristics' of; age, disability, gender, race and ethnicity, religion or belief, sexual orientation and transgender status (Home Office 2010). Legislation has not only progressively widened to include other groups to whom legal protection is now afforded, but also developed a wider conception of what discrimination can be, including the concept of indirect discrimination (Equality and Human rights Commission 2010).

However, some areas of discrimination and disadvantage continue to be afforded a higher profile in criminal justice policy than others, for example, there is an abundance of policies on 'race', gender and age (in relation to youth, less so in relation to older offenders), whilst issues of sexual orientation, disability and class have received less attention. Of particular relevance to this book, given the gendered associations of emotion (see Chapter 2), are the theories of masculinity and crime that have evolved from explorations by feminist criminologists of the gendered nature of crime (Smart 1977, Messerschmidt 1997, Buckley 1999, Gelsthorpe 2002, Cowburn 2005, Heidensohn 2006, Petrillo 2007). These theories have identified the particular characteristics of being male in this society that lead to greater criminality amongst men; approximately 80% of all arrests and court sanctions are for men (Ministry of Justice 2011), and the highest rate of offending for the most serious (indictable criminal offences) is among 17-year-old young men (Office for National Statistics 2012). Men commit serious violent crime and are also the primary victims of violent crime, in much greater numbers than women (Wykes and Welsh 2009). Men commit the majority of sexual crimes and the greatest proportion of these offences is committed against women. According to Home Office statistics, of 14,449 recorded rapes in 2005/06, 92% were against women. In terms of domestic violence, whilst women are occasionally violent, it is overwhelmingly men who use violence against female partners (Dobash, Dobash et al. 2000, Heidensohn 2002). Research evidence suggests that sexual and violent offending is supported by patriarchy or male dominance in social relations (Brownmiller 1975, Dworkin 1981, Silvestri and Crowther-Dowey 2008).

Other protected characteristics have, belatedly, been brought to the attention of public-sector agencies through examples of discrimination in terms of disability (Independent Police Complaints Commission 2009), sexuality and sexual orientation (Groombridge 2006, Chakraborti and Garland 2009), religion (Spalek 2002, Chakraborti and Garland 2009) and age (Gelsthorpe and McIvor 2007; Knight, Dominey et al. 2008). Class is not a protected characteristic under the Equality Act 2010 but is identified by a number of writers as a significant diversity issue and area of discrimination within criminal justice (Gelsthorpe and McIvor 2007; Knight, Dominey et al. 2008).

Intersectionality

In a challenge to the 'hierarchies' that have evolved around issues of discrimination, the diversity debate has begun to incorporate the concept of 'intersectionality', which refers to multiple discriminations and in particular arises from feminist research identifying the different inequalities and identities that affect women's lives (Bagihole 2009, Seidler 2010). As this theory highlights, inequalities intersect in complex and varied ways (Bagihole 2009). In terms of criminal justice, gender is a diversity strand that intersects with other identities to create complex patterns of advantage and disadvantage. For example, the majority of defendants through the criminal justice system are male, white, working class and young (although there is a disproportionate number of black males and females in prison (Ministry of Justice 2011)), and, as explored later in this chapter, the majority of leadership and management roles within criminal justice are occupied by white men (Equality and Human Rights Commission 2011).

Power

What is generally missing from the debates about discrimination and disadvantage is an understanding of the emotions that can hold prejudice and discriminatory beliefs and attitudes in place and the differential ways in which power operates to reinforce these feelings and attitudes. If practitioners working within the criminal justice system are expected to treat offenders, victims and witnesses with decency and respect, this requires them to have some understanding of the way in which discrimination and disadvantage impacts on different groups within society and the way in which power operates to hold this in place. It requires them to understand the strong emotional attachments that people, including themselves, may have in maintaining the status quo, of resisting change in either the structures around them or their own personal belief patterns. Thompson's PCS[1] model has been used to teach generations of probation students to understand how power and discrimination can operate within three domains: the personal (P), the cultural (C) and the social or structural (S) (Thompson 2006). These three domains are very similar to the first three domains of social reality identified by Layder and set out in the introduction to this book (psychobiographic, situated activity and social settings: Layder 2006). Thompson talks about the different amounts of influence and power that prevail within each of these domains or levels from relatively minor at the personal level, to highly significant at the structural or social level. However, whilst this model provides a useful framework for understanding the operation of power, it does not explore the more subtle forms of power identified by Lukes or the emotional attachments people have to the maintenance of the status quo. Lukes argues that power should be understood as a three-dimensional intermingling of forces, rather than a one-dimensional process (Lukes 2005).

Lukes' third dimension of power identifies a deeper analysis, one that incorporates the power to influence wishes and beliefs and to make people want things against their own self-interest (Lukes 2005). Whilst Lukes makes no reference to emotions, it is in this third dimension that the power of the emotions to resist change, to accept organisational constraints or to hold on to long-held belief systems is the most pertinent. So, for example, female administrators in a largely male-dominated organisation may embrace and own the title of 'girls' from their male bosses, despite its implications of childishness and junior status, because it allows a level of camaraderie and humour to exist which any challenge to this label or their subordinated status risks destroying. This is an example of the complex ways in which we 'buy into' the status quo and how women, in this example, operating in the domain of 'situated activity' (relationships) (Layder 2006) are powerfully affected by the sexism inherent in these forms of hierarchical relationships, which they have internalised.

Who holds the power?

In their report *Sex and Power* the EHRC provides statistical evidence for the way in which gender continues to shape the demographics of who holds power in

British society, with white men continuing to occupy the majority of leadership and decision-making positions (Equality and Human rights Commission 2011). This report, supported by research undertaken by Silvestri and Crowther-Dowey (2008), confirms the criminal justice system as comprising agencies that are strikingly gendered. In terms of where the power lies in criminal justice decision-making, 77.6% of members of parliament (which constitutes the legislative body of the United Kingdom) and 83% of the judiciary are male (Silvestri and Crowther-Dowey 2008). In terms of policing, 79% of staff across all ranks in the police service are male (Silvestri and Crowther-Dowey 2008). Within the prison service, male officers outnumber females significantly (66% of total employees are male).

There is a considerable body of literature that identifies the ongoing limitations on women performing to their full potential in the workplace despite the evidence of their success in education (Itzin and Newman 1995, Bagihole 2009, Equality and Human Rights Commission 2011). Whilst men do not outnumber women in all the agencies, nevertheless, the overall development of criminal justice policy, for example, within the judiciary and the police (Silvestri and Crowther-Dowey 2008), is male dominated. The fact that 90.45% of all administrative support staff within the probation service is female is just one example of how women continue to occupy roles that are traditionally viewed as 'servicing' more senior staff and are generally less well paid (Silvestri and Crowther-Dowey 2008).

The probation service, whilst historically a majority male service (Annison 2007, Knight 2007), has seen the staff composition change quite radically since the 1970s. Women now constitute approximately two-thirds of the practitioner workforce (Ministry of Justice 2007). However, men continue to have a higher representation in senior management in the probation service, occupying 52.5% of chief officer ranks, 54.55% of deputy chief officers and 54.29% of assistant chief officers (Ministry of Justice 2007). Women have increased their representation at all senior ranks within the service quite significantly, but this is still not representative of the overall workforce and suggests the continuation of a glass ceiling (Davidson and Cooper 1992, Ryam and Haslam 2005).

The EHRC report acknowledges that the proportion of female to male workers in the probation service is comparable with the public-sector average of 65.2% female staff (Equality and Human Rights Commission 2011). This demographic context poses some interesting questions about the motivation of people to work with offenders. Research evidence indicates that women are generally more likely to be attracted to work that involves helping and enabling people to change, and that despite the more punitive rhetoric this is still the main motivation for people joining the probation service. Women are also less driven by financial and status incentives than men (Knight 2007). These findings were confirmed by work undertaken by Annison and Eadie in examining the views of trainee probation officers during and post qualifying training (Annison, Eadie et al. 2008). The statistical evidence is that men are more drawn to the uniformed organisations (e.g. policing and prison service).

Emotional attachments to values

A small-scale research study undertaken with recently qualified police constables, who had received extensive teaching on matters of diversity and difference on their university-based foundation degree course prior to qualifying, showed them to be unable or unwilling to resist the power of the police operational subculture when starting their first jobs. This culture undermined and to some extent mocked many of the 'ideals' promoted by the training (Alcott 2012). Alcott argues that despite the introduction of the Initial Police Learning and Development Programme (IPLDP) with seven learning requirements, one of which included

responding to human diversity and social diversity,

the strength of the operational subculture overruled this new learning (Alcott 2012:7). It seems that the police service in this study had underestimated the importance of the emotional attachments built within police teams and subcultures which undermined the training for its new recruits aimed at helping them to understand, and be committed to, principles of diversity and equality.

Gender and emotion

The most significant diversity issue that arose from the research for this book was that of gender. Whilst emotions are ubiquitous, assumptions are often made that they are more commonly represented within the female and can signal weakness and irrationality, and that both men and women aspire to control their emotions in the pursuit of rationality. Perhaps associated with this assumption is the evidence that women in general are considered to be more emotionally literate than men (Ciarrochi, Hynes et al. 2005). A number of writers have identified a process of gender socialisation through which they argue women are more likely than men to see the significance of emotional connections with others (Miller and Stiver 1997, Kram and McCullom 1998, Cherniss and Goleman 2001). Baron-Cohen identified that girls learn expressive language including more extensive and earlier vocabularies, reading abilities and word fluency than boys (Baron-Cohen 2003). Girls as young as one year have been found to react with more empathy and distress than their same-age male counterparts (Fischer 2000:30), which suggests a mutual dynamic between the ability to articulate feelings and empathy. Other research has found that women are generally perceived to have a greater emotional vocabulary than men and to have greater facility in using it (Langford 1997, Bunting 2005, De Coster and Zito 2010). Research by Glenberg et al. found that women understand sentences about sad events with greater facility than men and men understand sentences about angry events with greater facility than women (Glenberg, Webster et al. 2009). It is suggested that women have a greater tendency than men to have the personal and interpersonal skills to engage in relational learning and that collaborative and nurturing behaviour is also more often reinforced by women (Cherniss and Goleman 2001). However, Cherniss and Goleman, in their work on emotional intelligence in the workplace, devote only two pages to the implications of gender in developing emotional competence and emotional intelligence through relationships at work.

Fischer argues that men are, in fact, just as emotional as women, citing examples of male behaviour when watching sport, when angry, when trying to avoid embarrassment and so on and instead challenges the persistence of the dichotomy between the stereotype of emotional women and unemotional men (Fischer 2000). It also seems that once men choose to join organisations such as the probation service most of them are as likely as women to value the significance of emotional literacy (Knight 2007, Knight 2012). There was some evidence provided by the research respondents of a paucity of emotional vocabularies (alexithymia – Muller 2000) in male offenders, particularly those charged with domestic violence and of the work undertaken by them to enhance these emotional vocabularies in order to enable change in their offending behaviour. There was also some evidence of female practitioners finding some of their male colleagues to be less emotionally supportive and aware than their female colleagues (Knight 2012).

Modernity, the focus on 'hard' technical issues at the expense of the 'softer' philosophical and ethical ones (Dyson and Brown 2006), has tended to afford a greater superiority to reason and rational thinking than to emotional expression. It has also favoured a male model of being 'grown up' in preference to a female one (Steiner 1997). As Steiner argues, in modern society power is afforded to those in control of people and finance, who are often men; the model of a powerful person is generally a male one. Whilst it could be argued that emotional literacy is a vital component of personal power (Steiner 1997:3), it is not yet valued in the same way as other forms of autonomy and power in the workplace. Some emotional expressions are associated negatively with women (e.g. crying, being anxious, fearful (Katz 1999, Fischer 2000)) whilst other emotions such as anger, more commonly associated with men, rather than being seen as 'being emotional', are viewed as instrumental in achieving a goal. It is argued that women may cry rather than externalise the anger they are actually feeling and men may get angry rather than get in touch with feelings of vulnerability, humiliation or fear (Katz 1999). It is also suggested that it is often these emotional qualities that make women very effective managers, although other attributes such as assertiveness and self-confidence, more generally associated with men, are the ones most likely to lead to promotion in the workplace (Ryam and Haslam 2005). This may be one of the reasons why, despite the majority female workforce, the management of the probation service is still unrepresentatively male compared to the probation workforce as a whole.

Research findings

The three broad conceptual frameworks of gender, emotion and crime and their interrelationship have been theorised through different academic disciplines (philosophy, sociology, psychology, criminology, feminist research, etc.). However, apart from some contributions emerging from the second wave of feminist writings, in particular on gender and crime (e.g. Silvestri and Crowther-Dowey 2008), they have rarely been brought together in one place. The research findings highlighted some interesting perspectives and issues on this interrelationship and what gender means for practitioners who aspire to be emotionally literate, in terms of the offender population, the staffing and the decision-making within the criminal justice system.

The research participants largely reflected the current gender balance within the probation service, with 19 women and 9 men in the individual interviews (67% female) (Ministry of Justice 2007; Silvestri and Crowther-Dowey 2008). This was a fortuitous but unplanned outcome; the research participants were all volunteers for the study. The balance was more even in the focus group with three men and four women (57% female). Nineteen of the 28 research participants interviewed thought that gender was a significant factor in emotional literacy.

Men and emotion

The majority of the comments that related to gender were framed as women understanding the importance of emotion and the interconnectedness between people and of men tending to struggle more with these concepts. There was some frustration felt predominantly, but not solely, by female research participants at their male colleagues, with examples provided of male staff failing to understand the emotional content of a situation and also compounding difficulties for female staff endeavouring to deal with emotional issues. Others (both male and female research participants) considered that in a general sense

men (both staff and offenders) had more difficulty in understanding or expressing their emotions.

> He can't let you know that he is at breaking point. (Mary)

> They're men so they're not awfully good on the emotional front. (Amy)

Some of the frustrations expressed by female research participants included
male colleagues being unable to do more than one task at a time, being ego-
centric and not being good team players. There is some research evidence that
suggests women are generally better at multitasking (e.g. Paton and Dempster
2002). One respondent, Karen, gave a number of examples of how she found
some of her male colleagues to be both unaware and lacking in emotional
sensitivity:

> Some of my male colleagues … that I have got at the moment, I find very
> difficult sometimes … there seems to be an ego in some people and there
> seems to be … an inability to actually to do more than one task at once,
> they really seem to struggle with thinking and planning ahead, all that sort
> of thing, you know, 'I can do one thing at a time and I can do it at this pace
> and I won't or can't do it any other way.' (Karen)

Karen gives a further example of a difficult piece of behaviour from an offender
that was subsequently compounded by the lack of awareness and support from
her male co-worker:

> So often … men just do not see it the way we see it. I … came out of this
> debriefing session furious, at the break. I did the opening round and the guy
> (male colleague) said 'how're you feeling about being in this session today'
> and he (the offender) started going on about 'that bitch, my probation
> officer, she's a bitch' and I thought 'oh' … and my male colleague didn't do
> a thing, he just sort of stood there … (afterwards) I said to him, what did
> you think of that? And he said 'oh well he's an idiot isn't he?' But he didn't
> realise the impact that was having on me, and he said 'oh well didn't you
> feel supported?' and I said well actually 'no, I didn't feel supported'. (Karen)

The next respondent, Michael, also makes reference to some male colleagues
having 'egos' which again seems to mean being overly confident about their
own abilities to the detriment of being able to hear the perspective of others:

> About me … my persona. I don't get on very well with men … It's egos
> with men … bloody egos … that get in the way and I'm aware of it … and

I suppose it makes it more difficult for me to work with men (probation officers). (Michael)

Sandy, a female respondent, who was looking for emotional support from a male colleague after a particularly draining session with an offender, mirrored this experience. She eventually recognised that only a female colleague could provide the support she needed:

> Recently I had a guy who was exposed to abuse, it was over a long period of time, but it was about an hour and he was telling me … it was really horrendous and afterwards I was exhausted and I said to my (male) colleague that I wanted to talk about what had gone on and … about how it made me feel, and I knew the next day that I needed to talk to one of the women in the team, … because I think that it impacted on me differently … and I think my female colleagues would hear me differently … overnight, … I went home and I had a shower and I know that's indicative of washing it away and I wanted to come back in and talk about what I felt and actually my male colleague came in and said, 'well actually I don't think I got it right with you last night' … and we talked about that and I said 'no I don't think you did' and I said this is what I would have liked and so we're on that level. (Sandy)

A slightly different issue, also highlighted by Karen relates to discomfort in a male worker about discussion in a group on emotional matters:

> I was working with another … sex offender facilitator on a domestic violence programme and one of the men said something, 'that's too deep' because we had gone a little too … because we had started talking about insecurities. (Karen)

This suggests that the male colleague was anxious about exploring some emotionally painful and difficult issues arising from domestic violence. However, it is not necessarily just the male workers who find this emotional work difficult, particularly with the most serious violent offences:

> Another officer told me she was out of her depth (a date rape offence) … you need a lot of support, you have to learn through mistakes. (Tess)

Sophie highlighted a different pressure that this culture could place on male staff. The idea of criminal justice work being 'tough' and 'hard' and therefore 'men's' work also promotes a view that men have 'thicker skins' and are unlikely to be as distressed by emotionally painful situations as their female colleagues:

> I think the other thing is sometimes, another thing I want to say is, it's different for our male colleagues, ... there are generally speaking more women than men and I think sometimes there is a tendency to think, we'll give it to a bloke, we'll give it somebody that hasn't got, do you know what I mean? because they're not going to be as affected by that, so I think there would be that guilt for all of us. (Sophie)

To some extent this is supported by the emotion language used by the male and female research participants in which, marginally, the men provided less evidence of feeling distressed or affected by the work than their female colleagues. However, Michael expressed the view that as a male worker he was able to identify with some of the men he worked with, demonstrating empathy and feeling comfortable with this:

> It needs people ... to know it's alright to get alongside a criminal ... someone who's committed horrible things ... giving people permission to be empathic and also for men ... to be able to identify with some of the thinking that these people have ... often as a man I can identify with the thinking but to be okay with that. (Michael)

Michael's comments suggest a more complex picture than just that of a gender divide around emotional literacy. They identify a more fluid or postmodern position, with the potential for both men and women to be emotionally literate or illiterate. Karen, despite her frustrations exemplified earlier with some of her male colleagues, also understands the need for male workers particularly in the group work programmes:

> Yes, but I'm not saying that all women should do this work because we need the men. (Karen)

Jack and Jack, in their research with lawyers, identified that most boys through childhood learning, gain a vision suited for a world of advocacy, stoic detachment, autonomy and suspension of emotional judgement (Jack and Jack 1996). There may be a risk that even the most emotionally literate men in the probation service will still, because of their gender, be stereotyped as more able to undertake the 'tough' work of controlling and managing high-risk offenders than the 'soft' work of emotional literacy, and that this 'tough' work is the most important.

David offers some analysis of why he thinks that men might struggle in the emotional arena. Whilst he is referring here specifically to men as perpetrators of domestic violence, he is also expressing it as an issue that he believes is common for men in general:

> Men have a fear of expressing their own vulnerability. They may show violence outside the home and within ... it is gender connected. (David)

Whilst much of the research on domestic violence indicates that men use their anger very effectively to gain and maintain power and control over women, David is suggesting that to change this requires a much more in-depth exploration of their emotional world than merely addressing the anger and control (Dobash, Dobash et al. 2000).

As demonstrated earlier, whilst some of the female research participants expressed some anger with 'unaware' or emotionally illiterate male colleges, two research participants were keen to state that in their experience there was no significant difference between the emotional literacy of probation staff (male and female), and that in their view it was not an innate quality specific to women (Geoff and Heather). This to some degree accords with earlier research that suggested that whilst men as a group might be deterred from joining the probation service because of its perceived 'helping and enabling' role, once particular men had made the decision to choose this career, they are as likely as women to have and to value these skills (Knight 2007). Some of this is clearly influenced by the view of these staff that they were in a 'helping' profession, where emotional literacy was of significance:

> I think one of my male colleagues who ... is absolutely spot on emotionally, because ... the stereotype that women ... might be better, at emotions or safer with emotions, I really do think that that is a socialised process, I don't think that is an innate process at all. (Heather)

Many of the female research participants described their appreciation at being able to talk about feelings with their colleagues and friends and saw their male colleagues as less able to do this. A number commented that male workers might be willing to express some emotion in a one-to-one situation with a colleague but not in a group (Tony, Angela, Sandy, Janet, Maggie, Jai and Heather). The prevailing culture of masculinity seems to inhibit men, in particular, from viewing emotional discussions as appropriate in a work context (Cordery and Whitehead 1992). However, some of the female workers also recognised the importance of trying to maintain a perspective that did not lead them to generalise about all men, from having worked with a few who had very deviant thinking and behaviour patterns:

> There is a tendency to tar all men with the same brush. (Indira)

> But I do try and sort of keep it in perspective, not all men are like that. (Maggie)

Women and emotion

A number of both male and female research participants identified 'being emotional' as a negative female stereotype, and as having sexist connotations. Those who spoke about such female stereotypes identified that negative labelling had sometimes had the effect of making the woman (worker) feel that she had been overreacting or could make her feel 'put down' or considered to be less knowledgeable.

As just one example, Amy, expresses a view about how her gender has made her feel through more than 30 years of working for the probation service in relation to her identity:

Invisibility is a road that women travel down. (Amy)

And in relation to her sexuality:

I remember a middle-aged officer told me to 'be careful what you wear when you go into prisons' there will be 250 eyes trained on you when you go on the wing' ... masturbation fodder for those men. (Amy)

Amy felt she had had to contend with a lack of recognition or status compared with her male colleagues, whilst also be the recipient of unwelcome sexual attention in certain contexts, in particular prisons. Other research participants also made reference to the way they considered that women working in specific areas of probation practice, including prison work, and with sexual and domestic violence offenders in the community, faced particular challenges that were different from their male colleagues.

This negativity sits alongside the view that women in general are more emotionally literate than men (Ciarrochi, Hynes et al. 2005). There is evidence that because of gender socialisation women have a greater tendency than men to see the potential of growth in connection with others and to have the personal and interpersonal skills to engage in such relational learning (Jack and Jack 1996; Cherniss and Goleman 2001). Associated with this is seen to be the willingness of women, more often than men, to express their vulnerability, to demonstrate a range of feelings, to actively listen, to nurture and to collaborate which is behaviour that is more often reinforced in girls and women than in boys and men (Cherniss and Goleman 2001:273).

A number of research participants expressed views about women in general being more emotionally literate than men. The following from a male respondent:

I think women are far more in touch, kind of in-tune with their emotions, and they deal with them so much ... more appropriately than men do, well that's how I feel, as men we are told, as my Father would say, you know, boys don't cry, and my Father was very much a man's man and ... so was his Dad and so on I suppose, but for me and I've got a son myself and I'm very different with my son and actually I'm very affectionate with him and he is with me and if he is upset, I can tell when he is upset and he will talk about what's going on, but we were unable to do that so much as kids and stuff ..., well, I think over time that will change, men are becoming more in-tune with their emotions and stuff ... again when I talk to a lot of offenders I would say that, you know I try to understand, you know. (Damien)

Damien's comments resonate with other research (Cherniss and Goleman 2001), and in particular the work of Hochschild, and subsequent writers building on her work, which has exposed the role of women in undertaking the majority of the emotion work in both the home and the workplace (Hochschild 1983, Ciarrochi, Forgas et al. 2001, Bunting 2005, Garey and Hansen 2011). There is a continuing association of women with a caring role; women are thought to be natural caregivers (Rivas 2011) and Damien is reflecting this in his recall of his family life as a child. His description of his father as a 'man's man' implies someone who is strong, tough, in control and probably silent on emotional matters. He is also describing how he has made the decision to interrupt this generational pattern and behave in a different way towards his son and also towards the offenders he works with.

Pat demonstrates some ambivalence and again reflects a more fluid picture:

I suppose society views women as much better listeners, there are more women in probation nowadays than men ... I would say that women are better listeners, maybe not quite so judgmental as men, you know, but then there are men that can listen and men that can't. (Pat)

Only one female respondent expressed some negative views about her own ability to recognise or value emotions:

S. 'it gets in the way, this is an awful thing to say isn't it, and it takes time up.'
C: 'So for you it is a negative thing?'
S: 'Yes it is I'm afraid.'

(Sophie)

Another respondent, Sandy, expressed a slightly cautious view that maybe emotional literacy could be taught but concluded that those workers who had had to address powerlessness and identity issues for themselves related, for example, to being members of oppressed or marginalised groups were more likely to have acquired these skills. This does suggest a view of emotional literacy as a learnt skill as much, if not more than, an innate skill based on gender:

> I think they could be if they got the training, I think most of the men come in and they haven't had the training and I think ... I don't know, not all women have either, but I think somewhere along the line, because the world isn't constructed for us, we have to learn how to manage it differently and all those rights that I think some men have, albeit they don't know it, they come up against it when they are dealing with emotions. I also think that, because in our team there are two Asian women and myself, who is a lesbian, we come with other packages really, so what we come with is a difference that allows us to engage differently again now, that's not to say that everyone, lesbian or Asian will be able to do that but it does seem to be. (Sandy)

Impact of the work on male and female staff

Here Tony, as a male treatment manager, explains his awareness of the impact of undertaking sex offending work, on women in his team:

> Let me see if I can give you an example. When we work with the men ... we ask them to describe their target or who might be a target for them and they would describe people in a particular way ... might be boys, other men, girls, or maybe women ... they will say ... the object of my fantasy or who've I've offended against ... or abnormally sort of fitted this sort of image ... petite or cherubic or large breasted or whatever it might be ... or wearing particular clothes etc. And in supervision and as a team, we have team supervisions and team meetings ...that's a clear point that must be difficult for ...particularly the women in the team ...because most of the men have offended against girls or women, not all of them but the majority have offended against women ... two thirds. (Tony)

Tony is suggesting that the impact of, in particular, working with sex offenders and domestic violence abusers is disproportionately felt by female workers who he considered were more likely to be the target of the often misogynistic beliefs, attitudes and fantasies of these men. For some staff, particularly women, in working with domestic violence perpetrators, there was a sense of feeling attacked or targeted because of their gender. Six of the research participants, (five women and one man) made reference to the particular issues associated with working with domestic violence perpetrators (Howard, Kim, Angela, Sophie, Gill, Karen), with a number identifying this form of work as more difficult than work with sex offenders because of the particularly powerful misogyny attached to this crime. For some research participants this issue increased the strength of their emotional response to this work:

> I find it more frustrating working with other groups e.g. domestic violence. Surprise I suppose ... in terms of some people's kind of like schemas ... really entrenched. (Kim)

> I find domestic violence the most challenging very, much, much harder. (Sophie)

> Yes, the other thing that I'm not so keen on in my role is the impact that I feel working with domestic violence men ... they are not my chosen area to work with and it is like ... I have to do that because of the needs of the service, and I ... personally I find it, I feel quite attacked, I find it, in the group, in a way that doesn't seem to happen with sex offenders. (Karen)

For others the gendered nature of crimes such as domestic violence and sexual offending linked to their own or others' experiences had made this work too difficult to contemplate without shutting down their emotions in some way. Research participants who identified themselves or someone close to them as former victims of, in this case, domestic violence, indicated how hard they found working with male perpetrators of this crime:

> If you had to work with some of the offenders we have, it is very, very hard to separate, you know, if you are working with a sex offender and you've been sexually abused or you know somebody who has, it can be difficult, domestic violence, it is absolutely massive, you know, it is very difficult to kind of you know how you do that, I think you become immune. (Gill)

Sophie views domestic violence offenders as more entrenched in their views and therefore more difficult to work with; she also acknowledges her own victim status:

> I think it's because generally speaking, most domestic violence perpetrators are men and I am a woman ... and I'm a victim ... so I'd rather supervise a sex offender any day than a domestic violence person ... only because I think ... I think I'm going to have less impact on very, very entrenched attitudes, I'm not suggesting that sex offenders don't have entrenched attitudes, however, I've got things that I can do to sex offenders, you know what I mean ... I've got constraints on them, if I can't change their thinking, I can certainly monitor their behaviour ... that's what I feel anyway. (Sophie)

The potential for this group of men to provoke very strong feelings of anger, particularly in the female workers, was highlighted by Karen who, despite these feelings, demonstrates a degree of self-regulation such that she maintained communication with the group and challenged the man concerned:

> I do a domestic violence group ..., less often than sex offenders ... but I had an experience with a domestic violence group last week and frankly I could have, ... marched that man out of that room and said, go outside, you are a pig, and that was because he was behaving in the session like he behaves in his life generally ..., he was, ... everything, very, very rigid thinking, very misogynistic ... 'I tell her, I tell her, I tell her, I tell her' so that made me really angry, so I said to him, ... 'where's the discussion?' and just posed that and then brought in the group and they were saying, 'you've got to listen to her man, you've got to listen to her'. (Karen)

Janet expresses a great deal of anger about their misogyny:

> Yes, sometimes I can really hate the way they actually use women as sex symbols, pieces of meat and talk about them in such a derogatory way ... you know, it makes you angry. (Janet)

She goes on to give examples of this:

> A lot of the time, very minimising, denial and blaming the woman, 'it's all her fault, she just goes on and on ... I earn the money, her job is to look after the kids, it's nothing, it's not hard work' and ... think a lot of the time people use them like, you know, they talk to you as if you were a piece of ... material object, it is theirs to be owned. (Janet)

The targeting of the female staff in particular is undoubtedly one way in which male offenders try to regain some power and control in a relatively uncomfortable and powerless situation for them. Sandy expresses similar concerns about being targeted as a female worker by male offenders but describes her strategy for dealing with this:

> I mean I used to find it in prison, when I ran groups there, you were often the lone female worker so you'd have two male colleagues and eight to ten offenders, and you always get the men who, where there are issues about women, you represent them all so there is all that really subtle putting you down and that used to drive me mad and I used to say to them, 'what is it you're doing?' and then they get really irritable, really angry with you and I say 'this isn't okay' and then they get ... I used to think that, they're not going to put me

down and they're doing what they've always done and trying to take control over me and that's the one bit I won't let happen in a group. (Sandy)

Howard, rather than finding the work intimidating, was just clear that he thoroughly disliked men who had committed domestic violence offences:

I hate men who commit domestic violence ... I'd rather concentrate on sex offenders but I'm available in emergency ... always willing to help if I possibly can...I just don't like overbearing misogynistic bullies and that's what the majority of men who perpetrate DV are ... fundamentally I just don't like them – nasty unpleasant people. If I can avoid them I will. (Howard)

The female staff were endeavouring to hold onto their emotional literacy whilst under attack, and on occasions feeling unsupported by their male facilitator colleague(s). Karen identifies a further gender difference in the way members of the group respond to the male and female facilitators:

I think if you're, ... the woman in the group, if the female facilitator says something, not all men, but ... you will get one, it is usually one in the group who challenges you, and says 'no that's not right, I don't agree with that' whereas they will be very accepting from a male colleague. I feel it is much easier for the men working with men who have done domestic violence to ... not become confrontational, but to try and get them to think in a different way, and I, ... I've really, sometimes it affects my mood and I ... if I didn't have to do domestic violence work I wouldn't do. (Karen)

She expresses concern that in some group work situations the male offenders were more inclined to accept a challenge from a male worker than they were from a female worker and she was unhappy that her male colleagues were not always sensitive to this or willing to 'back up' the female worker's position. Karen saw that on occasions the ability of the male workers to build rapport with the male offenders, for example, by wearing a Manchester United football scarf, left the female worker feeling marginalised. These examples from Karen highlight not just the limitations, as she perceives them, of the emotional literacy of some of her colleagues, but also the direct impact it has on her in terms of her own working practices.

Indira explains the particular issues for female staff, when subtle forms of sexism are expressed by offenders in the group, in deciding whether to respond and how. None of this is part of the formal protocol for the programme; it requires judgement, emotional clarity and an unpacking of the sexism:

Just challenging them ... behaviours that might not be as overt ... they are covert and subtle. It made me feel uncomfortable when J said 'so and so will be joining us soon' ... the men quickly said 'women are always on the phone nattering'. You can ignore that or you can have a five minute digression from the manual and open it up. As it stands it's quite a light hearted thing but underneath there are attitudes ... to victims ... it addresses a range of issues ... also for the female staff. Sometimes we make a judgement call about innuendos and subtle statements – sometimes you ignore it and other times ... if it's going to be helpful in an overall way ... you address it. (Indira)

Of particular significance to some research participants was the co-working relationship between male and female workers in a group work situation. Here Karen is describing the skills she believes she has in building rapport with sex offenders in the group work programmes she runs but she is also clear that her relationship with her male co-worker is very important in this process:

I am very good with building rapport with men and I think it does depend on your male co-worker. A lot depends on your male co-worker. (Karen)

Some research participants identified benefits of being female in the workplace, enabling them to gain emotional support from colleagues more freely than their male counterparts:

I mean in our office we're quite ... chatty, it's mostly women ... the majority of women have children so we do the whole juggling thing, so it's understood, and you know it does fall into sort of, we are quite touchy feely and understanding. (Sophie)

I do feel that as females, as women, we do have the luxury of talking more about, with our friends about things and ... (Jai)

An older female respondent considered that her age and her gender were an asset in breaking through certain barriers erected by offenders (Heather). She felt able to voice emotional issues and be respected for this in a way she suspected would be harder for younger and/or less experienced workers.

Conclusion

This chapter has reflected on issues of diversity, power and emotions within criminal justice. It has offered an overview of some of the statistical evidence for continuing discrimination and disadvantage and how this impacts both on offender populations and on career opportunities for staff within the criminal justice system. There is continuing evidence of how black and ethnic minority offenders, victims and staff are treated differently within the system and a growing awareness of how other protected characteristics such as sexuality, disability and age, can also be subject to discriminatory or disadvantageous treatment. However, in relation to this current research on emotional literacy the most striking diversity issue was that of gender and this chapter has placed a particular focus on its relationship with emotion and emotional literacy.

All of the research participants in this study recognised the importance of emotional literacy, in terms of relationship building and an ability to 'read' situations, but views were expressed about women generally being more able in this respect than their male colleagues. There was no evidence of male staff complaining about a lack of emotional literacy in female staff but there was evidence that some of the female research participants found their male colleagues to be less aware of the emotional impact of the work, and sometimes actually obstructive when it came to understanding and responding to emotions in offenders and in colleagues.

4

Values: Positive and Negative Emotional Control in Work with Offenders

Practice example

Sarah is a 48-year-old black female imprisoned for an offence of grievous bodily harm against a security guard in her local shopping centre. She had been demanding a refund on an item of clothing that did not fit her, and on being refused she became angry and aggressive. The security guard asked her to leave the shop and she attacked him causing a broken arm and lacerations to his face. In prison she has continued to be angry and aggressive, particularly in relation to the limited contact she is allowed with her 12-year-old daughter who is being cared for by her mother. The prison officers find her very challenging of their authority and believe that she needs to be 'put in her place' and learn to accept the prison regime. Some of them have been heard to describe her in stereotypical terms as an 'angry black woman with a chip on her shoulder'. The wing governor learns, during an adjudication with her, that she was subject to considerable violence as a child. He decides to convene a meeting with wing staff for them to discuss how they might work with Sarah in a way that reduces the opportunities for conflict and that reflects an understanding of some of the underlying reasons for her behaviour, whilst also aiming to improve the situation for everyone. He suggests that rather than relying on a stereotype to define Sarah, his staff should endeavour to treat her with respect and, whenever they feel themselves being 'wound up' by her behaviour, to step away and take stock of the situation, or ask another colleague for assistance, before intervening further. The governor offers support to the staff in achieving this approach with her and refers Sarah to the probation service for help with managing contact with her daughter and in her anger management.

Key learning points

- Negative emotions, unchecked, can allow practitioners to act in punitive and unreflective ways with offenders

- We can hold stereotypical views of people different from ourselves and form 'emotional' judgements on the basis of these views rather than on the evidence
- Criminal justice organisations generally have statements of principle about how offenders should be treated – these statements need to be operationalised by managers who understand their significance and can work in an emotionally literate manner with their staff
- Punitive control is not acceptable in human rights terms, but it is also unlikely to be the most effective way of managing an offender
- Endeavouring to hold a non-judgemental attitude is more likely to encourage the treatment of offenders with respect and decency

Introduction

Emotions, or feelings, are central to our experience of social life and our interactions with others. They also play a significant role in determining and sustaining our beliefs, values and attitudes. Emotions are closely associated with the development of morality and ethical principles (Batson 2011, Chapman and Anderson 2011, Greene 2011), and are seen as crucial in the process of moral and ethical decision-making. All of this has particular resonance in a criminal justice context. People hold strong views on the 'right' or 'morally correct' way to respond to crime and criminality, and emotions are frequently to the fore when such issues are debated. Victims, witnesses and bystanders of a range of criminal behaviour may find themselves consumed with powerful feelings about crime and victimisation, and holding strong opinions based on these feelings. However, we expect criminal justice workers to be able to retain a degree of professionalism and emotional detachment when they are confronted with similar behaviour. A police officer may have to deal with an abusive and angry teenager, or a distraught and humiliated victim of domestic violence; a prison officer could be confronted with a suicidal prisoner or a belligerent 'lifer'; a drugs worker may be provoked by a demanding drug user or a probation officer whose report to the court is believed by the defendant to have directly contributed to his being sent to prison may have to face the offender's anger and blame.

Such workers are likely to experience a range of emotional responses, with varying degrees of intensity, to the situations with which they are faced when working with offenders, victims and witnesses. They will also hold values and beliefs about these different groups of people that have evolved through their own life experience and social conditioning, their diversity, identity and status in the world and through the organisational culture and rules within which they operate as practitioners. Organisations within the criminal justice system (CJS), in order to manage such powerful emotions and beliefs, promote values for their staff, which are now commonly based on human rights, as core to their operational practice. These are likely to include treating all people with decency and respect, and valuing their diversity. Whilst these are commendable principles, making them operational in the face of the many complex emotions aroused by crime and criminality is altogether more challenging.

The research for this book generally indicated that the values of the probation participants were part and parcel of the empathy that they felt and expressed towards the majority of offenders with whom they worked. They had joined the service because they believed they could make a positive contribution to helping people to change their lives, and their values informed this motivation and provided a foundation for their emotional literacy. This raises the question of the extent to which being emotionally literate is also a moral endeavour, a skill that requires an underlying value base of concern or compassion towards recipients of a service.

As set out in the introduction, emotional literacy is seen to include a number of elements; motivation, self-awareness, self-regulation, empathy and social competence (these are explored in more detail in Chapters 5 and 6). It was also suggested that emotional literacy can be identified on a continuum from the superficial to the more complex, dependent on the context as well as the staff role. The first three elements, motivation, self-awareness and self-regulation, should in fact be viewed as essential components for all practitioners working in the CJS, in allowing and enabling them to manage themselves in their working environment in such a way that their own emotions do not dominate their work agenda. Ideally it also provides them with a degree of insight into the emotions of the recipients of their service, whether or not they wish or are able to respond empathically to these emotions. Work by Berking, Meier et al. (2010) highlights how police officers are routinely exposed to situations that provoke intense negative emotions in them, and how important it is that they have effective methods to regulate such emotions. Training in emotional self-regulation significantly enhanced their ability to tolerate negative emotions, support themselves in distressing situations and manage emotionally challenging encounters (Berking, Meier et al. 2010). A worker who lacks motivation and energy for their work, who has little self-awareness and therefore a limited ability to monitor and regulate their own emotions appropriately, is likely to be more at the mercy of these emotions in the day-to-day conduct of their job.

The theme of this book is the use of emotional literacy as an effective skill for practitioners who are engaging with, motivating and working towards enabling change in offenders. However, in the absence of clear policy and operational guidance, there is a risk that negative and 'punitive' emotions may come to the fore when workers try to enforce such change. This chapter considers how different working credos or values ('punishment', 'efficiency' and 'caring'; Rutherford 1993), and their associated emotions, that under-pin practice with offenders and victims within the CJS can impact on the practitioner role. It will explore some of the complex and tangled web of feelings, beliefs and values that informs how people operate in a criminal justice work context. It will consider how workers exercise differing degrees of interpersonal emotional control in their day-to-day work with offenders on a continuum from the benign to the more malign and exploitative forms of emotional control (Layder 2004). There is potential for workers to function at any point along this continuum in their work with offenders, and it is suggested that these processes are largely idiosyncratic and subjective, and remain unregulated and unmanaged within the context of organisational objectives and policy. Evidence from the research data suggests that pro-bation staff use their belief in the importance of being 'non-judgemental' towards offenders as a means of tempering the feelings that are aroused in them by their work. A philosophy of 'non-judgmentalism' in all criminal justice work could offer a means of avoiding the worst excesses of punitive emotional control and of fostering a more benign form of emotional control which links to the skills of emotional literacy.

Organisational values

It is now standard practice for organisations within the CJS to set out state-ments of purpose including their aims and vision for the future. Such state-ments are likely to include principles or behavioural expectations of their staff. Sometimes these are couched in the language of equality of opportunity and valuing diversity. Increasingly, within the public sector in particular, the prin-ciples on which staff are expected to base their practice draw on the concept of 'human rights', which has evolved from a search for common ethical values across societies (Klug 2000). Phrases such as 'treating people with respect' and 'with decency' are appearing in many of these agencies' vision statements. One of the most significant principles of international human rights law is that you lose rights only to the extent that it is necessary and no more than that, to protect the rights of others and the broader community. For example, the right to free speech must be tempered to take account of other rights or values, such as not to be slandered or subject to racial hatred. Canton suggests that the new focus on human rights should provide the opportunity for all organisations within the criminal justice arena to spell out some common principles and values for practice.

> We need a clearer understanding of the substantial question of what is due to offenders and victims, what it is to treat them fairly and well. (Canton 2011:41)

Canton goes on to argue that these rights do not have to be deserved and are not contingent on our individual identities; the 'sole and sufficient credentials are to be human' (Canton 2011:41).

A human rights approach would postulate that punishment involves some limitations of these rights, but such limitation should not go beyond the requirements of a legitimate penal purpose. Respecting the dignity and lifestyle of others, even when they have offended against the laws of society, is increasingly seen by all criminal justice agencies as the appropriate response of staff working for them towards offenders. This does not necessarily require staff to 'like' or even 'care' very much about offenders, but it does require them to hold back, or temper, any negative emotional responses that they might feel towards them.

The probation service

The probation service, as a public-sector criminal justice organisation, has traditionally gone beyond this. The probation service was established as an organisation offering 'welfare' and rehabilitation to offenders (see McWilliams 1983, McWilliams 1985, McWilliams 1986 for a history of the evolution of the service). Many early probation workers took their values from their Christian beliefs and saw their work as a distinctively moral endeavour (Canton 2011). The evolving educational link from the 1960s onwards with social work, and its associated values, encouraged probation staff to believe that positive change in offenders would take place via a relationship built on respect, a withholding of negative judgements and concern for the individual, and as 'the institutional expression of some of the values that ought to characterise a decent society' (Canton 2011:45). Canton argues that excesses of punishment are likely to be corrosive for any society and that the probation service has historically represented humane and welfare-orientated values that uphold a belief in the capacity of an individual to change through their own volition. Canton also argues that values are intimately connected with practice; they define *how* things are done as being no less important than the outcomes.

A number of writers have grappled with the impact on these values of the change from a primarily 'welfare' service for offenders, to a service delivering 'punishment in the community' (Vanstone 2007, Whitehead 2010, Canton 2011). The modern probation service has moved a considerable distance from its roots as a welfare service to offenders, and its current philosophy and aims are now focused centrally on the protection of the public from the risk posed by offending behaviour. The current published list of values of the National Offender Management Service (NOMS), one of the largest organisations within the CJS, incorporating both the prison and probation services states that 'in delivering offender management services, we will:

- Be objective and take full account of public protection when assessing risk
- Be open, honest and transparent
- Incorporate equality and diversity in all we do
- Value, empower and support staff, and work collaboratively with others
- Treat offenders with decency and respect
- Embrace change, innovation and local empowerment
- Use our resources in the most effective way, focusing on customers and delivering value for money for the tax payer'

These values reflect the language of human rights by emphasising the importance of 'decency and respect' in work with offenders. They are also articulated in the principles set out in the European Probation rules (No 5.) (Council of Europe 2010) and defined as respecting the human rights of offenders, and of working to the highest national and international ethical and professional standards. They reaffirm the point made earlier by Canton that

> in implementing any sanction or measure, probation agencies shall not impose any burden or restriction of rights on the offender greater than that provided by the judicial or administrative decision and required in each individual case by the seriousness of the offence or by the properly assessed risks of reoffending. (Council of Europe 2010: principle 5. P2)

Within the NOMS value statement, there is, however, no additional mention of the need to demonstrate care or concern towards offenders or to be 'non-judgemental' which, as identified earlier, was a core value held by the research participants (Knight 2012). As will be explored further in Chapter 8 on organisations and emotions, the above statements could be seen to promote a degree of emotional detachment, neutrality and objectivity; a holding back on negative emotions but with no particular encouragement to enhance or express the more positive emotions of empathy, compassion and concern towards offenders. This brings NOMS more in line with a range of other criminal justice agencies such as the police and courts, rather than continuing to assert the probation service as a distinctively 'welfare-based' or humanitarian organisation (NOMS 2012 – updated 15/11/2012) (NOMS 2012).

The Police Service

With regard to the police service, the National Policing Improvement Agency (NPIA) similarly confirmed a link with human rights stating that all actions should be compatible with the European Convention on Human Rights (1950). It recognises that the implications for the police of not acting

> fairly, professionally, honestly and with integrity are substantial given the scope of the police to infringe on the freedom and rights of individuals.

The 'Policing Pledge' similarly makes reference to the importance of treating people with

> respect, dignity and courtesy – to act with self-control and tolerance. (NPIA 2010)

Such values suggest the need for emotional self-control and emotional neutrality rather than any more proactive engagement of empathy or concern, as might be expected of workers in a potentially more therapeutic setting such as the probation service. The need for 'self-control' suggests that police officers are required, at the very least, to conceal or not act on any negative emotions they might hold towards offenders, and to manage their emotions effectively to achieve that end. The Metropolitan Police also include in their 'community engagement objectives' the need to:

> Maintain and develop the perception of diverse communities of how helpful, friendly and approachable the police are. (Metropolitan Police 2013)

These value statements suggest that both NOMS and the police service are keen to demonstrate their openness, responsiveness and desire to treat people well. However, even where there are clear organisational policy statements, and legislation to treat offenders with decency, to prevent discrimination and unfair treatment, this is generally insufficient to ensure good practice. For example, despite legislation to outlaw race, sex or disability discrimination there can be little meaningful exercise of these rights if workers find ways of subtly undermining their co-workers or their service users on such grounds (Klug 2000). Similarly, there have been some alarming examples of the institutional failings of organisations within the CJS to respect the diversity and human rights of offenders and victims (Macpherson 1999, Keith 2006, IPCC 2011). Courts of law can impose sanctions against breaches of human rights, but the values underpinning such rights are part of much broader culture of pluralism, tolerance and broadmindedness (Klug 2000).

Emotion and values underpinning criminal justice practice

In developing the links between emotions and values, it is possible to view emotions as a significant driver in determining both positive and negative orientations towards offenders. Of particular relevance, given the nature of certain crimes, is research on the formation of moral judgements on the basis of feelings of disgust (Schnall, Benton et al. 2008, Pizzaro, Inbar et al. 2011). As indicated at the beginning of this chapter, emotions are closely associated with the development of morality and ethical principles (Batson 2011; Chapman and Anderson 2001; Green 2011). Whilst the organisation might specify that its workers will treat all offenders with decency and respect, how meaningful is that principle in guarding against the powerful force of disgust in a worker faced with managing a sex offender, for example? In the probation service it has traditionally been accepted that a worker who has been a victim of, or closely associated with, sexual offending, will not be asked to work with such offenders unless they have had an opportunity, through counselling, to adequately process the experience and feel sufficiently robust to undertake such work. It is unlikely, however, that such choices will be available to all criminal justice practitioners in all settings. They may not have been a victim of such offending but, nevertheless, retain powerful feelings about the wrongness and harmfulness of such behaviour that dominates and restricts their ability to work with such an offender. In any worker/offender transaction or relationship the power will almost always lie with the worker to determine the quality and meaningfulness of these encounters. A worker holding unexamined feelings of anger, disgust or fear towards particular offenders is likely to find their practice is contaminated or at least strongly influenced by these feelings, albeit these may be at the unconscious level (Murdin 2010).

When the emotions underpinning our values and beliefs come to the fore we may be overwhelmed by the need to assert our own personal beliefs about what should happen to offenders and victims. Discussions with friends and families and the sharing of opinions on crime and society's response can be a source of heated and engaged debate. However, criminal justice practitioners have an obligation to carry out their *practice* with due regard to the stated values of their organisation.

Working credos

Notwithstanding how organisations present themselves to the public through their statements of 'principles' and their general commitment to human rights, diversity and equality of opportunity, Rutherford suggests that the values and beliefs that shape the work and concerns of criminal justice practitioners are 'working credos' and that they fall into three clusters:

1. *The punishment credo*, described as the 'punitive degradation of offenders'
2. *The efficiency credo*, described as a concentration on 'management, pragmatism, efficiency and expedience'

3. *The caring credo*, which identifies an attitude towards all service users in the CJS based on 'liberal and humanitarian values' (Rutherford 1993, p. viii)

Such a taxonomy can be helpful in locating the potentially different positions of different workers in the system. The values of staff undertaking practice in a range of settings will be crucial to the manner in which the actual practice is conducted and the extent to which these values are informed by powerful and deep-rooted emotions (Canton 2011). However, the connection between values, beliefs and the underlying emotions that sustain or enhance them is relatively under-theorised in criminal justice, although Haidt has written more generally in this area (Haidt 2001). People who choose to work in the CJS may do so for altruistic and ideological reasons, for example, wanting to work with, and help, people as victims or offenders, or wanting to further the cause of social justice in society. Such people may lean towards a career in the probation service, or in one of the voluntary sector organisations established to support and help offenders and victims. Such people are likely to present as holding a caring credo. People may also join criminal justice agencies with other motivations such as a desire to see processes are carried out efficiently and fairly (efficiency credo) or they may have unresolved negative feelings that could become translated or transferred into their working practices with offenders (punishment credo).

Interpersonal emotional control

The CJS is concerned with public protection through the managing and punishing of crime, and, therefore, unsurprisingly, the majority of workers in the statutory sector and in some of the third-sector partner agencies are required to employ techniques and practices that exert a degree of control over offenders. The nature and extent of this control varies depending on both objective factors, that is, which agency and what role, and subjective factors, that is, the individual's own values and beliefs.

Layder's theory of 'interpersonal emotional control' provides a framework for understanding how we all use emotions in our day-to-day lives to exert a degree of control of our social world.

> To know oneself, to be 'roughly' in charge of one's emotional responses, is necessary in order to win influence and exert control in the wider social world. The ability to influence others and control them 'benignly' depends on being able to 'read' the feelings, and respond to them in a way that creates mutual satisfaction. (Layder 2004:13)

Layder argues that you can only influence the minds and hearts of others through personal control, and that the level, amount and quality of personal control influences the shape, intensity and direction of emotions and feelings (Layder 2004:34). Layder suggests that benign control plays a central role in social life and underpins many social skills and personal qualities including emotional intelligence. This understanding of 'benign' control challenges the assumption that any form of 'control' is necessarily wrong or negative. Layder argues that it is an intrinsic feature of all social life. Such benign control endeavours to take into account the interests and views of others. Benign control is intended to influence or persuade and may not always be successful; communication is based on a two-way process. In contrast, a dominant stance sees the more powerful person overriding the interests of the other.

Layder offers a view of the principles types of control (Figure 4.1). He suggests that forms of emotional control to the left of the diagram represent the normal or 'healthy' forms of control through to the pathological on the right-hand side of the diagram.

> There is a continuity between what are regarded as legitimate, socially acceptable types of control and those involving more anti-social and 'unhealthy' aspects. (Layder 2004:62)

Translating these concepts into a criminal justice practice context, it is apparent that 'control' and indeed 'emotional control' is likely to play a very significant role both in managing and in seeking to change problematic (criminal) behaviour. Many criminal justice workers spend much of their time attempting to exert such control over people who may be compliant or resistant or a mixture of both. The extent to which this may be described as either 'benign' or 'pathological', or somewhere in the middle, opens up some interesting dilemmas for consideration. The majority of work undertaken by the probation service and voluntary sector organisations within the CJS could be viewed as the exercising of 'benign' control. In contrast, the 'dominant stance' is more likely to be seen in operation within the police and prison services where on occasion

> the aim of domination is total control of the 'other' in which their autonomy is completely suppressed and negated. (Layder 2004:60)

Layder offers examples of such total domination that include kidnapping, hostage taking, torture and violence, that is, involving criminal activity. However, in a criminal justice context, prisoners and 'suspects' may have to have their autonomy legitimately 'suppressed' and 'negated' in the interests of public safety and protection. Layder suggests that the settings in which, what he refers to as 'legitimate positional authority', may take place are likely to be more formal and less intimate or personal, and can be seen in operation in hierarchical organisations like government bureaucracies or the armed forces. He makes no

68

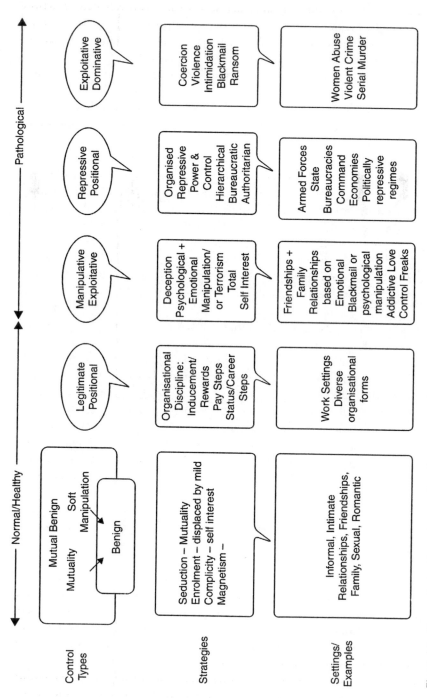

Figure 4.1 Types, strategies and examples of interpersonal control

specific reference to workers in a statutory sector such as the police or prison service, but this concept could be aligned to the work of these organisations where, for example, at the point of arrest, or in the case of a prisoner's behaviour becoming a risk to self and others, such authority is exercised.

At the far right of Layder's continuum, 'repressive-authoritarian control' is presented as the direct counterpart of positional control in the context of legitimate authority (p.64). Layder describes pathological control as a place where all hints of altruism and empathy are pushed into the background and the controller's interests are to the fore. Evidence of pathological control of vulnerable adults was seen in the exposure of the Winterbourne View scandal where staff used a range of repressive techniques to control behaviour in adults with learning difficulties (Department of Health 2012). The sole objective is to gain compliance from the recipient.

Punitive control

Punishment, defined through order of the court, typically involves some hardship or loss of liberty or rights, as a censure for wrongdoing (Canton 2012). In the British justice system this is generally exercised through loss of liberty (via imprisonment), completion of unpaid work (in the community), attendance on programmes designed to tackle offending behaviour (in prison and the community), financial penalties or a range of 'suspension' of sentences or 'binding overs'. Punishment is a form of communication; it condemns the conduct of offenders as wrong and aims to persuade them to face up to the implications of their behaviour (Duff 2007). Punishment is additionally an emotional process and can invoke a range of powerful feelings in its recipients, such as fear, anger, anxiety, resentment, humiliation and shame. It can also provoke a mixture of feelings in the practitioner tasked with enforcing it, including revenge, regret, shame, anger and embarrassment. Generally these feelings, of both recipient and enforcer, are seen to belong to the individual.

Recognising staff within a criminal justice organisation who hold more punitive ideologies towards offenders may or may not be of concern to the organisation. Such people may exhibit a punishment credo and in certain settings, for example, the police and prison service, such a credo may be viewed as understandable or indeed acceptable, as a working ethos. A significant number of prison officers in Crawley's research (Crawley 2004) considered themselves to have become 'harder' and more 'desensitised' to the distress and suffering of others. Whilst the corollary to this could be indifference, the punitive context of a prison environment may also invite a punitive response in the absence of any official encouragement for concern or empathy towards prisoners. Prisoner officers in Crawley's research feared that 'kindness' could be mistaken for 'weakness' (Crawley 2004). Crawley also gives examples of depersonalised language used by prison officers such as 'bodies' rather than people, the use of a 'body book' and the use of negative language to describe the prisoners such as 'scum', 'cons', 'toe-rags' and 'nonces' which, she argues

create spaces in which inhumane treatment can occur. (Crawley 2004:153)

The punishment credo, potentially exercised through the controlling, coercing, humiliating or manipulating of offenders and the imposition and/or threat of external controls and sanctions, draws on ideas that originated with Durkheim (Garland 1990), and incorporates the belief that the criminal law should be an expression of the values of the society and be about denouncing and condemning criminal behaviour (Canton 2011). It does not require any degree of understanding of why the behaviour has occurred. Staff working within more controlling environments, such as prison establishments, may be more likely to believe in, and potentially exercise, a punitive credo. This could be seen as a legitimate stance to take given the generally punitive nature of imprisonment. It is of interest, however, that significant numbers of prison officers in Crawley's research equated their role as more akin to that of a nurse or psychiatric worker, not least because they found themselves having to deal with increasing numbers of emotionally disturbed, mentally unwell and/or drug-dependent prisoners (Crawley 2004).

What might be termed a 'heavy-handed' approach to managing or responding to an offender is an example of where the punishment credo, based on a belief that offenders are deserving of an unlimited quantity of punishment, could allow workers to impose interpersonal emotional control at the more repressive and dominant end of Layder's continuum. Within the prison regime Crawley has identified the unspoken 'feeling rules' of the organisation as those of 'emotional neutrality' or detachment, in the workforce (Crawley 2009). However, she acknowledges that staff struggle to achieve this, for example, that some officers held a degree of resentment towards prisoners (p.104) and some were willing to admit to assaulting uncooperative prisoners (p118). It is suggested that whilst such heavy-handedness might be understandable, particularly when workers are faced with very challenging and sometimes frightening behaviour, it fails to recognise the human rights of the offender and illegitimately imposes additional punishment to that sanctioned by the legal system and court process.

Efficient control

Some workers may hold a more instrumental approach to their careers and be seeking employment that offers a degree of job security and status. They may be motivated by an efficiency credo. The efficiency credo, potentially encompassed within a managerialist approach to the work (Raine 2007), priorities the setting and meeting of targets over other, more qualitative processes (Rutherford 1993). Such an approach could apply to workers in any setting and is likely to be strengthened by feeling and believing in the importance of a degree of emotional detachment or neutrality towards the job. Those operating with an efficiency credo may care little about the individuals they work with but, nevertheless, believe in the efficacy of following due process and operating in a fair and dispassionate manner, such that the extent of their emotional control is minimised. Such an approach may result in a competent meeting of targets, but could prove inadequate to the task of really engaging or digging below the surface of why offenders commit crime and how they might be motivated to change.

Caring control

The practice of workers operating within a caring credo may be found in a range of organisations, predictably the probation service and voluntary sector organisations whose principle aim is to achieve behavioural change. With the move towards 'punishment in the community' and the more managerial focus of the probation service, the caring expectations of its workforce have, however, been considerably eroded. The probation service can no longer claim to be the caring arm of the penal system. In fact, caring can also be found in some of the more 'controlling' criminal justice establishments including the prison service. Crawley identified some prison officers as feeling considerable sympathy for prisoners (Crawley 2009:151).

Within the probation service the caring credo has traditionally been exercised through the philosophical approach of 'advise, assist and befriend', which was the cornerstone of early probation practice (Monger 1972). It continues to be a significant influence in motivating current recruits to the service (Knight 2007). However, an altruistic motivation is not the prerogative of recruits to the probation service. People entering the police and prison services, or the legal profession, for example, may also join for ideological reasons related to a wish to create safer communities and ensure justice is carried out fairly and equally. The main drive for all these staff tends to be a desire to make things 'better'.

Of these three credos, the caring credo may sometimes prove to be more emotionally controlling than the punishment credo, and offenders may prefer neutrality, or efficiency, to an overbearing emotional warmth that could feel manipulative. 'Sentenced to Social Work', written more than three decades ago (Bryant et al 1978), warned of the dangers of well-intentioned probation staff encouraging courts to impose probation orders on the grounds of the offender's social work 'need', when equivalent offenders lacking such 'need' were given lesser sentences on the tariff. A caring credo may not be straightforwardly benign and may not always be perceived by the offender to be beneficial to them. Layder suggests that despite our best intentions in encounters or established relationships we are inclined, alongside our altruistic intentions, to engage in a 'spot of innocent manipulation' which we 'camouflage' in what we consider to be their best interests (Layder 2004). In such a process we push our own views and interests at the expense of the offender's. Workers may care a great deal about the offenders they work with but also believe it is acceptable to impose and exert considerable degrees of emotional control and manipulation over them in order to 'protect the public', or they may be unaware or unconscious of their own personal needs that drive such manipulation (countertransference (Murdin 2010)).

Where does the probation service sit?

Amongst all the criminal justice agencies the probation service has historically experienced the most tension between the exercising of a punitive credo and a 'caring credo, between 'care' and 'control' (Foren and Bailey 1968), with oscillation at both policy and practice levels between the need to 'punish' and 'control' and the need to 'help' and 'change' (NOMS 2006). An examination of current operational policy in the probation service suggests that these tensions continue to exist. The policy is outlined in the Offender Management Model (OMM), which includes the four-tier framework against which all cases can be mapped. This describes four broad 'modalities' for working with offenders:

- Punish
- Help
- Change
- Control (NOMS 2006)

The allocation of resources is undertaken against these modalities and the decision about which modalities of intervention are relevant to each individual offender depends on an assessment of the level of risk of reoffending and of the potential dangerousness of the behaviour, using the Offender Assessment System (OASys) (Canton 2011). It is specified that all cases will require the implementation of the 'punish' mode, most will require 'help', a proportion will require 'change' and a few, described as the dangerous and very prolific, will require 'control' (NOMS 2006).

The concept of 'punishment' in this context refers to giving effect to the sentence of the court, as opposed to a particular kind of painful or retributive sanction such as imprisonment. Broadly speaking, 'punishment' and 'control' are seen to be exercised through the enforcement of community orders, ensuring offenders keep to the conditions of their orders, give up their free time to attend programmes or complete unpaid work, and by returning them to court when they are in breach of these orders. 'Help' and 'change' is undertaken through the provision of a range of instructional, therapeutic and practical programmes either provided directly or via partnerships agencies. The extent to which probation staff will be able to handle the emotional tensions and moral dilemmas that exist between these different strategies of 'helping', 'punishing', 'changing' and 'controlling' the people they are charged to supervise is largely ignored within operational policy. Prison service staff can also be designated offender managers of prisoners, and be required to operate with the same or similar models of intervention, but not necessarily with the same level of training as their probation officer counterparts.

As described in the introduction, in the discussion on Dowden and Andrew's work, Core Correctional Practice (CCP) makes reference to a set of required staff characteristics. These include:

1. Effective use of authority
2. Appropriate modelling and reinforcement:
   a. Effective modelling
   b. Effective reinforcement
   c. Effective disapproval
   d. Structured learning procedures
3. Problem solving
4. Effective use of community resources
5. Quality of interpersonal relationships:
   a. Relationship factors: the programme staff possessed any of the following characteristics; warm, genuine, humorous, enthusiastic, self-confident, empathic, respectful, flexible, committed to helping clients, engaging, mature, or intelligent
   b. Skills factors: the programme staff used directive, solution-focused, structured, non-blaming or contingency-based forms of communication with offenders (Dowden and Andrews 2004: 208)

The emotional balance held by the practitioner between these characteristics as they work with offenders has not been clearly explored or defined in contemporary probation literature, although some similar tensions have been identified in research with prison staff which has examined the conflict between providing support and maintaining authority and control (Tait 2011). In relation to the first CCP staff characteristic of effective use of authority, there is the potential for the 'firm, fair and clear use of authority' to be filtered through a punitive credo in a hectoring and authoritarian manner or through a caring credo in a more supportive manner. Characteristic 2, 'modelling of prosocial and anti-criminal attitudes', could be undertaken in a moralistic or evangelical manner, or through the provision of positive and caring models of alternative behaviours. Characteristic 3, the 'teaching of concrete problem solving skills' could be undertaken in a didactic (potentially authoritarian) manner or an interactive and enabling way. The final, and identified as the most important, characteristic of forming of 'warm, open and enthusiastic relationships' (Dowden and Andrews 2004), is perhaps the closest to a caring credo underpinning emotionally literate practice, but such relationships could, nevertheless, vary depending on the values and skills of the worker; from patronising, authoritarian or insincere, to ones based on humanitarian values of respect, a non-judgemental approach and equality of opportunity. It appears that current policy offers the practitioner no real guide to the emotional management of these characteristics.

Research findings

One of the skills identified by Dowden and Andrews is that of 'non-blaming' (Dowden and Andrews 2004). The most significant research finding for this book, in relation to how the research participants managed this complex balance between 'caring' and 'controlling' and the resulting emotional tensions, was to endeavour to withhold judgement on the people they were working with. A resumé of the findings are presented here, with the suggestion that for all workers in the criminal justice context, an ability to withhold judgement is a sound premise on which to carry out their organisational requirements. A police officer, conducting an interview with a challenging offender, has to seek not to 'judge' the person's guilt until all the evidence has been collected, regardless of their emotional response to the person's difficult behaviour. A prison officer, tasked with bringing a prisoner to court for trial, should work to keep that prisoner safe and secure, regardless of the person's guilt or innocence, which can only be subsequently confirmed by the court process. When dealing with a convicted prisoner's request for an additional visit from their family, the decision should not be based on the officer's feelings about the prisoner's crime but on the criteria provided by the prison for deciding on such a request.

Withholding judgement

However, 'non-blaming' or 'withholding judgment' is a complex and demanding process. Cherry talks of the need to empathise but not collude (Cherry 2010), although she acknowledges that this is a tightrope that practitioners walk every day, the demonstration of emotional literacy alongside the need to 'suspend' or 'conceal' what some might perceive to be very normal emotional reactions to unpleasant and sometimes disturbing behaviour. Whilst the history of probation practice and its alignment with social work training and values has encouraged a non-judgemental approach, as Biestek suggested, this generally refers to a holding back of judgement on the person's guilt/innocence or responsibility. Biestek, writing more than 50 years ago in the 'Casework Relationship', was one of the first to set out the principle of holding a non-judgemental attitude in work with social work clients. He defined it as:

> The non-judgemental attitude is a quality of the casework relationship; it is based on a conviction that the casework function excludes assigning guilt or innocence, or degree of client responsibility for causation of the problems or needs, but does include making evaluative judgments about the attitudes, standards or actions of the client; the attitude which involves both thought and feeling elements is transmitted to the client. (Biestek 1961: 90)

Biestek identified 'judging' as placing blame on a client and declaring 'him' (sic) either by words or by non-verbal indicators, as somehow responsible for the problems he faced or on his dependency on the social worker. He argued that the responsibility to 'judge' was vested in certain authorities (such as courts and tribunals) but judgements by people without that authority constituted a violation of human rights. He related this back to the early days of social work in which a client's 'worthiness' or 'deservingness' was a consideration in giving or withholding help, implying this was now inappropriate. Interestingly, this attitude still prevails in much political discourse in relation to all offenders, and particularly in relation to sex offenders, who are generally seen as undeserving of help (Harrison 2010).

Probation workers have always been encouraged to make evaluative judgements about the current attitudes and behaviour of the people they work with. Directives arising through the What Works literature, the OMM (NOMS 2006), and CCP (see above) actively encourage a demonstration of disapproval of antisocial behaviours and the promotion of prosocial attitudes and behaviour (Farrow, Kelly et al. 2007). Workers are also required to make judgements about the behaviour of offenders in relation to their potential 'dangerousness', the harm they might cause to others and the risk of their further offending. It may be a small step from these evaluations to acquiring a negativity or punitiveness associated with how it makes the worker 'feel'. However, an approach informed by both motivational interviewing (Miller and Rollnick 2002) and person-centred counselling (Rogers 2004) would argue that being 'offended' at the words or indeed the behaviour of a person – in this case an offender – merely closes down the opportunity for communication. It is suggested that the worker needs to recognise that the negative behaviour being portrayed is unlikely to represent the whole of the person (Mearns and Thorne 2008).

Amongst the research participants, Lynn explains her understanding of this:

> Basically you respect them even though you don't like how they behave in some way, and as I say, you demonstrate that in some way in how you behave from the beginning to the end of an interview. (Lynn)

Whereas Heather provides a more nuanced example of some careful judgements she feels she needs to make about when and how she might express her disapproval with something the offender has done:

> I think that to be angry with someone you have got to feel quite safe in the relationship with them and they've got to know that you are angry with what they have done, not them, otherwise you are just repeating the anger that they have had on them all their lives and it is not very productive. (Heather)

The achievement of this understanding and the withholding of feelings where appropriate may require a considerable degree of emotional resilience. Aruna refers to the need to 'grit her teeth' implying that she holds back from expressing her disapproval or annoyance with some effort, which may, of course, be apparent to the offender through her non-verbal behaviour (Biestek 1961):

> Frustration because you are being respectful towards them, you're being nice and polite and everything and they're not being the same to you, you treat them how you would want to be treated and they don't want to do that, you just kind of find yourself gritting your teeth and thinking, okay, let's try and change tack then. (Aruna)

David provides an example of how he aims to communicate via his own behaviour rather than condemn the offender's behaviour:

> In the programme we model emotional communication and respectful communication. (David)

And Janet describes how she endeavours to work with respect despite the difficult message she wishes to convey and the fine balance between creating safety for learning but also providing the challenge to change:

> I don't think you can go to someone you don't know and say 'look, this is the way you swear at home but you know we really do find it' ..., you can't just stand there and say 'right, stop using that language', or you might say, 'look you might use that language at home, but here we feel quite uncomfortable about it and would you mind minimising that'. They think 'oh this

person is treating me with some respect so I'll not do it', but sometimes it's not safe to do it and I don't think they feel safe not to do it and I don't think we should make them not feel safe, not to challenge. (Janet)

Twenty of the research participants, without prompting in the interviews, highlighted the significance of this 'non-judgemental' approach towards the offenders they worked with (Michael, Amy, Tony, Indira, John, Robert, Victoria, Pat, Maggie, Damien, Aruna, Mary, Gill, Jai, Geoff, Hannah, Nick, Heather, Karen and Lynn). They understood the significance of working with people whose behaviour could be unacceptable and who may also be different from themselves, not just because of their offending behaviour but also their identity or 'diversity', for example, their race, gender, sexual orientation, age and class (Knight, Dominey et al. 2008). They were very engaged by the need to not 'judge' these behaviours or differences negatively although they were not always clear about what it was they were not 'judging'.

Holding a non-judgemental attitude is seen as of particular significance in work with offenders because of the nature of their often negative and damaging behaviour which lends itself to public condemnation (Garland 1990, Trotter 1999). It is considered an important ethical approach in all helping and counselling professions:

> To be acceptant of each facet of this other person which he (sic) presents to the therapist. (Rogers 2004)

It has many of its roots in psychotherapy (Rogers 1943; Truax and Carkhuff 1967) and is sometimes referred to in the therapeutic literature as 'unconditional positive regard' or 'non-possessive warmth' (Mearns and Thorne 2008). It has, historically, been a key component of both social work and probation education and practice. 'Society' may want its criminal justice workers to uphold an ethos of condemnation (Durkheim cited in Garland 1990), and adopt a punitive credo (Rutherford 1993), but historically the underlying message to individual probation workers has been to treat offenders as human beings in need of help and to resist the urge to judge and condemn (Canton 2011). It is argued here that this approach is in fact relevant and appropriate to all criminal justice workers not just those in a 'helping' context.

Victoria and John are both clear that being non-judgemental is essential to building relationships. Victoria sees it as not demonstrating any 'bias' whereas John sees it as modelling a different form of relationship:

> I suppose going back to the point about not being judgmental would be one thing, I don't think you can build up a relationship with anybody if you are .... expressing any sort of biased opinion about something. (Victoria)

> For a lot of people you are probably the first person that they've got to work with in a non-judgemental environment ... their upbringing as well ... how damaged they are ... I think just being able to model that sort of relationship can be therapeutically beneficial. (John)

Although John goes on to explain that this is not an easy position to adopt:

> An ability to be non-judgemental about individuals ... to sort of really try and consider where someone is coming from as opposed to just reacting to what you are seeing in terms of their behaviour ... which is not always easy to do. (John)

Given its importance to the research participants, the integration of this 'non-judgemental' attitude within practice raised a number of important questions for them that inevitably impact emotionally. Whilst the principle might be commendable, how the worker implements this when faced with a particular offender is likely to be more idiosyncratic and subtle; for example, demonstrating empathy towards an offender who has behaved illegally and maybe also 'immorally' in the worker's eyes. Some research participants articulated a need to distinguish between the person and their behaviour whilst also recognising the inherent ambivalence and difficulty with this position:

> But I do have a deep belief, ... Charlotte, I do have a very deep belief that ... I think it is something that my granddad taught me when I was a little girl and he used to say that there was good in everybody, and if you can't find it you are not looking in the right place. (Heather)

> I would never be disrespectful ..., to whoever was in front of me, whatever they did ... and you've got to, after knowing the person and building a relationship with the person from whatever they did, it's your job after all, you then have to deal separately with what they've done, of course there's overlaps but that's, that's I guess the difficulty really isn't it? (Robert)

Gill sees it as a positive challenge:

> The fact that we do work with some very unpleasant people and you know, sometimes it's how you separate your own personal views on somebody from what somebody has done and your job, I suppose the 'personal/professional' dilemma really ... on the one hand that can be a challenge in itself but on the other hand it's part of the job that I love doing. (Gill)

Indira also draws a distinction between making judgements about risk and about the person, and she refers to the importance of respect:

> The work isn't about judgment … it's about risk but not personal judgement. I hope I give them no messages that I respect them less than another human being. (Indira)

This position is also identified in some of the more recent approaches to work with sex offenders that recognise the importance of tapping into an element of optimism in an offender's life, through the use of 'strength-based' models of practice, rather than a constant focus on the negative elements (Ward, Devon et al. 2006; Day, Casey et al. 2010). It is reflected in the desistance literature, which identifies the importance of positive emotions in the process of desisting from crime (Farrall and Calverley 2006). It is suggested that the worker needs to recognise that the negative behaviour being portrayed is unlikely to represent the whole of the person (Mearns and Thorne 2008).

Some research participants acknowledged quite honestly that it was hard to be non-judgemental and/or gave examples of when they had in fact been judgemental, either because they believed it was the right thing to do or because their feelings had got the better of them. In particular, feelings of frustration or irritation, which they acknowledged, could get in the way of being 'non-judgemental'. Pat admits with some considerable honesty how her feelings can be strong:

> Yes, I want to smack some of them right in the face, especially one at the minute and I'm not alone because everyone (laughs) says to me (laughs) he's horrible you know, so, I have that, I really (laughs) want to punch (laughs) somebody but you know. (Pat)

Pat's annoyance and irritation, whilst understandable, could give non-verbal signals to the offender that may lead him/her to feel 'judged' and therefore not free to talk about himself/herself (Biestek 1961:92). Similarly, Sophie is willing to acknowledge how her feelings of disgust can have an impact on how she presents her challenges to an offender, and the importance of weighing up when is the right time to challenge rather than just in response to an emotional feeling, leading to a moral judgement being generated within the worker:

> Sometimes I can be too challenging and that's going to … negatively impact on what they are likely to be going to say to me and that is a failing of mine and it comes from some form of disgust obviously … I think of their offence really … and that's something that I … don't always necessarily think that … it's always wrong to be challenging, I think that you have to be challenging

but I think that ..., you have to choose your moments and perhaps not ... during a PSR for example. (Sophie)

Some research participants were honest enough to share examples of when their more negative emotions had affected their response to certain offenders and what they had done to try and rebalance this. Lynn linked her feelings of disgust with a sense of disappointment that a particular offender could behave in this way:

I was once terribly disappointed with a bloke who, he was on a parole, not just disappointed but really quite disgusted as well. What else, it wasn't disgust but, yes it was almost disgust. It turned out that he had raped an old woman. (Lynn)

This illustrates how workers make an emotional investment in the relationships they build with offenders such that further reoffending of any sort, or as in this case of a particularly violent and unpleasant sort, can impact on and damage that relationship. Karen describes how she was persuaded, almost against her better judgement, that a particularly challenging offender did wish to learn how to communicate better. She also demonstrates how she struggled with her understanding of the potential for racism and discrimination in the judgements about who gets to stay on the programme and who leaves:

He persuaded me that he wanted to communicate better with his children ... and I felt that was enough for him to be on this programme, and also he was a black male and I don't want to discriminate further against him and ... so I'm thinking that we've got a white lad that's hostile and angry, but we'll have him and we've got a black guy who is hostile and angry and we won't have him. (Karen)

She concludes by reflecting on her ambivalence about this particular offender. She senses that he is beginning to show glimmers of understanding about the need to talk; she recognises he is a dangerous offender, but also that he is a father and that there are children who need to be protected from his unresolved anger and failure to communicate. Karen's observations illustrate some of the dilemmas workers have in deciding who can be worked with, who has the potential to change and how to continue to engage despite the sometimes appalling behaviour being demonstrated by the offender. Karen identifies her emotions (anger) but also her values – that he should not be discriminated against just because he presents as an 'angry black man'. She is able to acknowledge that he is showing some signs of wanting to change, and that he is a father.

Rogers suggests that the major barrier to interpersonal communication is our natural tendency to judge, to evaluate, to approve or disapprove, the statement of the other person or the other group (Rogers 2004:330). This can be accompanied by strong emotional feelings and can be particularly evident towards offenders who have committed acts of violence and abuse towards children and women (Harrison 2010). The extent to which a worker can ever be truly 'non-judgemental' when faced with very dangerous and damaging offending behaviour from an offender who also engages in, minimisation, denial and lack of cooperation, is of course, questionable. What is of more significance is the extent to which the worker learns to use and manage these feelings appropriately.

Howard demonstrates an example of a judgement on sex offenders that seems to justify any form of intervention if, in his view, it ultimately protects the victims:

> How am I going to fuck with his head to make him do it ... (laughs). It's what L. and I describe ... some elements of the programme as being ... head fuckery of the highest order ... something I quite enjoy doing ... not very academic but it works for me. (Howard)

Some research participants were critical of colleagues who were not able to hold back from being judgemental:

> But I had seen other people and I think they can be ... sometimes and again, this is not a criticism. But sometimes they don't listen and are sometimes too quick to jump on that behaviour and the problem in terms of, for me in terms of doing that, you set a precedent in terms of that interaction because next time they'll feel that .... that they can't ever express their emotions because that is a taboo thing to do with you and that it can't be had, and your reaction to it is so extreme that it will either result in you terminating the interview immediately or just not being willing to hear it. (Nick)

Whilst in the majority of social relationships there is a level of mutual emotional 'management', influence and control (Layder 2004), in unequal relationships such as those between worker and offender, there is the risk of the control becoming pathological and exploitative (Layder 2004:104). Menzies' study on the use of social defence systems within nursing (Menzies 1959), reviewed by (Lowdell and Adshead 2009), was the first to identify that professional carers might actually have negative feelings towards those they care for, that caring is not the highly idealised activity it seems to be, but that these feelings are frequently ignored or unacknowledged (Lowdell and Adshead 2009). This has implications for staff who, if they are not allowed to articulate and reflect on the negative judgements they may feel, have the potential to exercise 'malign' or 'repressive', as opposed to, 'benign' control in their professional relationships (Layder 2004).

The aspiration towards 'non-judgmentalism' by the majority of research participants may be admirable, but its exercise is challenging and complex. Fine judgements are called for, particularly in the field of sex offender work, but these can remain susceptible to the emotional state of the worker. From the evidence presented within the data it appears that matters of judgement are not suspended but are put to work and in most cases with the offender's interests at heart; for example, anger can be demonstrated in the context of a good relationship (Heather). However, there is scope for more repressive approaches to be adopted by workers which may go unscrutinised by the organisation.

The examples provided here of working with a non-judgemental approach are all from a probation context and it is acknowledged that in different criminal justice settings the issue of 'care' or the need to build empathic relationship may not be so obviously present. However, the ability of an individual worker to regulate their emotions, to suspend the desire to condemn or 'sit in judgment' on the offenders they work with is seen to be an appropriate position for all workers to adopt, in the knowledge that the real 'judgement' should be taken through the appropriate legal sanctions.

Conclusion

This chapter has considered how some of the public-sector organisations within the criminal justice sector have developed principles or values which guide their staff's practice, and how increasingly these have become based on principles of human rights. Whilst these principles are generally very worthy they do not guide the worker in how to manage any underlying emotional ideologies towards the work. They tend to assume an emotional neutrality in the workforce which in fact is very hard to achieve and may, as will be explored in subsequent chapters, be unhelpful in the furtherance of relationship building and working towards change in offenders. It has been suggested that the values that practitioners hold are underpinned and sustained by emotions and emotional reactions to the behaviour, power and status of themselves and others.

The most significant finding from the research was the importance placed by research participants on adopting a non-judgemental attitude towards offenders, as the most appropriate way to achieve the common goals of treating people with decency and respect. Interestingly, this is not a value or principle identified in either the NOMS or the policing statements set out earlier in this chapter. The particular issues to be considered for criminal justice practice relate to how workers should or might regulate and manage the feelings engendered by close proximity with offenders and exposure to 'popular punitiveness'

(Bottoms 1995). The 'holding back' on negative judgments is presented as a significant emotional challenge within probation practice, and is likely to be the case for practitioners in all other criminal justice organisations. The research data illuminates some of the struggles that the research participants had in handling the negative feelings that emerged in response to aspects of their work and how they relied on the value of non-judgmentalism to try and control these feelings. As Lowdell and Adshead's work illuminates (Lowdell and Adshead 2009), the issue is not so much the negative feelings, to which most research participants admitted, it is how these feelings are acknowledged, processed and conveyed to, or hidden from, the offender, and with what effects, that ultimately determines the quality of their work and how emotional resources are supported and sustained.

If an organisation expects at the very least an efficiency credo to be held by its staff, and in some instances also a caring credo, then how might staff who hold negative ideologies towards offenders be enabled to reflect on these ideologies and their underpinning emotional roots? With reference to Rutherford's 'working credos' there was little evidence of the research participants holding either a punitive or an efficiency' credo, although some expressed frustration at offenders which they acknowledged could lead them to behave more 'punitively' than they might wish, and some referred to colleagues with more punitive attitudes. The majority expressed a commitment to working with offenders that incorporated a set of humanitarian values related to how they believed people, as clients of a public service, should be treated (Mawby and Worrall 2011). Their primary orientation appeared to be towards 'welfare' rather than 'punishment', a caring rather than a punitive credo (Rutherford 1993). However, many offered evidence of the extent to which the managerial climate of the modern service was most supportive of the efficiency credo (Rutherford 1993).

5

Developing Emotional Literacy in Practitioners

Practice example

Phil joined the prison service after a stint in the army and then working for his father as a car mechanic. He decided that the prison service would offer him job security, a reasonable salary and the chance to take on an important role in society. He was surprised to find that he actually liked some of the prisoners for whom he was responsible although there were always a few who could be very troublesome. On one occasion, when he was running an offending behaviour group work programme with a probation officer, he became disturbed to see a prisoner shuffling in his seat and then admitting to having bullied a younger prisoner on his wing and calling him 'so gay'. Phil felt angry with the prisoner for his behaviour and thought he should be punished for this act of aggression towards a vulnerable prisoner. He tried to conceal his anger in the group but afterwards decided to tell his probation officer colleague that he had felt himself 'boiling up' in the group and he planned to report this man to the governor. He was surprised when his colleague acknowledged the legitimacy of his anger but suggested that instead maybe they could talk with the prisoner concerned, who had been honest enough to admit to his aggressive behaviour. His colleague thought there might be some potential for mediation between the two prisoners. Phil recognised that had he shown his anger in the group he would have effectively silenced the prisoner making the confession and closed the door on the potential to do some work with him on his attitudes and behaviour. He agreed to his colleague's plan of action although wanted also to inform the wing Governor of their decision.

Key Learning points

- Being able to regulate strong feelings that can arise in the course of work and subsequently reflecting on their implications is a key element of emotional literacy.

84

- Being able to articulate our own feelings (emotion vocabulary) is a prereq-uisite of being able to help others (e.g. offenders) articulate and reflect on their feelings and behaviour.
- Understanding the significance of non-verbal communication, language and metaphor in the expression of emotions

Introduction

The concept of emotional literacy has been developed primarily in an edu-cational context (Killick 2006; Sharp 2001). It is associated with emotional intelligence (Goleman 1995) and five elements defined by a range of authors relevant to both are self-awareness, self-regulation, motivation, empathy and social competence (Killick 2006). In this chapter the focus will be on the first two elements; self-awareness and self-regulation and are identified within Layder's social domains of psychobiography (the individual) and situated activity (interrelationships) (Layder 2006). With reference to the research data, some of the ways in which those working within the criminal justice system can become 'self-aware', learn about their emotions and develop an ability to articulate and regulate their feelings will be explored. The research revealed a turbulence of feelings, which highlighted some of the differences and tensions between their inner, largely invisible and 'underground' world of emotion (Scheff, Stanko et al. 2002; Layder 2004) and the organisational systems that represent the public image of their practice. Some of the substance of this inner emotional world is illuminated through an exploration of the words, meta-phors, emotional expressions, non-verbal indicators and reflections employed by the research participants. The chapter also examines some small gendered differences in the use of language.

Research findings

Knowing yourself; how the research participants described their emotional lives

'Knowing yourself' is not a prerogative of the probation practitioner, although self-knowledge has been recognised historically as of considerable significance in any form of therapeutic work with offenders (Smith 2006; Vanstone 2007; Monger 1972). 'Self-awareness' is seen as a prerequisite of emotional literacy (Sharp 2001; Killick 2006). It is argued that we first need to know and under-stand our own emotions if we are to recognise and respond to the emotions of others. The self-aware person is described as having a good understanding of what motivates them, where their feelings come from, what triggers these feelings, how they are expressed through physical sensations and non-verbal communication and how they are thought about, appraised and verbalised

(Frijda, Manstead et al. 2000, Freshwater and Robertson 2002, Ansbro 2008). Killick describes self-awareness as:

> Knowing one's own emotions at any one time. Recognising a feeling when it is being experienced and being aware of the thoughts that have led to the experience of the feeling. (Killick 2006: 42)

A number of writers have identified some key themes in relation to self-awareness which include having a positive self-regard, an extensive feelings vocabulary and reflexivity, which is defined as an ability to reflect on feelings and behaviour (Sharp 2001, Killick 2006, Sparrow and Knight 2006, Howe 2008).

Emotion vocabularies

The role of language in the construction of meaning is particularly important in relation to emotion experiences. An 'emotion vocabulary' suggests a wide-ranging lexicon specific to the emotional world. Beginning with Darwin in the late nineteenth century (1872), researchers have endeavoured to come up with basic sets of emotions and have tried to distil these from looking at language. Generally these 'basic' emotions are considered to be:

- Joy
- Distress
- Anger
- Fear
- Surprise
- Disgust (Ekman and Wallace 2002)

Kagan suggests that most emotion words are not sufficiently able to describe the subtle differences in how a person feels (Kagan 2010). The concept of 'basic' emotions proved to be only a very rough taxonomy within the research project and whilst participants mentioned all of the six basic emotions they were not predominant and they used a wide range of additional words to express their feelings (Baron-Cohen 2003).

An analysis of emotion words using Baron-Cohen's concept of negative and positive emotions highlighted the fact that the research participants expressed a much wider range of 'negative' feelings (some 25 feelings were identified as negative) and generally had more to say under this heading than under the 'positive' heading. The most frequently identified 'negative' feelings were grouped as sadness (44), fear/anxiety (29), anger (17), frustration (18) and upset (14). Many of those who identified feeling frustration located this more frequently in their attitude towards 'management' rather than towards

offenders, finding the managerialism and target-driven culture of their organisation an immense source of frustration. Some expressed the stronger feeling
of anger towards management although in almost equal proportions it was also
towards offenders who had committed particular unpleasant offences and/or
had proved particularly resistant to their interventions. Some (five) acknowledged feelings of disgust at offences that offenders had committed, and how
hard it was to try and detach these feelings from the work they had to do with
that person. Sadness was a feeling expressed by a considerable number of the
research participants.

Gender and language

A small number of gender differences in the use of language was apparent
from the data although insufficient to claim any strong generalisability. There
was some limited evidence that the female research participants used more
emotion words to describe themselves than the male research participants
(an average of 5.4 words for the females and 4.6 for the males). The strongest
of the 'positive feelings' were a sense of satisfaction, enjoyment and happiness
in the direct work with offenders and of feeling empathy and concern towards
them. The female research participants used slightly fewer positive words and
slightly more negative words than the males. A significantly larger percent-
age of male research participants (44%) were likely to find humour and fun
a positive emotion aroused by the work than the females (10.5%). However,
84% of the female research participants used words related to enjoyment and
happiness whereas only 55% of the male research participants used such words.
Interestingly, 44% of the male research participants used the word 'kind' to
describe how they felt towards their work and only 26% of the female research
participants used this word. Some females used terms related to uncertainty
(21%), disbelief (10.5%) and embarrassment (5%) whereas none of the male
research participants used these terms.

These small gender differences suggest either that the female research participants gained slightly more enjoyment from their work, alongside carrying
more negative feelings, including greater measures of ambivalence and uncertainty about the work, or that they were more willing to describe these feelings
in an interview. This is in contrast with their male colleagues who expressed
less enjoyment but found more humour in their work and saw themselves as
kind. They did not express the same level of confusion or uncertainty as their
female colleagues. This does reflect other studies that have examined the differences between how men and women describe their feelings in the workplace
(Oakley 2005, Glenberg, Webster et al. 2009). However, it is acknowledged
that the differences in this study were slight and interpretation of this area is
complex.

Talking about emotions

When talking about emotions, the research participants conjured up a complex mixture of the familiar and the obvious, alongside a certain bewilderment that it was so hard to explain and define. None of them had any difficulty in recognising the significance of emotion in their lives but the very nature of its 'unpredictability' and to some extent its 'uncontrollability' proved challenging for research participants to both acknowledge and articulate. This may be another reason why, despite its ubiquity, generations of writers within the social sciences have struggled to incorporate the concept of emotions within their research and writing, and that it is only relatively recently that it has begun to gain some centre ground (Layder 2004).

The research participants had to find words to explain or conceptualise their feelings. This inevitably involved them in a process of appraisal or reappraisal of previous occurrences in their lives which offers some explanation for the hesitancy of their language and their non-verbal behaviour during the course of the interviews (Berkowitz 2000). Some of the research participants were clearly unused to being asked about their 'feelings' and un-practiced at articulating, in words and in a work context, how they thought about their feelings (Oatley 2009; Ansbro 2008; Kagan 2010; Izard 2010). Questions about the meaning of emotion proved a challenge for many of them. Fourteen of them gave clear indications of pausing to think, and struggling to find appropriate words.

Karen acknowledged that the very nature of 'emotion' made it difficult to articulate:

> I think that what emotion means to me on a deep level, it can mean not being able to express how you feel. (Karen)

Whilst others were just identifying their struggle to conceptualise the meaning of the different words used to describe the subject under discussion:

> it's, sometimes I have difficulty understanding ... – differentiating between emotions, feelings and moods. (Jai)

All of the research participants had acknowledged the significance of 'emotion' in the context of the work they were doing by agreeing to participate in this research and the majority subsequently confirmed this during the course of the interviews.

> They (emotions) are a crucial part of my job, helping people to identify them and understanding the importance of them. (Hannah)

Some moved on to make the connection between thoughts and feelings, or how they believed that their feelings were mediated by cognition (Gendron and Barrett 2009). One very experienced worker described how she had to dig beneath the surface to reach the feelings beneath the words, an example of Layder's underground emotion work (Layder 2004):

> Well it is just getting in touch with your feelings about something. It goes beyond the thinking ... It is fascinating how often you ask people, how does that make you feel? And people instantly move into how they thought or what they did. But I would say, but what was the feeling that was there? (Lynn)

The majority of research participants decided that 'emotion' was about 'feelings', lots of different feelings and getting in touch with feelings. Other explanations included the idea that emotions were 'pure' (Victoria), that some were soft and others stronger (Janet), that they were normal but irrational and could creep up on you (Michael) and that they were an immediate reaction to something that could not necessarily be controlled (Victoria). Lynn talked about the 'rawness' of emotions and being in touch with what your body or heart is saying to you. As the interviewer I was asking the research participants to identify the 'internal conversation' that goes on when we are thinking something through, when we are endeavouring to see ourselves through the eyes of others and anticipating how they will respond (Layder 2006:74). Language or 'symbolic communication' creates the conditions for a much more subtle and complex form of interaction between people than might normally occur (Layder 2006:74). Others who have written in this area suggest that talking with others about emotional experiences may, in the course of the interview, cause them to redefine or even change their own emotion experiences (Fineman 2003, Coupland, Brown et al. 2009). The process of having your feelings understood and validated by an empathic and non-judgemental listener can enable appraisal and cognition to take place (Rogers 2004; Hennessey 2011).

For a minority of research participants their range of emotion words and their engagement in the interview was more controlled and distant. Robert used only one word to describe his emotions at work, which was 'kind' and he was not able to describe any particular emotional experiences within the work environment:

> I've not really been upset ... in terms of face to face ..... no I can't, nothing springs to mind. (Robert)

The use of metaphor

Much of the language used by the research participants to describe their understanding of emotion was metaphorical and offered some powerful symbolism of the mind/body connection and the differences between a sense of the innateness of emotions and the cultural contexts in which they are shaped. A metaphor can be a way of uncovering or revealing what is going on under the surface of a discourse. A great deal of a person's emotional life is conveyed through metaphor and sometimes they can be quite apocalyptic or cataclysmic such as 'exploding' with feelings (Cameron, Maslen et al. 2009). In the following extract Pat conveys the notion of the 'underground emotion work' (Layder 2004) that is going on whilst the outward appearance of calm is maintained:

> You're like a duck on the water, underneath you're paddling like mad but you're calm on the surface. (Pat)

As Pat's quote reveals, in order to do her job in certain difficult circumstances she needed to work extremely hard, even perhaps 'frantically', as the 'paddling like mad' image conveys, whilst outwardly conveying to the world calmness, stillness and competence. Layder refers to the outward appearance of smoothness and of nothing untoward going on, which actually conceals a complex mix of emotions and influences going on underneath the surface of the encounter (Layder 2006). Our language is riddled with metaphor and it could be argued that all language is, to a greater or lesser extent, a metaphor for understanding how we think, feel and relate to others (Cameron 1999).

'Being emotional'

Most research participants provided examples of feelings provoked by face-to-face work with offenders. Some talked about times when their emotions had been close to the surface and sometimes very overtly expressed. Some indicated that they had been in tears or obviously angry. Others indicated that they had been nearly in tears, and with hindsight thought that the offender would have noticed, but, nevertheless, they kept some control on their distress. One described going 'red in the face' such that the offender would notice, but otherwise controlling her responses. Some admitted to showing other non-verbal signs such as 'sighing'. Sandy gave an example of how she could not always predict how she might feel in a given situation:

> I remember reading about a guy, it was awful abuse but the bit that made me really sad was reading about the state of the beds that the children had slept in, it had nothing to do with him, they had maggots in and I think, that bit really frightened, upset me because I was quite prepared for the sex stuff that I had read, dealt with that, but I suppose those things catch you when you least expect it. (Sandy)

This suggests Sandy had 'prepared' herself for unpleasant revelations about sexual behaviour but was caught unawares by the poverty of the family situation. Howard referred to how a dreadful sexual offence did not have an impact on him whereas a different offender's behaviour did. The suggestion he makes to explain this is that he found one man likeable and another made him feel angry. There may have been issues of unconscious transference of feelings between them of which he was unaware (Rogers 2004).

Damien identified a powerful roller coaster of emotional states in himself and Maggie described feelings that were almost overwhelming and which arose from the risks she feared a particular offender posed. She was worried about this offender and the road in question that she refers to below is where he lived. She provides an example of the degree of responsibility and anxiety felt by many workers that has to be 'contained' or 'lived with' throughout their daily lives and not just when in a face-to-face situation with an offender.

> Yes ... well one incident did happen one evening when I was leaving W ... they had blocked off the road, the main road to get out and my heart was just going: dooff, dooff, dooff, dooff and I thought, 'Oh no, that is right near so-and-so's house that is', and I was worrying about it all the way home, and I was thinking, 'Oh God', as soon as I got in and then I had to phone up the next morning and find out if it was his house. (Maggie)

In some instances this sense of 'being emotional' was defined as a personal characteristic – that some people were naturally more 'emotional' and displayed their feelings more frequently, but for others it was just something that could 'spill over' for anyone, in times of particular stress or distress. This latter group of research participants saw people as normally living within certain parameters of social conduct and 'being emotional' meant moving outside these normal parameters (Berkowitz 2000). Some also considered it to be an extreme expression of feelings such as being very weepy or very angry (Jai and Karen).

Some talked about 'being emotional' in relation to themselves:

> And again, sometimes for me it bubbles over. (Angela)

The metaphor of 'bubbles over' has an association with Descartes notion of a hydraulic theory of emotion, which viewed feelings as mental fluids that circulate the mind (Evans 2003). The use of this metaphor suggests that Angela feels her emotions are unpredictable and fluid. Whether an emotion occurs in an 'out of control' manner because it exists independently of free will and thought process is debatable (Lakoff 1987; Theodosius 2008). The idea that emotion can 'bubble up' may suggest that it is something 'out of control'.

However, Hochschild argues that we should not let language, through the use of metaphor, define emotion as having autonomy and agency; she suggests it is dependent on how we represent it through language (Hochschild 1998).

Research participants also gave descriptions of how they saw 'being emotional' in relation to other people. Robert conveyed a sense of disapproval:

> Whether good or bad, there's lots of people who shout and scream, 'oh my god, this is happening' and whatever ... I am not one of those people, I tend to kind of ... deal with information myself and kind of, I'm not very expressive outwardly about things. (Robert)

Whereas Heather, whilst recognising the negative stereotype, actually welcomed it:

> But when people talk about being emotional we tend to use it in a negative way rather than see it as somebody in touch with certain feelings and that can be a positive. (Heather)

The overall picture painted by the research participants was that 'emotionality' or outwardly florid expressions of emotion were not welcomed within the probation service and were viewed as both negative and in need of control. It was also seen by a number as having an association with mental ill-health which they felt was largely unacknowledged within the service:

> And it shouldn't be taboo, and this is in terms of ... you know when people are off with stress or their mental health is not particularly good, ... some people have good mental health and some people don't, and it is almost like there is a stigma around mental health. (Gill)

Emotionality was seen by some research participants to carry a negative gender stereotype (Langford 1997, Ciarrochi, Hynes et al. 2005).

Non-verbal indications of feelings

In addition to words there are important non-verbal indicators of feelings conveyed through body language, that people may have greater or lesser self-awareness about (Howe 2008). Darwin first emphasised the importance of these signals in 'Expressions of the Emotions in Man and Animals' (1872/1998). He referred to gestures, including sets of facial and bodily movements caused by internal mental states seeking expression, as 'emotional expressions' (Darwin and Ekman 1872/1998, Gendron and Barrett 2009). Darwin explained emotional expressions as habits or reflexes prepared by evolution to enable the person to deal with the situations with which they are confronted (Darwin and Ekman 1872/1998). There are also cultural differences in body language, which can convey different meanings in different contexts. Non-verbal communication can be invisible to people who have not learnt how to read the signs, and this is particular evident for people on the autistic spectrum (Baron-Cohen 2003).

An understanding of the non-verbal aspects of communication in building relationships and engaging offenders in the change process was referred to by a significant number of research participants. In particular they saw eye contact as a very socially significant piece of non-verbal communication. Lack of eye contact can indicate a lack of interest, disapproval, a lack of confidence or even untrustworthiness (Thompson 2009:116). Michael acknowledges this:

> Body language and eye contact – very important messages I'm trying to give to someone. (Michael)

Howard was able to acknowledge the negative messages he recognised he was conveying:

> I knew immediately at the time. I acted on my emotions at that time. I think sometimes my voice – sometimes – my body language might portray I'm frustrated – the men might call it anger. I'd call it frustration. (Howard)

Reflexivity: understanding the impact of feelings

Self-awareness may be judged largely by the ability of the person to reflect on their behaviour and emotions. Probation students are taught about the significance of reflective practice (Schon 2003, Thompson and Thompson 2008), and are encouraged to write reflective accounts and learning logs which include reflections on their feelings and responses to the work in the belief that honesty, particularly in relation to mistakes made, is the best learning tool (Knight and White 2001). However, the best learning usually occurs when there are opportunities to 'catch' the feeling that occurred in a particular situation and affected the person's behaviour, before the feeling passes or is dismissed. For example, a flash of fear or defensiveness felt by the worker in an interview might be disguised and subsequently 'forgotten', but with the right opportunity the trigger for, and meaning of, this feeling and its impact on the worker's ability to give their full attention to the offender could be reflected upon in a subsequent supervision or mentoring session.

Reflection was a significant focus of the research interviews, albeit there were inevitably limitations on how much the research participants might reveal of their 'inner conversations' with themselves (Layder 2004). In a number of interviews (Sandy, Victoria, Karen, Hannah, Janet, for example), there was a noticeable increase in emotional openness as the conversation progressed indicating that the interaction between interviewer and interviewee was opening up a safe emotional space for disclosure to occur (Truax and Carkhuff 1967; Herman 1997; Rogers 2004). One of the ways this 'opening up' was judged was by the answers the research participants gave to a question that invited them to talk about any time when they felt their emotions might have 'spilled over' into their work more than they would have wished. Research participants gave some quite revealing accounts. For example, Amy said:

Probably there's a level of hostility in the way I'm dealing with them. (Amy)

This indicated a willingness to acknowledge the potential impact of her negative feelings on some of the men she worked with. Howard was candid enough to admit to having lost his temper with one man:

I hauled a man out of the group from this very room – to give him an enormous bollocking about lying in the group. I knew he was lying – about his offence – that was precisely the wrong thing to do – I knew immediately at the time. I acted on my emotions at that time. (Howard)

Howard's language is full of metaphor; he is unlikely to have actually manhandled this offender from the room, but his powerful and rather aggressive choice of words 'enormous bollocking' is male-orientated. This event is presented as largely feelings-driven and he is aware, on reflection, of the inappropriateness of his behaviour.

Self-regulation of emotions

The concept of 'emotion regulation' – the control and moderation of emotional responses – has long been of interest to philosophers, scientists and researchers (Barbalet 2011), although it has emerged as an independent field of study only in the last decades of the 20th century (Gross and Barrett 2011). Regulating and managing emotions in the context of day-to-day living is something that all people undertake to a greater or lesser extent as part of normal social interaction and has important consequences for health and adaptive functioning (Tamir 2011). Some of the more extreme life events such as loss, death, conflict and celebration, for example, may heighten the presentation and expression of emotions (Goldie 2009). A career in the criminal justice arena will bring practitioners into more frequent contact with some of these major life changing events through the narratives of the offenders (De Haan and Loader 2002), and is likely to make heavy demands on staff in terms of the need to regulate their own emotions.

Regulating or managing emotions is the second element in becoming emotionally literate. It is described as the ability to use the knowledge generated by reflexivity and self-awareness to manage feelings effectively and to be able to make positive changes to personal behaviour (Killick 2006). It includes the ability to manage a feeling in order to change a pre-existing emotional state (Hochschild 1983), and as an evaluative process it involves people taking a stance about their emotions and the consequences of any subsequent actions (Frijda 1986).

Learning how to regulate emotions

As the research participants developed their comments around the concept of emotion and how they described their emotional lives, they identified ways in which they felt they had learnt to regulate or manage their emotions at work. A significant number of them (20) felt that in the early stages of their career their feelings had been much nearer the surface and less 'processed' and that it was mostly only through life experience and the passage of time that they had learnt to recognise and manage their emotions more effectively. This 'maturation' of emotional control is a recognised process – the ability to recognise and understand what we feel can take a lifetime (Harré and Parrott 1996). For a number of research participants the learning about the significance of emotions and emotion regulation in order to enhance their work skills was largely 'on the job', through observation of others – an 'apprenticeship' model. Some research participants gave examples of how they believed they might have initially done it the 'wrong' way but then learnt, through 'trial and error', to do it the 'right' way with an acknowledgement that this was not always an easy process. The indications are that some felt less able to control their feelings when they started their career, and saw this as something of a problem:

> In the early days I cried at court. (Mary)

Geoff describes how the overall learning process around feelings has resulted in a levelling out of the extremes of emotion that he might have experienced in the early years:

> I think years and years ago I would have had a whole range of quite strong emotions. I would have been quite angry, I would have been disappointed, I would have been sad, but … I would have been elated when we had a result from somebody you know, when a light-bulb went on, … but … I think that has subsided over the years. (Geoff)

Geoff conveys a sense of the 'passion' in him, involving both positive and negative feelings, being eroded by the passage of time and work; he does not indicate if he feels any regret about this loss. Other research participants described strengths of feelings at certain points in their work and an acknowledgement that they needed time, or assistance, to regain their composure and their equilibrium and return to the professional role required of them. This was a further indication that they had some concept of the need to be 'professional', which they aspired to via a process of control and management of their feelings.

Some gave examples of how they had just learnt through life experience:

> Most of my learning (about emotions) has come from my own personal experiences. (Tess)

> I think to summarise, it really is something that you learn from experience, you can't be trained in it in any way, it would be nice if there could be more acceptance of it at the training stage and the relevance of it ... you have to learn to control it when you are dealing with people that we deal with ... and forget it when you go home. (Pat)

Howard talked about how he learned to regulate his emotions, indicating that he had a notion of how this should be achieved through a mixture of maturation, control and cognition:

> So the personal skills that I bring from my life experience – I was 36 when I joined probation ... I've been around the block a few times ... because when I was young I was particularly feelings driven – they were the most important things in my life and they kind of dictated the way I made choices to behave – the choice part of it – the thoughts that militated the way that I behaved were fairly indistinct and not very well developed. Now as an older person with the benefit of life experience and learning – that I've chosen to change the way I live my life – and to militate some of those feelings with thoughts. (Howard)

Howard's use of metaphor; 'been around the block a few times' suggests a different form of learning; a 'street' apprenticeship that he believes gave him the skills necessary to do his current job. Other research participants identified learning about emotions, and emotional control that had arisen almost incidentally, as a by-product of being involved in delivering accredited offending behaviour training programmes (Ministry of Justice 2010). They had gained vicarious learning for themselves by reflecting on the courses they had been on to deliver the programmes, or on guidance in the manuals, about the emotions of offenders. John made reference to how a group work programme which helps offenders get in touch with their feelings had helped him to learn about his own emotions, metaphorically 'as he went along', implying a journey of learning (Cameron and Low 1999):

Hannah, in the next quote, accepts the need to prevent her emotions, aroused by the nature of the offending behaviour, from 'getting in the way' of dealing directly with the person:

> If their offences are very serious, that can invoke really strong emotions in you ... of disgust and anger, ... and just incomprehensibility, really all of those things but ... when you then deal with the person you mustn't let that get in the way, because it is about dealing with that person and helping them move forward. (Hannah)

Geoff, prompted by me, provides a further example of his understanding of the nature of transference and the need to regulate his feelings as a result. He also knows what to do with his feelings subsequently, which is to discuss them in supervision:

> G: 'There might be something that occasionally is slightly stronger than that...where I might become angry with someone but not within the group, that might come out later.'
> C: 'You contain it?'
> G: 'Yes, because that is where it belongs, because I am irritated – I am aware I am not angry with the man, I am irritated, but I am angry about other things and so supervision is the place to take that.' (Geoff)

David referred to a very difficult early life experience that he had been able to successfully 'work through'. His 'success' in dealing with this distressing early life experience had resulted in him being able to maintain 'calmness' in almost all work situations, an aspiration of being 'professional':

> I don't get angry very much myself – I am generally calm; it is rare for me to get upset. I once was engaged in some therapeutic work with colleagues when I recounted an experience I had as a child – but I think my colleagues were more upset to hear it than I was to tell it – I had largely worked through it. (David)

All these responses indicate an assumed 'correct' way in which emotions should be managed and controlled within the work context. In the above responses 'calmness' and 'control' come through as goals of emotion regulation, the inference being that strong or unregulated emotional expression would not be appropriate in the work setting. Fineman suggests that we may not show what we feel because we are aware of the delicate balance to be sustained between showing what we feel and destabilising a social order (Fineman 2001). The research participants appeared to have imbibed a belief about emotion regulation through a life process and a sense of what being 'professional' entailed.

Fear of emotion

These first comments about emotion regulation begin to build a profile of workers seeking to 'calm', 'control' and 'moderate' their emotional responses in order to meet the perceived needs of 'professionalism'. However, underlying this assumed need to maintain a 'stable social order', there was also, for some, a certain fear or anxiety about emotions. Layder refers to an 'ontological insecurity' that the self is subjected to, which can lead to generalised feelings of insecurity and a frequent desire to hide or conceal this from others:

> It is quite scary as to how you can control all that. (Gill)

> We're not robots so I think emotions are very hard sometimes to manage (Janet)

Sophie raised an issue that had come up in a training session of potentially being aroused by depositions containing graphic accounts of sexual behaviour and how difficult this would be for anyone to admit to or seek help with:

> One of the ... things that came out of one of these sessions was that, it would take some guts to admit, one of the officers said that you have to recognize that sometimes if you are reading depositions (deps) about sex offences, that sometimes people might become sexually aroused but to say that in ... that kind of setting ... kind of like, phew, ..., but, it isn't anything that I would explore I don't think. (Sophie)

Sophie expresses admiration at the bravery of anyone who might acknowledge the arousal of their own sexual feelings, but also her fear of articulating such concerns for herself. In this context Sophie's fear is of the specific and inappropriate (in a work context) feeling of sex arousal. This was the only statement that came close to any acknowledgement of sexual feelings despite the majority of the research participants working directly with sex offenders, and is perhaps an indication of some of the inhibitions on discussing emotional, and in this case, sexual, feelings in the work setting.

Not all workers demonstrated the same levels of concern about or fear of emotion. Janet reflects positively about her approach to regulating her own emotions. She demonstrates her understanding, similar to the other research participants, of the perceived need in a work context, to 'hold onto' her feelings and not give them full expression but she presents as feeling comfortable with this:

> I've been near to tears before but I've never actually done it but ... no, I've held onto it so far, but I've probably got a bit flustered and a bit red in the face and my body language has probably changed you know ... but on the whole I think that I manage them quite well. (Janet)

Strategies for self-regulation

The challenge for the research participants is the judgement of what to do with the feelings that have arisen in them as a result of a particular situation; for example, an offender's behaviour or attitude, or an organisational demand or edict or the extent to which they understand the reasons or triggers for the feelings that have arisen within them. The feelings may be directly related to the current situation or they may contain elements of transference from earlier or previous difficult experiences in their own lives. The greater their self-awareness about the potential causes of their feelings the more choice they are likely to have in the strategies they employ to regulate these feelings (Mearns and Thorne 2008).

Analysis of the data suggests that the research participants used three broad strategies to manage their emotions in the workplace. These strategies were not mutually exclusive and some research participants described using more than one strategy at different times:

- Controlling, suppressing or masking, such that they did not spill over directly into their work (Goffman 1959/1990)
- Detaching – consciously avoiding the feelings (Crawley 2004)
- Integrating, that is, incorporating their emotions within their practice – having a 'helping relationship with self' (Rogers 2004; Mearns and Thorne 2008)

Controlling, suppressing or masking

A significant number of research participants (18) considered that emotions, particularly those deemed 'inappropriate' to the context, were something that could not easily be controlled, but that, nevertheless, had to be controlled and concealed, even 'masked' in order to do their job, and remain 'professional'. Thirteen research participants used the word 'control' when describing the management of their emotions in the workplace and they had a range of strategies for achieving this. For some the idea of 'being emotional' meant being 'out of control' with the associated fears of powerlessness and vulnerability. Some saw the gradual development in managing their emotions as the necessary control of a messy and irrational aspect of human behaviour.

> I've learnt in my work to control them more. (Victoria)

Aruna demonstrates a progression from 'panic' or fear of her emotional response, through to control and 'management':

> First time you get somebody you kind of panic, you're not really sure what to do, but with practice the more you can deal with it, your emotions, the more you know how to deal with it … the last time somebody kicked off almost … and was getting quite angry and verbal and blaming me and everyone else for all his problems … you know if you raise your voice, then they'll raise and you raise and so on, so it is about making sure you remain calm and making sure that my voice stays at a certain level and it doesn't raise, I listen to what they've got to say and take on board and if they still rant and rave I just repeat my point, and the fact, that okay I understand your feelings, I can't change that. (Aruna)

Aruna demonstrates the premise of the majority of research participants, that 'calmness' and control of her own emotions are essential in volatile situations such as this. She also uses assertiveness techniques (e.g. repetition of certain statements (Cherry 2010)) to maintain her stance, which she acknowledges works in some situations but not others. Aruna's strategy is to remain calm and, if necessary, terminate the interview. This position is likely to be supported by the health and safety policy of her agency with regard to angry and abusive offenders, which would prioritise her own safety and that of colleagues.

In addition to controlling them, a number of research participants saw emotions as needing to be masked, suppressed or hidden, which suggests the erection of a defence or screen between how they were actually feeling and how they presented themselves to the outside world; Goffman refers to this as 'impression management' (Goffman 1959:203). He identifies it as the attributes that are required for the work of successfully 'staging a character' 'and talks of people undertaking a 'performance' and 'playing a part' (Goffman 1959:28). He considers that at one extreme the performer could be fully taken in by his (sic) own act and could sincerely believe that the impression of reality he is giving is the real one. At the other end of this continuum the performer may not be taken in by his own act and can be 'seen through' by others; Goffman labelled this a 'front' (Goffman 1959:33).

Hochschild also describes the process of emotion regulation as a form of acting and that this is undertaken on either a surface or a deep level. In 'surface acting' the person endeavours to change how they outwardly appear through their body language; for example, a 'put-on sneer, posed shrug, controlled sigh' (Hochschild 2004:35). She describes surface acting as the ability to deceive others about what we are really feeling without deceiving ourselves. In contrast, 'deep acting' involves deceiving ourselves about our true emotions as much as we deceive others (Hochschild 1983:33). In this case the 'actor' learns to believe in the emotions they are expressing through 'conscious mental work', 'psyching themselves up for a particular activity or event' (Theodosius 2008:18). In 'deep acting' feelings are actively induced, suppressed or shaped. This raises a question about the point at which regulation of emotions may lead to insincerity or inauthenticity, pretending to feel something that is not actually felt, and whether or not the offender identifies this and with what consequences. Alternatively, it may cease to be self-deception if the worker convinces themselves of its truth to their current situation. It is also an approach that can lead to a genuine connection in which the feelings of both participants are sincere.

For the research participants, being in control of feelings also meant putting them 'on hold', and to some extent acting as though these feelings were not impinging on them:

I've got to put my feelings on hold ... hopefully it doesn't show. (Jai)

In this example Jai is describing surface acting in which she makes a deliberate attempt to conceal her feelings but recognises, by her doubtfulness, that they may still leak through. She also admits to feeling discomfort at showing, or presenting, any negative emotion despite clearly holding some quite strong negative emotions:

He was blaming her all the time and her behaviour, and those kind of things make me frustrated and angry and it was one of those cases you know, I kind of let it show, usually I kind of control ... my responses in front of a group. (Jai)

Other research participants gave examples of the need to conceal and mask their feelings, in other words 'perform a part' or put on a 'front'. Tess felt she needed to do so in order to protect the offenders she worked with from her own negative feelings about their situation:

Generally I would try to conceal, if I feel it would be inappropriate for them to see how I was feeling, particularly with the hopelessness ... with the anger aspect. (Tess)

In the following exchange between myself and Pat she described how she initially 'masked' her emotions but in the process felt she had 'become harder'. She was initially performing 'surface acting' but this had moved towards 'deep acting':

C.   'You talked about masking feelings sometimes, what were those feelings that you masked?'

P: 'Well I masked but over the years you become a lot harder ... at the beginning I was close to tears with a lot of things, even in child protection when they had to take a child away I was really close to tears but I had, you know, you become tougher and I had to toughen up to be fair ... so you have to hide you know, every emotion really because you have to be this sympathetic ear ... because if you screw that up they're not going to tell you anything again.' (Pat)

Despite this declared 'hardness' her final comment suggests that she is balancing a desire to be 'professional' and unemotional, with a belief that only by keeping her own emotions on hold will she enable the offender to express his real feelings. Rogers argues for the creation of a 'helping relationship with myself' (Rogers 2004:51), by which he means a sensitive awareness and acceptance of his own feelings that then offers a better chance of forming a helping relationship with another.

Drawbacks to strategies of control

Whilst maintaining a 'front', and controlling and masking emotion may be an essential skill in the probation workers' strategy (e.g. the expression of disgust at the narrative of a sex offender would effectively terminate all effective communication), it also has some potential drawbacks. In masking an emotion the worker may have insufficient time, resource or opportunity to reflect on the causes of the feeling (self-awareness). They may be unaware of the potential for such repressed feelings to leak out and infect or corrupt their exchanges with another person (Rogers 2004). Rogers suggests that if, as a therapist, he is experiencing an attitude of annoyance towards another person but is unaware of it, then his communication will contain contradictory messages (Rogers 2004:51). The words are giving one message but in subtle ways he will be communicating the annoyance he feels and thus confusing the person and making (him) distrustful, although that person may also be unaware of what is causing the difficulty.

In this next quote, Sandy is explicitly recognising the importance of an understanding of self as a prerequisite to being able to work constructively with others and the potential dangerousness of workers who lack this self-understanding:

> I think most people come into this job because they have something to fix often and I would have said some years ago that I didn't, ... then I realised that I did and so I went and sorted it, but then I think what happens is that you learn from those skills, and I would quite like them to have the opportunity to fix because quite honestly some of them are dangerous. (Sandy)

Detaching and distancing

A significant number of research participants chose to consciously distance themselves from the emotional world of the offender (Tony, Angela, Robert, Victoria, Pat, Aruna, Sophie, Mary and Gill) and disengage their feelings from what they were hearing. There is evidence of this as a general strategy in many organisational contexts (Du Gay 2003). This form of detachment is primarily focused on protecting the individual from excessive emotional demands and stresses in the working environment and can be an important strategy for avoiding 'burnout'. Some described it as a process of 'getting tougher' which could mean an emotional resilience or an emotional distancing or immunity:

> Unfortunately I think you do become a little bit hardened to it so it only really affects you on the extreme cases and I so think you get a little bit desensitised to issues. (Mary)

Mary's comment indicates some fear on her part that she may miss or lack sensitivity towards certain aspects of the lives of the offenders' she was working with. Robert gives a good example of a form of surface acting that enabled him to detach his feelings from the distressing circumstances of the people he worked with (Hochschild 1983). He even makes reference to acting:

> Yes, it was sort of a conscious decision because when I first started doing the job I realised that people can tell me quite shocking things and it can really get to you if you take them on board, the reality of it, it can be quite shocking so I kind of see myself walking through the door as if I am going to a theatre or television set and I am kind of participating in it in some kind of way ... you go through the pain barrier and you start dealing with difficult cases. I ... try to kind of switch off that ... part of my brain in a way, try not to become emotionally involved ..., I find it easier to go home and not worry about what people are telling me and ... so I don't actually feel too much. (Robert)

Robert uses metaphors in his explanation of how he manages to self-regulate and control his emotions. He talks of work with offenders as 'going to a theatre' and 'participating' presumably in some form of 'play' or 'drama' (Goffman 1959/1990). He talks of going 'through the pain barrier' which implies something quite frightening and painful to him such that he tries to 'switch off' the part of his brain that might actually feel this pain. He is also clear he does not wish to take 'troubles home', implying they should be left behind at work.

Aruna uses another duck metaphor to suggest that she was untroubled by the emotional context of the work:

> But I think that I'm more, 'water off a duck's back' nothing really bothers me that much, I don't think I let things get to me, they don't bother me that much. (Aruna)

Sophie was honest enough to admit that she found it distracting and time-consuming if an offender became emotional, by which it seems she meant 'upset', rather than, for example angry, in an interview:

> They become emotional, but unfortunately if it's not actually related to what I am trying to write the report about, it is also quite time consuming. (Sophie)

Nick recognised he had gone through a process of desensitisation or conditioning as a form of protection:

> But we work in an environment where we, the files contain some horrific ... you know offences, but I don't know, I think sometimes you can become quite blasé you know almost conditioned in a sense. (Nick)

This 'conditioning' is an expectation of prison staff. Displays of emotion in the prison context are seen as leaving the worker open to manipulation, collusion with and exploitation by the prisoner; with a presumption that no prisoner can be trusted (Crawley 2004). These are the same (mostly) men with whom probation staff work and the transfer of such strategies, whether consciously or unconsciously, to probation practice is not such a leap to make, particularly for probation staff seconded to work in prisons and/or responsible for significant numbers of prisoners and parolees.

Drawbacks to strategies of detachment

The problem with detachment as a strategy is two-fold; the worker may, through standing back from emotional engagement, fail to harness the

motivation of the offender and secondly fail to pick up on important signals and information about the offender's state of mind and attitudes.
Chamberlayne identifies an emergent pattern of emotional retreat by professionals at key moments of interaction, which she argues can reinforce
a sense of social exclusion in the 'client' at the point at which there is a
chance of doing something positive about the real and underlying problems
(Chamberlayne 2004). Some research participants were able to acknowledge
that being 'detached' could mean showing insufficient empathy (Janet and
Sophie), and that this had begun to change for them with experience and
confidence; they felt they could show more.

Managing emotions within practice

The third strategy came from those research participants who seemed more
comfortable in their discussion of emotions for both themselves and the
offenders they supervised. These were staff who talked about strong emotional
support at home and/or with work colleagues and who, in many cases, had
experienced counselling or counselling type support in other employments or
through personal interest.

> I've never been in a situation where my own house isn't reasonably in order.
> (Indira)

This group of staff seemed to appreciate the understanding and management of
their emotions as an important part of their personal growth and development.
This view is supported by writers who argue that emotional learning and maturation are central to professional competence and that this involves personal
growth and development (Akerjordet and Severinsson 2004). These research
participants felt they had less need to control, mask or detach from their feelings and were more able to 'be themselves' and act naturally, albeit still retain-
ing their awareness of professional boundaries. They were able to maintain a
degree of congruence between their feelings, the feelings of the offender and
the interaction between them such that they were generally able to integrate
their feelings within their practice and make appropriate judgements about
how they used their emotions as part and parcel of their skill repertoire (Haidt
2001, Rogers 2004). They talked about 'working it through' and their observations included examples of reflective practice (Schon 2003), where the research
participants acknowledged their feelings and reflected on when, where and
how these feelings might be best regulated:

> Most of the time I'm okay but just occasionally I think – you showed them
> something there that you shouldn't have done ... it's a fine line – we are

saying to people – it's okay to show emotion it's fine, but actually some emotions are best suppressed at times – it's a very fine line. (Michael)

If they (the depositions) are particularly bad I will feel angry, outraged, feel like ripping his head off. For me it takes about 24 hours for that to settle down – not always. Thereafter I'm in role – so I then make my way back if you like, to emotions that are centred in some level of compassion, understanding. (Amy)

Amy is admitting here to very strong feelings of anger generated by reading details of a particularly unpleasant offence and the need to give herself time to regulate these feelings such that what she takes into the actual interview with the offender is empathy and compassion, rather than disapproval and anger.

Tess demonstrated a willingness to understand what might have triggered the offender's feelings and not to take them 'personally' although she acknowledges that sometimes she feels things after the interview, suggesting she has the capacity to regulate her feelings regardless of the potential provocation. Nick demonstrates an acute awareness of the legitimacy of an offender's anger in the face of his (Nick's) inability to resolve the difficulties with his parole application. He avoids the temptation to rise to defensiveness or anger in return:

You know, he threw a few sort of expletives at me and he said, 'you're useless, what have you done for me?' you know, and I sort of came away from there thinking he was right in a way because I have tried to do those things but ultimately I have run into a brick wall myself really in trying to make this happen. (Nick)

Sandy's emotional response to the very distressing early life experience being relayed to her by the offender is understood by her as legitimate and congruent to the situation in which she was working, namely, a one-to-one interview. However, she also recognises that whilst she might have experienced similar feelings if she had heard this account in the context of a group work programme she would have made the decision to conceal her feelings. This illustrates a degree of management by Sandy of the expression of her feelings dependent on the context.

No, at one point I had tears in my eyes when he was telling me and he saw them, I don't have a problem with that … I think, because that's just about being congruent in that situation isn't it, but I wouldn't in a group necessarily because I think that is very different … to managing eight, nine people, so one person is in, I mean, they know when it affects us I think. (Sandy)

A considerable number of research participants saw self-regulation as part of their personal growth and actively sought out ways of becoming more aware and better able to manage their emotional lives:

> I think that, from someone who was quite detached from their emotions ... to actually someone who would kind of ... well I wouldn't say I was kind of an overly emotional person, I would say that I was more in-tune with that, I'm more understanding, I remember doing ... when I was in the prison service when I first joined I did a load of psychometric tests, and one of things that was flagged up for me was ...that I was very, that I showed very little empathy ... It was yes ... I suppose at the time it was absolutely right. (Damien)

Conclusion

This chapter has examined the ways in which research participants articulated and thought about their feelings and has offered some analysis of the use of language in the construction of meanings in relation to emotion. Across the interviews a wide emotion vocabulary or range of language and metaphor was employed. There was evidence that some research participants were more aware than others of the impact of their non-verbal communications. For most of these research participants the triggers for their emotions and strong feelings was immensely variable. There was some limited evidence that the female research participants used more emotion words to describe themselves than the male research participants. The gender differences in the expressions of positive and negative emotions, whilst small, do have some implications for recruitment, training and ongoing support to staff, who continue to be a majority female group. In particular it seems that the female staff may carry a greater burden of anxiety and concern in relation to their work than their male colleagues, although it is acknowledged that they may have been more willing to express these feelings in the research interview than their male colleagues.

Two significant findings were the volume of negative feelings and the extent to which research participants were able to articulate and reflect on, the impact of their feelings on themselves and the offenders they worked. Some of the research participants were clearly unused to being asked about their 'feelings' and unpractised at articulating in words and in a work context, how they thought about their feelings. The use of metaphor was an example of the sometimes veiled manner in which emotions are described.

The chapter has also considered the range of ways in which the research participants explained how they learnt to 'regulate' their emotions. This was mostly through general life and work experience although some had acquired specific learning from the training materials provided for accredited programmes. Some referred to a 'journey' of learning and for one (Sandy), this was particularly related to her identity as a member of a minority group and the work she felt she had had to do on understanding herself, her emotions and her place in society.

There was some evidence of a rather generalised fear of emotions within research participants that caused them to wish to suppress or hide feelings when they emerged, some to the point of being able to largely exclude emotions from their practice. Three different strategies employed by research participants to manage and regulate their emotions in the workplace were grouped under the headings of 'controlling', 'detaching' and 'integrating', with examples given of each of these strategies and a critique offered. The overall conclusion is that the choice of strategy for regulating and managing emotions in the workplace is a subjective one that depends on the person's previous life and work experiences and is largely unaided and unsupported by the organisation. It is located largely within the social domain of their 'psychobiography' as an individual and subjective process (Layder 2006). Workers who were able to integrate, and reflect upon, their emotions within their practice appeared most at ease with their emotional lives.

6
Building Relationships with Offenders

Practice example

Marina is a newly qualified probation officer who has been supervising Sadie, a young woman charged with credit card offences, committed jointly with her partner, Robert. Marina has worked slowly and gently with Sadie, recognising her vulnerability and her fearfulness, and that most of her offending behaviour has stemmed from her relationship with Robert. As Sadie's trust in Marina has developed she has begun to talk about occasions when Robert has been violent towards her. Marina has found this hard to hear, as she was herself a victim of domestic violence some years earlier and she finds herself telling Sadie about some of her own experiences. Her impulse is to tell Sadie that she must report Robert for his violence and she must leave him and go to a women's refuge in the town. Sadie is resistant to this and begins to withdraw in the sessions, becoming much less open with Marina.

Marina feels upset and angry at Robert's behaviour and frustrated that Sadie seems unwilling or unable to do anything to change the situation. She feels she cannot work with Sadie anymore if Sadie won't take her advice.

Marina's line manager suggests that Marina takes up the opportunity of talking with a mentor allocated to their team, about her feelings. In discussion with the mentor Marina remembers her own sense of powerlessness when in an abusive relationship with her first husband and recognises that this is probably what Sadie is feeling too. In her next session with Sadie, Marina encourages Sadie to talk about the things in her life that she enjoys doing and that make her feel better about herself. She concludes by emphasising that it is Sadie's choice what actions she takes in relationship to Robert and that she will support her whatever decisions she takes. She also encourages her to join a self-help women's group that is running at the local Women's Centre.

Key learning points

- Forming a close relationship with an offender within which trust is established and working to the strengths of the person can be an effective way of moving that person towards understanding and the motivation for change.
- Practitioners need to negotiate the emotional boundaries of the relationship. In sharing information about himself or herself with an offender the practitioner needs to be very clear that its purpose is to help the offender understand and learn, and it is not an avenue for gaining attention for their own needs. Too strong an emotional identification with an offender can be overwhelming for the offender; practitioner's need to be able to empathise but not overload the supervisory relationship with their own agendas.

Introduction

Building relationships between criminal justice practitioners and offenders is a process that occurs in a range of settings and with differing degrees of formality and informality. Almost all transactions, bar the very perfunctory, are likely to elicit a relationship of some sort, and of variable quality and meaning to the participants. Police officers work to build relationships with individuals in the process of investigating crime, and with communities and agencies that are significant in developing community safety initiatives. In terms of their interrogation of offenders and witnesses the establishment of a relationship may well be key to eliciting significant disclosures from people. Prison officers can be responsible for managing the well-being and safety of prisoners over many months or even years, and relationships built with prisoners can assist in the smooth running of the prison. Many voluntary and private-sector agencies in the criminal justice context, working in areas of victim support, drug and alcohol misuse, and homelessness issues, rely heavily on the use of the relationship, and they will increasingly take on work formerly undertaken by the probation service (Burke 2013, Ministry of Justice 2013).

For some criminal justice workers the relationships they build with offenders may be primarily instrumental, the need to gain information, or to ensure compliance to a prison regime, for example. As explored in Chapter 4 some relationships may contain significant elements of repressive interpersonal control and as such are not reflective of emotionally literate practice. This chapter examines the more benign and potentially 'therapeutic' role of relationship building in interventions with offenders to enable them to disclose information about their lives and to motivate them towards changing their behaviour. In examining some of the core elements of this process the chapter makes reference to the experiences of the probation research participants and locates this within the social domain of 'situated activity' (Ladyer 2006). It examines the perceptions of the research participants of their 'social competence' and their use of 'empathy' (Sharp 2001, Killick 2006), two further elements of emotional literacy through which they understand and respond to a range of emotions in the offenders they supervise. This includes their recognition of the significance of getting emotionally close to some offenders and of how they negotiated emotional boundaries to these relationships. It also considers their use of 'intuition', their recognition of the importance of non-verbal communication from offenders and the emphasis they place on the building of trust within the relationship in order to foster motivation and offender 'readiness to change' (Day, Casey, et al. 2010). Building trust, negotiating practical and emotional boundaries and enabling disclosure from the offender are seen as paramount in the accurate assessment and subsequent management of risk (Kemshall 2008, Kemshall 2010), which is further developed in Chapter 7.

Research findings

Social competence and empathy

The concept of 'social competence' covers a range of interpersonal and social skills seen to be core to all forms of criminal justice practice and with particular reference to the building of relationships. These skills include being able to listen with empathy, resolve conflict, negotiate, summarise, offer positive and constructive feedback and receive it oneself (Killick 2006). The socially competent person is considered to be:

> better able to handle and understand relationships and resolve conflict and disagreements. Socially competent people demonstrate improvements in social problem-solving and cooperative behaviour. (Killick 2006: 17)

Seventeen of the research participants, without any particular prompting during the course of the interview, expressed views about the significance of the relationship in all the work they undertook with offenders (Amy, Tony, Indira, Kim, Robert, Victoria, Pat, Sandy, Maggie, Damien, Aruna, Sophie, Gill, Jai, Hannah, Nick and Karen). They provided many illustrations of how important they considered the whole process of building relationships. For example:

> Trying to get some sense of that person – establish a relationship with them – you're not going anywhere without that. A sense of them as a person. (Amy)

Recognising emotions in offenders

In order to begin the process of building a relationship, either consciously or unconsciously, it is suggested that the emotionally literate person seeks to recognise and respond to a range of emotions in the other person (Goleman 1995, Sharp 2001). On being asked to identify the range of feelings and emotions expressed by offenders, most research participants found this easier than when asked to identify their own feelings. They struggled to think of 'positive' feelings expressed by offenders, identifying only nine themes in total including happiness, kindness, curiosity, persistence, openness, relaxed, thoughtful, honest and compliant. In contrast, all four of Ekman's basic 'negative' emotions were described (Ekman 2004), with anger/rage/hate being the most prominent and identified by 17 research participants. The second two largest negative categories were 'manipulation' and 'defensiveness', although manipulation is perhaps a strategy rather than a feeling. These were presented as approaches used consciously or unconsciously by offenders and seen by research participants to block or inhibit the genuine expression of emotions and to act as obstacles to productive work. Linked to a strategy of manipulation was a range of offender 'feelings' described by the research participants such as disinterest, opinionated, sarcasm, stubbornness and blocking.

The following examples illustrate some of the ways in which research participants described the negative emotions they saw in offenders:

> Talking about sex offenders, there doesn't seem to be too much anger, there tends to be denial and blame, justification ... minimalisation, quite a lot of that, trying to change the subject or manipulate you. (Robert)

> Anger ... frustration ... bitterness ... can't' be botheredness, whatever that might be (laughs) ... I can't think of the word for that, sometimes you know, disbelief, they can't believe they're really here, you know, emotions that are attached to denial ... emotions that are attached to being a victim themselves ... very rarely happy. (Victoria)

Some research participants saw these predominantly negative feelings as reflecting need and vulnerability:

> I suppose if I was to describe them generally I'd say they are quite a trusting bunch if you do your work right. They are needy, vulnerable – deviant obviously – defensive, sometimes they can be angry – not very often. Usually for not a long time. (Michael)

> Early on in the process – fear and trepidation – lack of assurance about what is going to happen to them. (Howard)

Other experienced sex offender workers also saw fear and anxiety behind the aggression and anger:

> They show ... oftentimes quite a lot of hostility, anger, big chunks of resentment, fear, anxiety and sometimes they are quite difficult to read – so

emotionally illiterate –and also have a huge amount invested in not showing anything to us or to each other – they are pretty closed down. But you
can see the fear and anxiety –creeping out in places. (Amy)

Research participants were dealing with, and interpreting, a great deal of negative emotion in offenders and their ability to respond positively to this seemed
to require considerable empathy.

'Standing in their shoes' – empathy

The most significant aspect of social competence is empathy. Killick defines
empathy as:

> Increased levels of social perceptiveness and improved ability in reading
> emotions and in sensitivity to others' feelings. (Killick 2006: 17)

It is seen as a central dimension of the therapeutic relationship (Mearns and
Thorne 2008). Bolton describes this as a 'gift' (Bolton 2005), something that
is freely offered by staff in particular work contexts, but which can equally be
withheld or not available. As explored in Chapter 4, this has particular significance in the probation field given the punitive ethos within which the service
operates and the level of negativity associated with offending. Howe identifies
empathy as being about acceptance and non-judgmentalism which links to
the emphasis placed on being non-judgemental by the research participants
and discussed in Chapter 3 (Howe 2008). Empathic people are considered to
be better at listening to each other and checking out or 'reading' the non-
verbal signals that can provide evidence of the emotional temperature of the
other.

Empathy has been promoted in recent probation literature as a significant skill within probation practice (Farrow, Kelly et al. 2007, Cherry 2010).
There is, however, little objective evidence to suggest that it is specifically
encouraged, supported or quality controlled within the probation organisation although there is some recent evidence of a new research interest in
this area (Knight and Clow 2010, Raynor, Ugwudike et al. 2010, Offender
Engagement Team 2011). Empathy was described by three of the research
participants as 'standing in their shoes' (Michael, Amy and Tony), and
viewed as a process of engagement in which they endeavoured to 'get alongside' the offender. Being able to 'stand in the shoes of' men who may have
been publicly reviled for their crimes and expressing a complex range of
negative feelings remains a largely invisible process. However, many of the
research participants were able to engage with the humanity of the person
through the use of empathy.

> People have a lot of baggage – to be aware of that ... show concern – empathy. (Michael)

Michael is reflecting his awareness of the potentially damaging and disadvantaged backgrounds, 'the baggage' of the offenders he works with.

These next two research participants demonstrate a degree of compassion for the offenders they work with:

> You're the only one who seems to value them in any way, or spends time talking to them or treats them like a human being. (Lynn)

> But the main thing that I want people not to want to lose is their self-respect and their self-esteem and you know, that is probably the hardest thing to try and build up in other people. (Heather)

Angela saw empathy as a process that involved breaking down barriers, redressing the power imbalance and recognising the commonality of human emotions. Robert recognised the importance of seeing the whole person and not just the offending part of their behaviour. Maggie provided an example of how challenging this could be:

> Yes, you know, you dragged her down the stairs and you ripped her hair out and you punched her, and you think like, 'Ooh!', but then when you meet them I suppose, ... you get to see the whole person rather than just that one aspect of them. (Maggie)

Nick articulated how he had gradually learnt to 'read' or understand the negative emotions of offenders such that he now handles things differently. In this next instance he is responding to the frustration of a prisoner:

> I think that when I first experienced that, I found that very difficult to deal with and I think that all... offenders have different feelings about how they would want somebody to deal with that situation because for some it is just an outpouring of frustration ... that has led to that point and ... there was a case in point on Monday when he was crying and because he was being abusive as well, the easiest thing for me to have done would have been to say that because you are being abusive I am going to terminate the interview and I didn't want to do that for a number of reasons. (Nick)

Nick is demonstrating how he has learnt to identify two different emotions in an offender (distress and anger/frustration) being expressed simultaneously. He implies that, with less experience, the challenge of being on the receiving end of this might have led him to respond to only one of the emotions (anger/frustration), to take it personally and to consider his own self-protection by terminating the interview. He would probably have been supported in such an action by the Agency's Health and Safety policy, but instead he chose to regulate his own feelings, acknowledge his agency role and reflect on the source of the feelings being expressed, demonstrating both compassion and altruism (Ekman 2008). The above example shows a worker acknowledging and containing the angry feelings of a prisoner. Other research participants gave examples of this 'acknowledgement' or 'validation' of feelings (Heather, Sandy, Indira and Angela). The ability to do this but not become overwhelmed with the intensity of the other's feelings is seen as a crucial counselling skill (Mearns and Thorne 2008).

Empathy was seen by some research participants as requiring a 'giving' of aspects of the self, which accords with Bolton's view of philanthropic emotion management as a gift (Bolton 2005) (see Chapter 8). The use of 'self' and of judicious 'self-disclosure' is seen to require skill and judgement, a careful balance needing to be maintained between self-disclosure for the benefit of the client/offender and self-disclosure that may be about the worker's own needs. The psychotherapeutic literature (e.g. Mearns 2005), provides guidance on the role of self-disclosure in counselling practice but there is little evidence that any consistent guidance on this is included in probation training or in supervised practice (Knight and Ward 2011). Also, as Nick's earlier comments suggest, the exercise of empathy in a probation context may be qualitatively different from that offered by a counsellor or therapist who endeavours to make himself or herself fully available to a client (Mearns and Thorne 2008). Research participants in this study gave examples of judicious self-disclosure:

Absolutely and where appropriate I do share things with, you know... with offenders ... if I feel it is going to help our ... professional relationship ... or they've got a worry about something, something that is obviously upsetting them and ... you know can kind of be empathic to that because you're human too. (Victoria)

However, Sandy recognises the risks of giving away personal information that might lead the offender to take advantage of her:

I mean I don't give very much of myself at all really, occasionally I might say that I drum, but that's it, ... and I'll talk about my car ... occasionally mention that I've got a cat but that's it, never mention anything that could come back. (Sandy)

Sandy is demonstrating her awareness of the importance of maintaining personal boundaries and judging when the sharing of mutual interests may be beneficial to the relationship or where it may stray into more risky territory. Gill indicates a lack of clear guidance from the agency about the appropriateness of self-disclosure and her need to work it out for herself. She sees it as a form of reciprocity, giving something back to the offender; giving enough to build a relationship but not enough to yield intimacy:

> But sometimes you can feel it is appropriate to share something on a personal level with people you work with. We would probably be told that it is not allowed, that we shouldn't be doing that, but I think, you know, that it has to be down to that individual offender manager to weigh that up ... we don't want the offender to feel sorry for us ... but we've got to show that we are human, that we are not just emotionally dead inside and that we don't really give a monkeys... (Gill)

If empathy is indeed a 'gift' then how workers decide when to offer it and when to withhold it remains a largely subjective and unregulated process. The demonstration of empathy and kindness towards offenders who may have committed dangerous and abusive acts requires an ability to 'put yourself in their shoes', whilst keeping sufficient distance to maintain awareness of the risks they might continue to pose.

Getting close

Some research participants provided evidence of the success they or others had had in building relationships with the most challenging and problematic people on their caseload. Three research participants made reference to the use of attachment theory (Bowlby 1969, 1978, 1980) in their work with sex offenders, and recognised that some offending behaviour was related to failures in early childhood attachments. They used this understanding to inform their belief in the importance of building strong emotional attachments with offenders. However, the extent to which it is appropriate to become emotionally close to offenders is far from straightforward. Some research participants cited examples of where the relationship had become of very great significance to the offender. For example, Damien was able to recognise, albeit with some initial reluctance and even embarrassment, that the relationship he had built with a particular offender had led to him becoming of central importance to this man:

> I asked him what was the most, what was really important for him in his life at the moment and he said I was ... I was took by shock really and I thought, what's that about? and he said 'well you really are an important part of my life' because I come in, we spend time together blah, blah, blah, and I think

I was kind of, suppose I almost brushed him away a bit, and took it as a, almost as joke if you like. (Damien)

Mary described a rather more ambivalent emotional attachment towards some offenders – as inevitable and unsurprising but also with some fear that it might not be appropriate. She recognised the significance of such an attachment:

I know there shouldn't be but with some people there is an emotional attachment, if you've been working with someone for three or four years, if there isn't some sort of an emotional attachment there then I think there is something quite wrong, but I think that you have to very aware of it if there is that attachment there, it is a responsibility. (Mary)

Victoria described occasions when she felt that the relationship was perhaps beginning to mean rather more to the offender than the professional boundaries dictated. Eight research participants made very explicit reference to their concerns about getting too close to offenders (Kim, John, Damien, Mary, Gill, Hannah, Karen and Lynn). Damien articulates, with some hesitancy, his belief that he was drawn in 'too far' with one particular offender and what this meant for him:

I did get quite, what's the word, quite attached to an offender in terms of the kind of relationship that we had ... that I could see that he was doing so well, I was so, kind of pleased that this guy was doing so well and then ... it all kind of fell to pieces ... and I was really was quite distraught by it all ... I really felt so disappointed, so distressed and that was it for me then, that kind of ... a level was drawn, of feelings of empathising so much with people and getting drawn into that, I couldn't go further anymore. (Damien)

As a result of the strong bond developed with this particular offender, when the latter reoffended Damien felt enormously let down and disappointed. He felt he had become 'too close' to this particular offender and had therefore been very distressed when things had gone wrong; implied by his use of the metaphor 'fell to pieces'.

There was other evidence of how research participants tried to protect themselves from what they perceived to be undue emotional involvement for fear of 'collusion' with offenders, collusion being defined as a 'secret or illegal cooperation or conspiracy in order to deceive others' (Stevenson 2010). It is a concept that carries considerable significance within the police and prison systems where there is seen to be a risk of 'collusion' between workers and offenders around the potential for illegal or subversive activity (Harvey and Smedley 2010). Within the probation context collusion is more likely to refer to values, attitudes and beliefs, the risk that the probation officer might collude with strong feelings and 'anti-social' beliefs supporting future offending (Cherry 2010). Unfortunately, fear of collusion can become an obstacle to building emotional attachments, when the real challenge is to be open and transparent about what is or is not permissible within the relationship.

In this next extract the risk of 'collusion' is related to becoming affected by the offender's unhappy early life experiences:

> Then they start to become ... angry at their dad and they're wanting you to, not collude with them but they're really wanting you to say yes, but you are angry at them too, and you want to say 'well what a bastard' but you can't and you just have to nod along, but you are furious as to what they have gone through ... you just have to sort of sit back and be careful of your language to be sure that you are not sort of agreeing or disagreeing with them, you are just understanding what they are saying. (Mary)

This is a good example of how Mary is regulating and controlling a number of quite strong emotions aroused by the offender's narrative. She makes a distinction between 'collusion' and 'understanding', the former suggesting an over-involvement in the emotional world of the offender, and the latter a more 'measured' response that contains the offender's anger rather than stoking it (Mearns and Thorne 2008).

Hannah has a different sort of dilemma which arises from her recognition of what she might have in common with certain offenders and her need to remind herself not to allow this to take over and lead her into closer emotional involvement than she believes to be appropriate:

> A lot of the time people that you meet on the sex offender groups are not your typical offender so often I might have more in common with them in terms of background and work and things like that so ... that does make it sometimes, easier to associate, because you have more in common with them than with some people ... I have got to be careful not to ... I want to say, not to like them too much. (Hannah)

The implication is that workers equate emotional closeness with the potential for collusion, and risk being swayed by this liking away from being 'professional' and doing the job 'correctly'. These examples highlight some of the challenging issues that can arise in work with all offenders but particularly sex offenders, and the potential for transference and indeed countertransference of feelings (Mearns and Thorne 2008). Research participants also acknowledged the difficulties for them in building relationships with some offenders, either because of the resistance they encountered from the offender or because the relationship had, in some way, become threatening or problematic for the worker. Offenders do not voluntarily enter into therapeutic relationships in the way that Rogers describes (Rogers 2004), and there can be enormous obstacles to building relationships with people who are resistant, angry, coerced and in many cases feeling powerless to influence the course of the relationship.

Negotiating boundaries

'Closeness' may be a good thing therapeutically but there are risks to both worker and offender if the closeness breaches certain boundaries. Boundaries are seen to be essential in all professional 'helping' relationships (Mearns and Thorne 2008). In order to manage the 'contract' and the relationship between themselves and the offender effectively the probation worker needs clarity about the expectations and boundaries of this relationship (Hennessey 2011). Whilst National Standards (Ministry of Justice 2011) guide the worker in establishing the practical requirements of the contract there are additionally matters of transparency, clarity and honesty that can carry emotional issues within them, some of which are further explored in Chapter 7.

Counsellors have to hold and maintain clear boundaries in their relationships with their clients but, with some notable exceptions (e.g. child protection issues), they are also bound by the duty of confidentiality and the therapeutic relationship to work at the client's behest and within the confines of that relationship (Mearns and Thorne 2008). Probation workers, as 'law enforcers', have to work primarily at the behest of the courts and the public in their work with offenders, and to take steps to deal with any breaches of orders. The power balance in probation relationships is significantly different from those within a counselling relationship where the client generally chooses and maybe also pays for the counsellor, and retains the power to terminate the relationship. The offender lacks this control. Probation workers following National Standards may have to return an offender to court for breach and re-sentencing which could involve imprisonment (Ministry of Justice 2011). The balance between 'law enforcer' and guardian of the official contract and 'therapist' offering an emotional relationship through which the offender may learn to trust and change is struck, it seems, through trial and error, experience, judgement and discretion, and is largely idiosyncratic to each worker and offender.

Research participants talked about how they negotiated the boundaries of the relationship and managed the interface between themselves, the offenders and the accountability inherent in their role. It was possible to detect some of the ambivalence they felt in managing these tensions. The quote below shows Pat describing herself in a somewhat contradictory way as both tough and lenient. She distinguishes her current role from the former 'social work' role and also indicates a willingness to accept the consequences of enforcement:

> I can usually get quite a good working relationship, I'm very tough but fair, they know where they stand from the beginning, you know I'm quite lenient but I've been called that, but no hesitation in so they know I think, where they stand ... I am an enforcer, I am not a social worker kind of probation officer. (Pat)

Pat is clearly associating social work with a 'softer' approach than probation and does not make connections with the enforcement role of social work in, for example, child protection cases and mental health.

Sophie identifies her preference for the clarity imposed by the particular boundaries of licence supervision:

> When you're supervising people on licence ... I am actually happier doing that because there is a clear relationship right from the start, this is it, you know, I am your offender manager and I will be the person to breach you if you whack up. (Sophie)

Whilst setting the contractual boundaries, such as expectations of attendance and behaviour, may be relatively straightforward, setting the 'emotional' boundaries is quite tricky territory to negotiate and may have to evolve as the relationship develops and as trust begins to build. There can also be more personal issues at stake when boundaries are being considered and this relates back to fine judgements around of self-disclosure:

> Well for me it is knowing my own boundaries, ... because I don't think everybody does ... in terms of the personal information you give out and your emotional boundaries, so that you will know that if you are angry you are not going to take it out on somebody and ... so that you know you can work safely with somebody because that's what I see as missing now, because a lot of people don't have those boundaries and tell clients all sorts of things, you just think, oooh ... and ... the way they ... people are around clients, a bit like mates and actually we're not, we've got a professional role to fulfil, and a professional function which doesn't mean that you can't have empathy or be kind or any of those things but you do need to have some sort of barrier there and that you've got to know otherwise you are in danger, at risk and you put the other person at risk and I think that's what I see is an issue. (Sandy)

Sandy is expressing her concern about colleagues who she feels lack clarity about personal boundaries and sometimes overstep them. Damien has concerns about some of his relationships:

> I've got a couple at the moment which I feel want to ....want me to be more than their probation officer in terms of you know, they almost want me to be their friend. (Damien)

Damien's fear may be of overstepping an emotional boundary of intimacy and where this might lead, or a behavioural boundary related to how they associate with one another. Probation workers build relationships with offenders often over quite lengthy periods and it is unsurprising that mutual liking and indeed affection can grow within some of these relationships. The key issue is how the boundaries are maintained and protected.

Non-verbal communication

The non-verbal aspects of communication in building relationships and engaging offenders in the change process were referred or alluded to by a significant number of research participants (Michael, Amy, Indira, Victoria, David, Sandy, Maggie, Damien, Aruna, Sophie, Gill, Jai, Geoff, Hannah, Nick, Karen). Some of their comments suggest that they are able to 'read' the clues given through body language that identify engagement or disengagement by offenders with the learning process. According to research undertaken by Mehrabian, 55% of our communication is conveyed through non-verbal means, 7% by our tone of voice and 7% by the content of the words, this is apparently of particular significance when people are talking about their feelings and attitudes (Mehrabian 1972). It is also suggested that if there is a lack of congruence between someone's verbal and non-verbal communication people are more prepared to believe the latter. People's gestures, facial expressions and other non-verbal behaviours are all seen to give indications of what the other person is feeling or of their intentions and a lack of congruence can indicate insincerity or a lack of authenticity and lead to an erosion of trust (Thompson 2009). A number of participants explained how they understood or became aware of the emotional state of the offender by reading these cues.

One of the experienced group workers articulated how she used a method she called 'scanning' to check out what was going on in the group. This skill was not one identified in the sex offender programme manual, but she had learnt from experience the importance of checking the 'emotional temperature' of the group by looking at body language and facial expressions. If she noticed any evidence of discomfort, or lack of interest, or agitation, for example, she would bring this to the notice of her co-worker so that attention could be given to it at an appropriate moment:

> Once we know from eye contact and body language – we are very good at scanning round the room – this lends itself to having a much more personal dialogue with the men. As co facilitator – if we see a man in distress we'll bring him out of the room. Although we've made an original judgement about them – they can't anticipate or we can't gauge how emotionally engaged they are. (Indira)

She went on to explain how she would raise such an issue with her co-worker in a way that did not create a major distraction or interrupt his leading of the group, but indicated that there was an issue that needed attention. Several other research participants also gave very clear examples of how they 'read' the nuances of non-verbal interaction and looked for signs of disengagement or disenchantment with the group process:

> One of the guys was new, unusually quiet and sat forward and he was really relaxed and reading everything that was on the board and really taking it in and watching us and looking at us and making a lot of eye contact and I thought, you're really listening, and then, (laughs) another guy was like this with his arms folded and I thought ... there's a blockade there, you could see his eyes were like wandering and he was huffing and puffing and that sort of thing, not interested at all. (Maggie)

Of significance in the general identification of emotions was the number of workers who described how they 'reflected back' or 'mirrored back' to the offenders what they observed to be happening in the interview or the group work context. This generally related to non-verbal cues rather than the content of what was being said. So, for example, in the case of an offender whose non-verbal signals were of disinterest, or annoyance, or upset, the worker might make an observation such as 'you seem to be finding this a bit difficult' or 'I can see that you are not happy with what has just been said, do you want to say what is going on for you?' This recognition of, and passing back of, a 'feeling' in a non-judgemental manner seemed to be quite a skilful practice that was primarily articulated by the experienced group workers, although some other workers, in one-to-one situations, also recognised the importance of 'reflecting back' rather than 'absorbing' the emotional reactions of the offender.

> One of the things I do try and do, is I try and reflect back emotionally what I'm getting from people. So I'm quite keen on reflecting back – 'it seems as if" or 'I've noticed you are doing this I was wondering how aware you are

of that' and – 'why do you think that might be' – and then discussing that with that person. (John)

In other examples research participants showed how they checked out their initial judgements about the non-verbal behaviour recognising that sometimes they might misread this. For example, they might suspect boredom or unhappiness at being in the group, but on asking discover it was more to do with tiredness (Victoria). Geoff gave examples of other non-verbal cues such as sweating, or flushing, recognising that the person concerned may not himself know or understand his physiological reactions to what was going on for him and it might need some careful exploration. Aruna recognised that clues about agitation in an offender needed to be handled carefully if the situation was not to escalate. Jai was aware of how offenders could emotionally 'leave' the programme, if the clues of disengagement were not picked up.

Accurate reading and understanding of non-verbal cues can be enabling for offenders in helping them to discharge some of the tension and distress they may be endeavouring to hold in. Nick gives an example of a situation when he made a conscious choice to respond to these cues knowing that in itself this also carried a risk of exposing very strong feelings that he would then have to deal with:

> He had come to the meeting very agitated. You could see that from the minute he walked in through the door. The prison officer said that to me, 'I could see from the minute he walked through the door and knew this was not going to go well.' I looked at his eyes and I looked at his face because you know ... you don't have to be that perceptive to see in somebody how aroused, you know somebody is, and I knew from that sort of minute but ..., if I did anything positive out of that I enabled him to go, okay, I think he released a lot of incredible amount of anger and frustration, and I might not want to hear it but then I also think to myself, where does he take that if he doesn't direct it at me? (Nick)

This is in contrast to what might be termed the 'Health and Safety' approach that some research participants referred to either in themselves or in colleagues they had observed, where the interview was terminated because of the level of the offender's emotional arousal and the worker's unwillingness to deal with it. However, here this is an acknowledgement by the worker that the anger was coming from elsewhere and needed an outlet, if it wasn't to spill out into other areas. In the next quote Indira picks up on an offender's distress and says only three words which offer him recognition and an opportunity to let out some of this distress:

> He just mentioned it to me in passing and I mentioned it to my co-worker. When we were doing a piece of work we started to realise that ... his offence

was against his own daughter. I said 'are you okay?' At this point he broke down – he hadn't wanted to be the monster – there were things he didn't want to do but he'd started to do. How aware he was – you make all your decisions in your waking moments but the extent of awareness – you can be listening and listening – what connections he was making I don't know. (Indira)

'Having a sixth sense' – intuition

Another element of empathy sometimes referred to as 'intuition', 'gut feelings' or having a 'sixth' sense came through in the data. Some research participants referred to having these feelings about what was actually going on under the surface (Indira, Sandy, Karen and Amy).

> Having that sixth sense – or anticipating in advance who are the likely candidates to find the work a bit more challenging. (Indira)

Indira uses it to reflect on the needs of particular offenders whereas Sandy, in this instance, is using it to take care of herself:

> That has taken me a long time to get there, I mean I have a really strong gut instinct, I suppose ... I mean my psychic ability, intuition whatever you want to call it, so I need to know when I need to protect myself. (Sandy)

Sandy is referring to situations in which she may be in some personal danger and she trusts her intuition more than other forms of judgement in such instances. This highlights some of the challenging issues that can arise in work with all offenders but particularly sex offenders. Karen relates it back to body language:

> Well ... they will be looking around, sometimes they will yawn, ... they are desperately trying to be engaged, body language ... silence ... I am also quite intuitive about picking things up between men ... when one man is frustrated with another man, ... and then I know that I need to intervene if one man is talking too much, so ... it is not just co-facilitating, it is watching the other group members as well. (Karen)

Prins refers to having a 'hunch' (Prins 1999). Gladwell defines it as the 'adaptive unconscious', the part of the brain that leaps to conclusions (Gladwell 2005). He argues this should not be confused with Freud's concept of the unconscious, but rather as an inbuilt 'computer' that is able to process information very rapidly and can sometimes offer better judgements than the more ponderous and mechanical processes that are frequently used within a managerial context. Whilst 'gut' feelings are felt by both men and women, 'intuition' is more commonly associated with femaleness, a 'woman's intuition', and it holds a mixed press, with a sometimes innate suspicion of this kind of rapid cognition (Gladwell 2005). When associated with a 'commonsense' approach to life it is generally seen to be a useful check in a range of situations. 'My gut feeling told me it wasn't safe to enter the room' and so on. It can also be derided as lacking logic or rationality and as being of dubious use in a professional work setting. In this context it has some associations with the concept of 'emotion' and 'being emotional' as explored in Chapter 5. Within a psychotherapeutic relationship, 'intuition' or identification of feelings generated within the therapist by the client is seen to be highly significant (Rogers 2004). Prins has identified it as a key tool in risk assessment and cites a former chief inspector of probation:

> I learned to trust my instincts (if a person frightened me he was probably dangerous) and to go with that knowledge until I had analysed it for what it was worth. (Sir Graham Smith, a former HM Chief Inspector of Probation cited in Prins 1999: 144)

Building trust

The significance of building trust within the worker/offender relationship was referred to by seven of the research participants as key to effective relationships (Amy, Indira, Gill, Karen, Jai, Nick and Heather). Trust is a fluid and broad concept, for example, an offender might be trusted to carry out certain tasks with reliability but not trusted in terms of potential reoffending. Offenders might find a worker trustworthy in that they are sincere and consistent, but they may not trust them to not 'breach' them or recall them to prison.

Some research participants were very upfront about their decision to trust offenders, by which they meant 'trusted' to tell the truth about their lives (Indira and Heather):

> We always validate the positive factors. In the first place unless they prove me wrong I'll trust them – I believe them unless they give me a reason not to ... I will receive information and also I'll have no reason to disbelieve the offender unless there are inconsistencies in their account. (Indira)

By showing empathy the worker has a route into building trust from and to the offender but Mearns warns that the establishment of trust in a relationship is a delicate and complex process and that in cases where the therapist is demonstrating great empathy the client may reveal too much, too quickly (Mearns and Thorne 2008). Heather demonstrates her understanding of how meaning-ful this trust can be, and the compassion and altruism she had invested in the relationship(s), which has built her own store of emotional resource:

> I just think that, I don't think we can pay one another a greater compliment than doing that, and that when people, particularly people who have not had that experience of trust in others, which a lot of our clients haven't had, a lot of relationships that they've been in have not been trusting ones and when they trust you enough ... the girlfriend had said that she thought that I really cared what happened to them and I did, and it really mattered to me that they felt that ... so when people trust you and let you in, in that sort of way, I ... think that is what has kept me in it all these years. (Heather)

Others identified that to build this trust required time:

> You are trying to relate to them so that, and you know, that is how you build relationships with people, you open up to them and hopefully you know, that trust that they are looking at from you, I mean we don't need it from them but a lot of them need it from us, a lot of them have had such unstable lives where they have never really been given any time, not been paid attention to, not that they crave it, but they may find that in you and like I said that can be a really, really long road. (Gill)

Gill also considered that in some instances there would be offenders who could never be trusted, which suggests the worker makes a judgement about this.

From the offender perspective, Mearns et al. identify what they refer to as the 'hardened' client who may have been in touch with a range of helping agencies before and be more resistant to establishing trust in the relationship or may be quick to discern inauthenticity, whether it exists in reality within the worker or not. The suggestion is that the client may want to gauge the counsellor's genuineness and willingness to engage in a non-defensive manner (Mearns and Thorne 2008). The establishment of trust might also be viewed as a risky commitment for any offender to make given the punitive ethos of the system and the risk of their trust being 'breached' through the enforcement procedures of the agency.

Conclusion

This chapter has explored some of the emotional components involved in building relationships with offenders within the parameters of the legal and professional requirements of community orders. Whilst all research par-ticipants to the study identified relationships as important some were more willing or able than others to dig below the surface of the contractual elements of the relationship as laid down in policy and reflect on the emotional challenges and contradictions inherent in this process. Issues of understanding emotions in others, not allowing your own emotions to intervene too powerfully, demonstrating empathy, getting close and building trust, whilst negotiating and maintaining boundaries, are all emotional processes that these research participants identified. What is perhaps most revealing is how variable and unguided these emotional processes are, with research participants endeavouring to find their own individual and subjective routes through. The research participants to this study generally saw emotional connections as positive and constructive, whilst recognising their power to be used in a negative manner. They demonstrated a degree of subtlety and complexity in the way they managed the empathic components of the worker/offender relationship. They were actively negotiating the tension between relationship building and the obligations to enforce compliance within a community order.

What is not evident from this data is the extent to which any offender really has a choice to resist such emotional relationships with workers. There may be a risk that an aloofness from engaging emotionally with a worker could lead to a judgement by the worker of non-cooperation or non-engagement with the treatment programme.

7
Using Emotional Literacy to Manage Risk and Change in Offenders

Practice example

Ted, a probation officer, has been working for a number of years with Ken, a 28-year-old sex offender currently serving six years in prison. Ted visits Ken in prison to discuss his parole application and the potential arrangements for release should he be granted parole. Ted previously supervised Ken on a community order, and during this time they had established a good relationship in which they developed mutual respect and a degree of trust. On this visit Ken is visibly upset and on being encouraged by Ted to talk begins to describe some of his early childhood experiences of being abused by his father and his current fantasies in relation to wanting to sexually harm a child who lives near to his parent's home. Ted is very disturbed by these revelations and goes back to the office feeling he will need to act on this. In discussion with his line manager they conclude that Ted will have to make reference to this in his parole report and that it has serious implications for any pending parole decision. In their view Ken is not yet ready for release. Ted recognises the temptation to just write the parole report and say nothing to Ken, who may not realise why his parole application is subsequently refused. However, he feels he owes it to Ken to be honest with him and so books another visit to go to the prison and talk with Ken about what he has to include in the parole report. Ken is very upset and accuses Ted of breaching his confidentiality and abusing his trust in him. Ted spends time talking with Ken and reassuring him that he wants to find a counsellor to help Ken begin to understand and talk about his own early abuse, with a view to Ken then joining a sex offending programme either pre-release or eventually on release from prison. Both of them find the session difficult and draining. Eventually Ted leaves feeling that he has done his best to help Ken whilst also acknowledging the risk he continues to pose. He is glad he has been honest but he fears his relationship with Ken has been damaged.

Key learning points

- Offenders can also be victims
- Sometimes the real risk an offender poses only comes to light when they feel sufficient trust in their relationship with their supervising officer to talk about difficult and painful matters
- How practitioners handle this information with both the offender and the 'authorities' can have a lasting impact on the quality of the relationship and on the practitioner's own belief in their role
- It takes courage and emotional literacy to maintain 'transparency' and integrity in practice when other work pressures and demands come to the fore.
- Challenging an offender too assertively when they admit to problematic behaviour can have the consequence of silencing the offender from revealing more

Introduction

This chapter offers some illustration of how the research participants used the emotional processes integral to relationship building, as described in Chapter 6, to negotiate the procedures involved in managing community orders, including assessing risk, and working to manage and reduce the risk of reoffending of offenders. It reflects on the process of managing and enabling change in offenders; including helping them to disclose difficult and sometimes very sensitive information that can inform risk assessment, and may increase the level of risk, as well as aiding the therapeutic process of change. It makes reference to some of the ambivalence felt by the research participants in handling these disclosures. A link will be drawn between work with high-risk offenders, with particular reference to sex offenders, and with child protection work, where the practitioner's ability to encourage, hear and contain difficult and sometimes very complex and painful thoughts and feelings in offenders (clients) requires highly sophisticated levels of emotional literacy (Munro 2011).

There is a dualism inherent in an understanding of offenders as culpable of criminal behaviour and also as potential victims themselves that can link to their readiness to change. For example, there are specific issues related to some sex offenders having experienced abuse themselves as children, and how a failure to engage on any level with this experience is likely to inhibit their ability to learn from and respond to programmes that demand they take responsibility for their own behaviour. It is argued that if the abused children of today are not to become some of the offenders of the future, then emotionally literate practitioners need to be able to interrupt these cycles of abuse at all stages (Fitzgibbon 2011). The chapter also considers how the research participants learnt to 'challenge' the offender's thinking and behaviour in the process of managing risk, and how open and transparent they were able to be in the enforcement of orders. The context for the work of these probation practitioners is 'evidence-based practice' (Chapman and Hough 1998) and Core Correctional Practice (CCP) (Dowden and Andrews 2004).

Evidence-based practice

The research for this book was undertaken within the probation service, an organisation that has been transformed from a primarily 'welfare-based' service to offenders to an organisation concerned with protection of the public through the assessment and management of risk. The evolution of 'evidence-based practice' and the move towards 'actuarial justice' which offered an apparently rational calculation of 'risk' was formulated on the following principles of:

- 'Risk': which asserts that criminal behaviour can be reliably predicted and that treatment should focus on the higher risk offenders
- 'Need': which highlights the importance of criminogenic needs (those factors which have a direct link to offending) in the design and delivery of treatment programmes
- 'Responsivity': interventions should be delivered in ways which match the offenders' learning style and engage their active participation
- 'Programme integrity': interventions should be rigorously managed and delivered as designed (Chapman and Hough 1998)

Of these principles, the risk principle has dominated policy and practice in recent years with the development of a range of risk assessment tools (Kemshall 2003, Kemshall 2008, Kemshall 2010), and with pressure on staff to complete detailed paperwork to track these assessments (Oldfield 2007). The assignment of offenders to categories of risk has become the central task, from which follows different levels of intervention, control and surveillance. The 'need' principle centres on factors closely related to offending behaviour rather than on 'welfare' need, which is seen as the remit of other community-based organisations or partnerships (Whitehead 2010). The evidence drawn on to formulate this evidence base indicated that the most effective forms of intervention were 'cognitive-behavioural group work programmes with a strong focus on offending behaviour' (Mair 2004: 26). These programmes, which emerged from effectiveness research (much of which was conducted in Canadian prisons), became the only form of practice regarded by probation managers as sufficiently evidence based to be defensible (Smith 2005).

The 'responsivity principle' sets the context for addressing the risk principle. How the research participants used their skills of emotional literacy in the furtherance of these two principles are examined in this chapter. Significant to these themes is an understanding of offenders as 'learners' as well as recipients of compulsory treatment. The inference of court-mandated attendance on accredited programmes that address offending behaviour is that offenders will be shown or instructed on the correct and prosocial way to think and behave. What is sometimes overlooked is that teaching and learning are different concepts and that in order for a programme to achieve the most effective outcomes and to create lasting change, the offender has to be ready for, and responsive to, learning. This is supported by a core value of probation that people have the capacity to change through their own volition (Canton 2011). Educational theory highlights the factors that promote learning and they are almost without exception related to openness, safety, positive emotions, mutual support and respect (Chamberlayne 2004). Coercion or manipulation in the learning process may achieve short-term compliance but is unlikely to achieve long-term change.

Within the framework of what is defined as CCP, building a 'therapeutic alliance' with offenders and using the process of this alliance to enable and help offenders engage in the change process is making something of a comeback (Dowden and Andrews 2004). This comeback is reflected in the evolving literature on 'desistance from offending' (Rex 1999, Maruna and LeBel 2010, McNeill, Raynor et al. 2010, Raynor, Ugwudike et al. 2010) and in the Offender Engagement Programme (OEP) now established within the National Offender Management Service (NOMS) (Ministry of Justice 2010). The government green paper 'Breaking the Cycle' (Ministry of Justice 2010) and its response published in June 2011 (Ministry of Justice 2011: 24) argue that punishments must be 'robust' and 'demanding' but also acknowledge the importance of the offender/worker relationship. Of significance in the green paper is the introduction of new National Standards for probation which allow for a return to greater practitioner discretion (Ministry of Justice 2011); much of which had been eroded by early versions of National Standards (Home Office 1992). This renewed focus on the significance of the practitioner/offender relationship provides the context for an examination of the micro skills of practice and for an exploration of the significance of emotional literacy.

Offender readiness to change

Responsivity is defined as those characteristics of an individual offender that are likely to influence how they will respond to a treatment programme and can include their motivation and the attention given by the worker to any diversity issues they may have (Chapman and Hough 1998, Farrow, Kelly et al. 2007). One of the potential obstacles to offender readiness to change is the extent to which the offender may or may not be ready within himself/herself to make the necessary changes to lead a non-offending lifestyle (Day, Casey et al. 2010). An assumption frequently made within the popular press, and also within much political debate, is that offenders are the villains, victims are the innocent parties and that a sharp distinction can be drawn between the law-abiding majority and the (relatively) few who prey on them (Canton 2011: 179). The simplistic presentation of crime in the media separates out the roles of offender and victim as discrete and oppositional, whereas in reality many people can occupy both roles at the same or at different times in their lives. There is strong evidence that offenders are a disproportionately victimised group and that many female offenders, in particular, have themselves been victims of abuse and violence (Boswell 2000, Rumgay 2004, Ward, Devon et al. 2006, Canton 2011). They are also very likely to have backgrounds of disadvantage, discrimination and poverty, which will have shaped their worldview and their experience. One outcome of the polarisation and stereotyping of victims and offenders, as Canton argues, is that offenders become ineligible to be victims (Canton 2011).

The What Works drive has tended to view the immediacy and impact of the offending behaviour as the core target for intervention and the majority of programmes are designed to tackle this through a cognitive behavioural model. However, psychotherapeutic literature, the recent work on 'desistance' and the potential for offenders to also be victims all identify a much more complex picture of how and when people are ready to make changes in their lives and how receptive they are to learning about new ways of being and behaving. The concept of 'readiness' is core to therapeutic work with voluntary clients. Mearns argues the client's 'readiness' will affect the speed with which trust is developed and the establishment and maintenance of this trust (Mearns and Thorne 2008). The idea of 'readiness', like the 'cycle of change' (Miller and Rollnick 2002), is however, a somewhat shifting process and court-mandated clients have a lot less choice, and potentially less motivation, than voluntary clients.

If workers are to enhance 'offender readiness' for those offenders who have been victims themselves there is evidence from the psychotherapeutic literature of the sorts of needs they are likely to present. Research on work with victims of abuse and trauma has identified five psychological needs of safety, dependency/trust, power, esteem and intimacy which should be addressed by the therapist when working with traumatised victims (McCann and Pearlman 1990). Dayton describes similar and additional characteristics including alexithymia, or lack of words to describe how you feel (Dayton 2000). Regardless of whether the probation worker can respond to the offender as a potential 'victim' as well as an offender, as highlighted in Chapter 6, demonstrating empathy for another person's predicament is seen as a crucial stage in building trust, and trust is seen as necessary for a person to be able to share 'risky', personal or particularly sensitive information (Mearns and Thorne 2008). This may be of particular relevance in the area of sex offending where the information to be disclosed is of a personal, intimate and quite possibly shameful (for the discloser) nature (Ward, Devon et al. 2006).

Research findings

Victim/offender dichotomy

Whilst the role of the probation officer is to 'challenge the offending behaviour', which in most cases means placing the focus directly on the culpability of the offender for their behaviour, this can be difficult if the offender is consumed with feelings of his or her own 'victimhood'. The following respondent demonstrates her understanding of the potential for this dichotomy and the fact that the decision to work with either or both of these 'identities' inherent in the service user is rarely straightforward.

> Through that work I found that some of the men who offended were victims themselves ... dual status ... victims and offenders. So that meant different types of support than for the men who just had this one sex offender status. The conflict in the groups was do you pay attention to the offender or victim status? (Indira)

The need to balance the confrontational, or holding to account for behaviour, with the need to engage with and motivate an offender towards change requires, according to Day et al., an acknowledgement of 'his' individual circumstances, life history and own perceptions of why he behaves in this way (Day, Casey et al. 2010). However, a number of research participants reframed the concept of offenders as potential victims to a 'poor me' syndrome which they perceived as offenders feeling sorry for themselves and being unwilling to engage with offence-focused work. For these workers this recourse to a victim status by the offender was seen as a ploy to avoid engagement with the main focus of the intervention or as a manipulation to divert the worker (Kim, Howard, John, Pat and Hannah). Kim explains the difficulties she experiences sometimes between her natural urge to be compassionate and her fear that this might convey the wrong message to the offender:

> In terms of the fact if I'm seeing people upset my instinct is to comfort so I have to be very careful ... you are not feeding into the 'poor me' ... I

think you should acknowledge them ... but it's ... important to detach ... you fear you might be colluding with that individual or feeding in to their 'poor me' stance that they might have – or if it's not genuine you might be demonstrating to them that you are allowing them to manipulate you. (Kim)

Howard associates evidence of mental ill health with a tendency to be self-absorbed:

Yes ... if they are depressive – it makes me think they are demonstrating 'poor me' and makes me ask questions about – 'what's that about?' (Howard)

John explains how his own feelings can come to the fore when he perceives the unwillingness of offenders to motivate themselves for change:

But I think it can be frustrating as well – people who present as a very kind of 'poor me' – have a victim approach to their offending and life-style. It can be very frustrating to work with people who find it difficult to motivate themselves to make changes. (John)

Hannah admits with some honesty that she has less sympathy for sex offenders, particularly when they present as self-absorbed:

I am I think quite good at empathising with them and try to see what they are going through, but I must say that, especially if they are sex offenders, I always think, 'well ...Tough!'... it sounds really, really rotten but maybe that is an added way of dealing with it, and as long as it is not a lot of 'poor me, poor me' stuff which you get a lot because that I don't have a lot of time for if it continues. (laughs) (Hannah)

And Pat acknowledges her irritation:

There's always some tears ... it's always self-pity though of course, 'oh poor me, poor me I've suffered', I do find that quite irritating to be fair ... and I do ... struggle ... to be sort of sympathetic in that circumstance ... to be fair, so that's another emotion I have to struggle with, irritation. (laughs) (Pat)

The common use of the term 'poor me' suggests this may be part of a collective understanding or indeed contemporary 'policy' that workers bring to their practice. These research participants will be supported by their agency and the policy on managing community orders, in having little time for offenders who present as 'self-pitying', given their main task is to challenge the offending behaviour. Where this line is drawn in terms of tolerance or even sympathy for the victim status of the offender is variable:

> I can deal much more with straightforward aggression and anger and ... what-have-you, but the sort of the moaners and the whiners, and the poor me-ers, I really, even they might be entitled to feel that, who am I to say that they are not? But I recognize that ... I have to name it and I have to actually say, look you know ... 'Honeybunch, is it my fault that you are here?' (Heather)

However, as Indira indicated above, if sex offenders have experienced sex abuse themselves, then a failure to engage on any level with this early abuse is likely to inhibit their ability to respond to a programme that demands they take responsibility for their own behaviour. Literature from the educational field suggests that in order to learn well, people need to have their own perspectives and positions acknowledged (Chamberlayne 2004). If all avenues for the expression of their distress are shut down to the offender, they may be unresponsive or not 'ready' for change. Not all people who commit offences of violence have themselves been abused although it is likely that they will have witnessed violence in their earlier lives (Morran, Wolf-Light et al. 2011). It is suggested that the worker needs to be open to the potential for this, which can be particularly challenging in work with domestic violence offenders:

> Practitioners have indicated ..., that their experience of engaging with domestic violence offenders on programmes faces them with a quality of resistance to engagement quite unlike their other experiences. While it is distinctly possible that this is a characteristic of angry or ashamed or callous men themselves, resistance is also diminished or enhanced by the quality of the connection or relationship between the man and the worker. (Day, Casey et al. 2010: 29)

Some of the research participants found working with domestic violence offenders the most difficult of all the work they undertook. This related to the nature of the offending, the abusive behaviour towards women and the men's general 'unreadiness' to change and confront their own behaviour, supported in their beliefs by a society where patriarchy and misogyny continue to have credibility (Romito 2008). Engagement with the potential victim status of these men is particularly challenging and in many cases actively discouraged (Dobash, Dobash et al. 2000). Whilst the rationale for this is clear, these men need to take responsibility for their misogynistic behaviour, a shutting down of all avenues for them to explore their own early experiences of violence may limit their ability to be ready to change (Day, Casey et al. 2010).

In a counselling context, Mearns and Thorne's five elements that can indicate a 'low' state of readiness to change are all of relevance in the struggle probation workers often have to engage offenders in a change process:

- Indecision about wanting to change
- General lack of trust for others
- Unwillingness to take responsibility for self in life
- Unwillingness to take responsibility in counselling
- Unwillingness to recognise or explore feelings. (Mearns and Thorne 2008:1 61)

In a probation context, particularly when there is a high risk of reoffending and of further serious harm, the balance between emotional support and encouragement to change, and coercion, may be problematic both in practice and in the monitoring of practice (Layder 2004).

Disclosure and risk assessment

In addition to building the motivation for change, emotional literacy can be significant in enabling disclosure that relates to future risk. Disclosure is what probation workers aim for in their initial assessments of risk in the reports they are required to prepare for court, parole and pre-release hearings and so on, and it can also be a key factor in future risk assessments. Whilst the report writer usually has access to the depositions and therefore has knowledge of the details of the conviction and the various witness statements, the perceptions and beliefs of the offender about the reasons for their behaviour are also crucial in assessing risk, judging culpability and planning an appropriate intervention (Harrison 2010).

One of the requirements of the worker undertaking the assessment and any subsequent intervention is to enable the offender to 'tell their story', to describe and ultimately take some ownership of their offending behaviour and accept responsibility for the harm they have caused (Farrow, Kelly et al. 2007). For some this may be an instantaneous process based on genuine remorse and a sense of guilt. For some this may only be gradually drawn out over a period of time, with help from the worker to construct a narrative of explanation. For others their willingness to accept responsibility may never be forthcoming, for example, because they believe or claim themselves to be innocent of the offence or because their sense of 'victimhood' is overriding all other considerations. The offender may in fact become subject to greater degrees of surveillance and control the more 'risk' he/she reveals through disclosing personal information. His/her resistance to disclosure could be interpreted either as a lack of cooperation or as a rational decision to resist the imposition of even greater control by the 'system'. The offender may have their own reasons for resistance, given that sex offending, for example, is viewed as especially shameful and abhorrent, the only power available to them in an unequal relationship. Motivational interviewing skills (Fuller and Taylor 2003), prosocial modelling (Cherry 2010), the skills of emotional literacy and the quality of the relationship are all tools available within the practice repertoire to encourage the offender to work through a process of minimisation and denial, as confirmed by Victoria:

> It's really important, but we have got a really good professional relationship and you know since then he has disclosed lots of other things for me, not for me, but to me, which have been really useful in managing his risk. (Victoria)

John took pleasure in the relationship because of the obvious and positive impact it was having in enabling the offender to disclose crucial information as well as satisfying agency demands in terms of public protection:

> I was working with someone yesterday – who is very reticent to discuss aspects of his offending but he has been able to step back and take a hard look at aspects of his offence and lifestyle at the time and he seems genuinely able to do that – very rewarding – therapeutic relationship almost non-forensic – he seems to have accepted he can tell me stuff within reason – things we already know about –and it's not going to impact badly on him – the more he is able to share and reflect and demonstrate some insights ... the more reassured the service is going to be. (John)

John comments that 'it's not going to impact badly on him' so he has already made a judgement that disclosures by this particular offender are unlikely to increase his risk of increased monitoring, breach or recall. However, personal disclosure may not always be as straightforward as this. The process of risk assessment continues throughout the life of the order and will be influenced by any future disclosure on the part of the offender. The depth and quality of the information about themselves that offenders are likely to share with their workers was seen by three of the research participants as very strongly dependent on the quality of trust that has been built up (Gill, Nick and John).

Many sex offenders embark on programmes of change in heightened states of denial and resistance (Marshall and Barbaree 1990). Depending on the skill of the group worker or offender manager, this resistance can be eroded with a growing awareness and acceptance of responsibility or, if this skill is lacking there may be an increasing resistance and refusal to accept responsibility with a perceived heightened risk of further offending. This next participant recognised the particular difficulties of expecting disclosure in an accredited group work programme environment where there were constant changes of membership and therefore a lack of trust in the group:

> It is cognitive behavioural, but, I think it is more educational really ... and also because it is modular-based, you will have different people coming in on different modules, trust can't be established in the same way. I think for change to take place, if you are exposing behaviour that you feel ashamed about then trust has to be there. (Jai)

Indira understood the importance of reflecting back what she had heard in order to aid the offender's own comprehension of the seriousness of his behaviour:

> They are also very shocked. They've come to realise the extent of their behaviour when you reflect it back to them. In order for me to note it down I'll say to them, 'so you're telling me that after a while you became sexually attracted to ...' 'And took this and this measure' ... 'Have I understood you rightly?' They'll realise fully what they've done. (Indira)

Perhaps one of the most difficult areas to negotiate for the sex offender worker is the permission to the sex offender to disclose sexual fantasies about potential harm to victims, which they may not have previously shared with anyone else (Ward, Polaschek et al. 2006). There is also an acknowledged risk that the offender may gain vicarious sexual pleasure simply from the act of telling, and the worker may become unwittingly caught up in complex issues of projection (Schaverien 2006). Ward et al. suggest that skilled workers should be able to encourage these revelations, hear the unpleasant associations and challenge the distortions, whilst also supporting and not condemning the offender through this process (Ward, Devon et al. 2006). This is a very challenging set of requirements.

Pat identified the need to be very direct with an offender but even when there was evidence of him being disingenuous she still endeavoured not to impose a judgement on him. She clearly had sympathy for the men she worked with despite their offences, and recognised the difficulties for some of these men in having to talk about very personal and intimate matters with a person in authority.

> I don't want to generalise but a lot of that group, are quite vulnerable ... I think most of mine are really, feeling isolated, vulnerable, ... not good at interaction

skills... Some think they are cleverer than you, and then it's very, very difficult because they want to buck the system. But some are ... I've got one in court today, you know, he went on the web and was masturbating on the web to people ... he was caught, and it involved a young child. In my interview with him today ... he is one those that are really, really shy, really difficult person to, and you have to talk about such personal things in that hour ... you know. (Pat)

However, this does pose its own issues for workers who may have difficulties in listening to these revelations:

Particularly one of my sex offenders was talking to me about the offence, and this was some way into the order ... and obviously disclosure, and there were things in there ... that ... I didn't feel particularly comfortable with ... but I had to kind of, not be emotional and not do the behaviour and keep that in and be professional about it so that, sometimes I find that difficult, to you know, deal with, ... and obviously I am a human being ... and I do have feelings and reactions to certain things. (Victoria)

Victoria is offering some insight into how complex and tricky such disclosure in relation to sexual behaviour can be to negotiate. As indicated earlier, sex offenders have many reasons not to disclose and to be particularly sensitive to any indications of negative or stereotypical labelling, hostility or lack of empathy from the worker (Roberts and Baim 1999, Ward, Devon et al. 2006). The preliminary evaluation of disclosures following mandatory polygraph testing identified the significance of an effective working relationship based on trust and confidence and that offenders were less likely to disclose information if the practitioner displayed a negative emotional response, for example, shock (Wood 2010). Victoria may, unwittingly, have been demonstrating some of her discomfort to the offender through non-verbal indicators. Probation staff may have their own reasons for not wishing, or being able, to hear disclosure of this nature including their own lack of knowledge about sexual matters, unresolved issues around their own sexuality, early and unresolved experiences of abuse and associated feelings of embarrassment, fear, anger or disgust (Wood 2010). Put together these obstacles to disclosure can be insurmountable and there are risks that worker and offender enter into a collusive relationship of mutual denial and minimisation about the serious nature of the offending (Prins 1999), or a conflictual relationship of challenge and withdrawal, neither of which is helpful in the disclosure and change process (Ward et al 2006).

Ambivalent investment

A further layer of complexity relates to managing contrasting and sometimes conflicting 'positions' and feelings at the same time, best described as 'managing ambivalence'. A worker may experience an offender's distress but also his accompanying abusive behaviour and language (e.g. Nick). A worker may grow to like particular offenders but have to constantly remind herself of the appalling crimes that they may have committed (e.g. Hannah). A worker may be angry or disappointed with the failure of a particular offender to learn from a group work intervention but at the same time remember that this person has deep-rooted difficulties with self-image and esteem. A worker may feel he has built a strong relationship with a particular offender only to be faced in an interview session with resentment, hostility and prejudice when he (the offender) seeks to blame the worker for some perceived failure of resources or support (e.g. Damien). Kaplan describes this sense of ambivalence as a situation in which an individual has the opportunity to simultaneously indicate both a favourable and an unfavourable attitude towards a given stimulus (Kaplan 1972).

Prins describes this as 'ambivalent investment' (Prins 1999). He suggests that this operates in three ways:

1. The worker may not have resolved earlier problems of having to come to terms with any revulsion and fear felt, and the result of this is to blind the workers to the realities of the case and make them unable to take the necessary steps to overcome blockages in therapeutic engagement.
2. Even if the worker has overcome this he or she then has to face the fact that they carry a great burden of responsibility for the welfare of the offender on the one hand and the community on the other.
3. The worker in his/her role has a considerable investment to see that things are going well ... which may lead to a degree of unrealistic optimism about the progress of the case and the need for intrusive supervision or monitoring (Prins 1999: 129).

One of the criticisms levelled at earlier forms of probation practice was that the worker was taking too close and collusive a stance with the offender at the expense of challenging their offending behaviour (Cherry 2010). As illustrated by Lowdell and Adshead's work with forensic mental health workers, the risks of avoiding the 'bad' behaviour, or denying the harm caused, may lead the worker to become drawn into a collusive relationship with the offender that condones his minimisation of the crime, or emphasises his own sense of victimisation within a given situation (Lowdell and Adshead 2009). Whilst, historically, probation officers tasked with 'advising, assisting and befriending' offenders might have sometimes held a non-judgemental approach that was too heavily weighted in favour of the offender to the detriment of their ability to see and challenge the offending behaviour, contemporary practice is expected to place an almost exclusive focus on the offending behaviour.

For some research participants (Damien, Aruna, Jai and Geoff), the need to understand was of crucial importance and allowed them to place their own emotional reactions to the offence almost to one side:

> People who have committed sex offences, I wouldn't want them to think that actually I think you're sick, and what you've done is wrong and I think you're disgusting, I think well, actually you've done something and I want to kind of unpick, I want to understand the reasons why you've done it ... and I want you to understand the reasons why you've done it ... and the impact that's had on people, and the impact that's had on the victim. (Damien)

Also, awareness that showing their feelings in this context would effectively stop the disclosures:

> I think it is, not being judgmental, not colluding, but not showing your horror at something that someone has done, because they are so tuned in and that would just shut the person off, so actually ... presenting as though this isn't the worst that I have heard and you know, that I am listening. (Jai)

Pat was honest enough to describe a situation in which anger at the man's behaviour and his unwillingness to see or accept the damage he was causing led her to erupt in a supervision session. She describes a mixture of regret at her outburst coupled with a self-justification on the basis of his offence, his intractability and his denial:

> He had an eight year old step-grand-daughter and ... she would come to his house and then he'd let her walk around in the nude and ... then she brought a friend and then he started taking photographs and in the end he did literally penetrate her, she was eight, and so he was ... denying and then he said she was being physically abused by her parents, mum and step-dad, they were hitting her and ... so she'd come to me and ... to get away from all that and I couldn't help so I said, 'so she's being abused by her parents and she comes to you for a break and you know, for a rest and you've sexually abused her', and he stood up, END OF INTERVIEW, and he wanted me to say 'stay', and I said 'yes, go, leave', and I put in my report that he had stormed out of the interview, but I knew I shouldn't have said that, you know. (Pat)

Hannah offered a good example of how disclosure can come when we least expect it, and she described her discomfort at hearing it, and what she subsequently did, which was to log it with the offender manager and agree to return to it at a future date:

> For example I did a post-treatment report on a sex offender ... and I had to review and ... there was just me and him and the offender manager and there was quite a lot of stuff in the report that he wasn't happy about ... but he came out with new stuff that he had never really, sort of about fantasy that needed to explored further and because he had never really gone there and he came out with all this risk, with terrible conflicting stories of fantasies and misconceptions about it. (Hannah)

Enforcement and transparency

In addition to working with an offender to encourage change and manage risk, workers have to operate within an enforcement policy that determines how and when the offender should respond to the conditions of their community order (Ministry of Justice 2011). Building a strong relationship with an offender and yet sometimes also having to act to enforce an order can, as described earlier, generate powerful feelings of ambivalence in a worker. Sometimes the issue relates to how to confront the offender with the implications of their behaviour in terms of a breach of the order and a return to court for re-sentencing. The risk is that because of the discomfort aroused by holding conflicting feelings simultaneously, workers will resolve these tensions by opting for one approach over another rather than being supported and enabled to hold the balance. Two research participants highlighted the difficulties they felt in hearing or receiving information that related to risky behaviour and how this would affect their assessment of the offender's risk (Pat and Tess). They recognised this would have an impact on the offender:

> You get a lot, of information at that stage and you just feel a little bit bad when you write the pre-sentence report and you know, then you quote them ... you know and basically, because then, when they go to prison. (Pat)

The sharing of this assessment with an offender can be a minimal process, undertaken in an official, bureaucratic manner that meets the requirements and rules of National Standards (Ministry of Justice 2011), or it can be undertaken as a much more interactive process that builds on the trust and integrity developed within the relationship and enables the offender to understand and 'own' the significance of their behaviour and its impact on others. These skills are a largely invisible, unquantifiable and rarely quality assured process. Several research participants (Amy, Indira, John, Lynn and Maggie), gave clear examples of how crucial they believed this transparency of process was in building relationships, in gaining the trust and cooperation of the offender and in enabling change, enhancing legitimacy and increasing compliance (Chapman and Hough 1998):

> The quality of the relationship is to be able to say to them 'I hear and I understand your perspective and your current take but my take is this' (Indira)

> The other thing I've learnt much more is to be upfront with people ... and what I've been asked to do ... e.g. risk assessments ... be upfront about the implications and the processes involved. Ultimately that's a much better way of working with people. I think you have to be transparent. (John)

One worker expressed quite graphically the frustrations she experienced, having built a relationship and established trust, at having to follow enforcement procedures and destroy that trust in the process:

> So the fact that you had to keep taking people back to court when you know that it was farcical but somehow if they could build this relationship, that it was working and that they could really feel that there was a chance that you could get some work in alongside them and help them change, and then you've suddenly got to take them back to court because they'd breached or something, because life was just too chaotic. So that was very exasperating. (Lynn)

The evaluation of the use of mandatory polygraph testing highlighted that some practitioners acknowledged the importance of an accepting attitude in encouraging disclosure but that this:

> Sometimes conflicted with their duty to act on information disclosed in a way that appears to punish the offender (e.g. by recalling an offender where a disclosure reveals an escalation of risk). (Wood et al. 2010: 3)

Challenging or enabling?

As suggested at the beginning of this chapter, the emotional 'approach' that workers take to offenders can have a significant bearing on their responsiveness to learning. As Day et al. argue, the therapist skills and style are central to the development of a therapeutic alliance (Day, Casey et al. 2010). They cite Marshall and Serran's (2004) research on work with sex offenders which suggests that promoting approach goals rather than avoidance goals is likely to increase programme effectiveness, and that the focus should be on promoting prosocial behaviour rather than the ceasing of anti-social behaviour (Day, Casey et al. 2010). The first key element of CCP is the effective use of authority and this includes the avoidance of negative responses such as arguing, blaming, criticising (Dowden and Andrews 2004), and 'interpersonal domination', confrontational enforcement or abuse (Andrews and Bonta 2010).

However, one of the key expectations of 'addressing offending behaviour' is to challenge distorted thinking and to use 'Socratic' questioning to highlight discrepancies and inconsistencies between what offenders think and how they actually behave (Farrow, Kelly et al. 2007). Within the learning context of an accredited programme a programme tutor is expected to identify and clarify the information that the offender brings to the session, and then to engage with this information in a way that encourages the offender to view it differently. In terms of risk management and intervention, research participants talked about the significance of adopting an enabling as opposed to a confrontational approach in their work with offenders. Whilst the behaviour under discussion could be very problematic they knew that to show disapproval and condemnation by adopting a very challenging style of communication was likely to be ineffective. Jai provides an example of this and stresses the importance of not humiliating the offender in the process:

> The manner in which people are challenged shouldn't be confrontational, so for me, challenge is about exploring what they have said more, and it is about ... looking for things that don't support what they are saying and ... using the group to get different perspectives, that might question where they are coming from, so for me it is a bit of a drip-drip effect and yes, it's not, it's about challenging in a way that doesn't humiliate and ... using people's own experiences. (Jai)

Workers are advised to encourage the offender to place himself in his victim's position (which ironically is a position many offenders may already have been in), and begin to reflect on the likely impact on her of his behaviour. This is seen to constitute a 'challenge' to his perceptions and beliefs but not in a condemnatory manner. What the worker is encouraged to achieve is to teach the offender to be more empathic (Cherry 2010). The research participants in this study provided evidence of practice that accorded with this view. Whilst many were keen to explain that their work inevitably involved a 'challenge' to a piece of behaviour or 'distorted thinking' in an offender, they saw how this challenge was managed and processed as crucial. Thus a challenge that simply rehearsed a disapproval or disapprobation was seen as unlikely to elicit anything other than a defensive reaction from the offender whereas a challenge that required the offender to think and reflect was seen as a positive process. They considered that the negative aspects of any overt or aggressive form of challenge would invariably result in the offender clamming up, or being 'backed into a corner'.

Janet considered that the effectiveness of the challenge was determined by the quality of the relationship that had already been established as well as the actual timing:

> I think sometimes with these men, you've got to know them to be able to challenge them well, I think at the start of the programme they come on, or any programme, they come on very embittered, they don't want to be there ... and it is the same when they are on probation supervision or on license, you know, they've done their time for the crime, why should you interfere with their lives, why should you tell them what to do .... I think it's – know when it is right, when it is safe, sometimes you need to challenge straight away if it is something that is completely not acceptable, but it's the way that you do it, you know some people can be from there to there in three seconds and ... it's not only putting yourself in danger but it's bringing out the worst of them as well you know. (Janet)

Some commented on their observations of colleagues who challenged more strongly than they would have done. Nick reflected on his experience of seeing challenging being done aggressively and leading inevitability to sanctions for the offender:

> So I would say that challenging is ... I wouldn't say difficult but it is an essential element of what we are doing I think. We challenge people's perceptions, we challenge people's attitudes and such like, but I think that sometimes we can ... and I reflect on this sometimes, we can sort of bulldoze our way into those sorts of situations (laughs), but again you know, I know some people that would have said again that they had terminated that... given him a verbal or other warning on license for using that word you know. (Nick)

Karen expressed discomfort about what she perceived to be unhelpfully aggressive challenging by one of her colleagues and went on to explain how she tried to repair the damage caused by an aggressive challenge from another colleague. She makes clear the distinction between holding authority and acting inappropriately:

> And we get feedback from offenders and if they don't like their offender managers, and it might be the offenders not the offender managers,

but ... we have a situation where we had someone who came into group the other day and he was furious, he had just seen his offender manager, he was absolutely furious, almost on the ceiling and ... the session was spent calming him down, and then when he had calmed down, what he said was 'look, I know that what he was saying was right but it was the way that he said it, he wagged his finger at me' and it made ... this fifty-year old man feel, really insulted and ... so it's that, it's how you are with people. There is a way of challenging people you don't have to wag fingers at them. You have the authority you don't have to show it always. (Karen)

Victoria was able to reflect on her own response to being challenged and make the connection with how this might make offenders feel:

I don't really like the word confrontational because I don't like confrontations they kind of make me feel a bit on edge so I can only imagine how they might feel. (Victoria)

Some (Damien, Mary, Gill and Hannah) described in detail how to 'challenge' really meant to try and 'unpick' or sort through the explanations that offenders were giving them of their behaviour in order to clarify the inconsistencies or lack of congruence between thoughts and behaviours, in a context where the behaviour under question carries a great deal of stigma and public shame.

And then I suppose just try to unpick things so try to ... build up a relationship for them to try and spill everything out. (Damien)

Sometimes the challenge was such that the offender could not contain his reactions to it, but, nevertheless, the strength of the relationship appears to be what 'held' him and enabled him eventually, once his feelings had subsided a little, to come back and continue to talk it through. The worker recognised that he could have misinterpreted the man's initial departure:

I thought, he's not going to come back in again in five minutes. I actually felt that if I had continued to challenge him, because he was going round in circles and you could see the rage in his face and, he said to me, 'five minutes, I just need five minutes' and ... I said to him afterwards that I wasn't going to be critical of you because you used that five minutes so constructively. The easy thing to say would have been; well he walked out. (Nick)

Research participants also talked about the use of humour as a way of tackling difficult or embarrassing issues and/or of lifting the otherwise rather flat mood (Tony, Howard, Kim, Geoff, Hannah and Karen). Geoff gave an example of how he had used humour to challenge a man to reflect on his honesty about, and responsibility for, his own sex offending behaviour.

A significant issue in relation to how these research participants chose to challenge the offenders they work with is the emotional subtext. A worker operating with a punitive credo (Rutherford 1994), as explored in Chapter 4, might seek to challenge more aggressively or with more confrontation, taking justification from the nature of the offending behaviour, whilst a worker with a caring credo, as the research participants to this study largely demonstrated, would aim to temper their negative feelings.

Conclusion

This chapter has covered elements of managing the process of a community order, as outlined in the Offender Management Model and National Standards. It has illustrated some of the emotional components of working towards change with offenders, including helping them to disclose important and often very personal information that can inform risk assessment and risk management. The implications of being honest and transparent in the way in which this information is to be subsequently handled, particularly when it may have a negative impact on the offender's liberty, have been discussed. Also explored are some of the tensions and ambivalences held and felt by the worker in managing these processes. Research participants were keen to build supportive relationships in order to enable disclosure but expressed some discomfort when this, or other events, resulted in them having to take enforcement action against the offender.

Given that the primary aim of a community order is to reduce the level of risk an offender poses, the core task of probation, and indeed any other of the 'helping' agencies within criminal justice, is to enable the offender to learn different ways of managing their lives. This requires the offender to be motivated and ready to learn and change. Research participants to this study recognised the importance of addressing this but overall insufficient attention has been paid to the issue of learning and the need to ensure that offenders as 'learners' are in the best place to benefit from the treatment or intervention being provided. An unexpected finding was that some research participants were resistant to the idea that offenders may also be victims, and need attention given to their own sense of victimhood. Historically, this would have been a significant focus of probation practice, quite possibly at the expense of challenging the offending behaviour. It seems this balance has shifted to the other end of the continuum where offenders are not encouraged to allow any trauma from their own past and present experiences to interfere with taking responsibility for their current behaviour. There may be a distinction to be drawn between genuine distress and confusion at past abuse and a mere 'rehearsal' or dramatising of past and present grievances that get in the way of current work. However, the distinction between these two may not always be clear-cut.

Also explored in this chapter is the extent to which a confrontational or challenging approach to offenders at one end of a continuum and a therapeutic, enabling or empowering approach at the other end affects the responsivity of the offender and any subsequent work undertaken with them in both assessing and managing risk. Research participants demonstrated a preference for 'soft skills' over 'hard confrontations'. Whilst they were mostly concerned to use their emotional skills in a productive and enabling manner, there is scope for the emotionally illiterate or unaware worker to use the authority in their role to 'challenge' in a negative way, to berate the offender for unacceptable behaviour or ideas and to not openly share any negative consequences of disclosures, including breach action, with them.

8
Emotions in Organisations

Practice examples

Claire has been working in her current offender management team for four years. She invests a great deal of emotional energy in her work and is very committed to the offenders that she supervises. Recently her workload has increased quite dramatically and so has the volume of paperwork she is expected to deal with. Claire feels frustrated that the quality of her work with offenders seems to be undervalued, but that she is 'jumped on' whenever her risk assessments are late in being completed. She tries to conceal her frustration but sometimes it spills over and recently she found herself in tears in front of the photocopier when her line manager was walking past. Claire felt unable to explain the real reasons for her frustration and told her line manager that she had a migraine. She subsequently went on sick leave.

Claire's management of her emotional skills could largely be described as 'philanthropic'; she cares about the offenders she supervises and is able to demonstrate empathy and kindness towards them such that she has built strong relationships and achieved good results in terms of successful completion of orders. Her management of her feelings in relation to her line manager is largely 'prescriptive' – she follows the rules that she feels are required by her profession, of concealing her true feelings and presenting a calm exterior whenever possible. The 'feeling rules' of her organisation do not encourage her to feel safe enough to talk about the real sources of her frustration for fear that she would cry when talking about her work and be seen as weak and lacking in competence.

Sam, in contrast, always strives to keep his feelings completely out of his working life. He prides himself on taking nothing home with him at the end of the day. He recognises that some of the offenders he supervises have had pretty dreadful lives and experiences but he believes his job is not to engage with their experiences but simply to supervise them fairly and consistently, and monitor their responses to the order. He represents an 'efficiency credo' in his practice. One of his offenders, Ashwant, is on supervision for assaulting his father, ostensibly for disagreeing about Ashwant's choice of career, as an art teacher. His father wanted him to follow his own profession of pharmacy. Ashwant is a compliant supervisee, keeping to his appointments and responding to all of Sam's questions about his work, his family life and his activities. However, Sam's emotional distance leads Ashwant to feel unable to explain to Sam that the real reason for his dispute with his father is the fact that Ashwant is gay. To all intents and purposes Ashwant keeps to the letter of his supervision order and Sam is able to tick him off as a successful case. The underlying reasons for his assault on his father are never addressed and subsequently Ashwant is back in court for another offence of assault.

Sally has been a probation officer for 22 years and is feeling very jaded and disaffected with the organisation and with her current workload. She is asked to write a pre-sentence report on a young offender, Justin, charged with a string of offences involving taking cars and criminal damage. Justin fails to attend his first appointment and arrives late for his second appointment. He is generally sullen and uncooperative in the interview and Sally finds herself getting very frustrated and cross with him. When it comes to writing the report she concludes that the service cannot offer any help to Justin because of his attitude, and subsequently Justin receives a custodial sentence of three months. When interviewed in prison Justin claims that Sally had been unsympathetic towards him when he missed the first appointment because his mother was ill and he had had to do her shopping. He believes that it was the negativity in her report that had resulted in him receiving a custodial sentence. Whilst Sally had legitimate reasons for feeling cross with Justin it is just possible that she allowed her feelings towards the organisation to spill over into her work with Justin and that she exhibited more of a 'punitive credo' in this instance, when a more neutral or indeed empathic approach might have elicited a better response from Justin. It is, of course, also possible that Justin has no intention of responding to probation intervention but it suited him at the time to find a focus for his resentment at the sentence. Nevertheless, Sally could have been helped to address her own frustrations in a more constructive way.

Key learning points

- Holding a 'caring credo' can enable practitioners to build strong and effective relationships with offenders. However, emotional investment in the work can be exploited by the organisation rather than supported by it. Such work requires emotional resources and emotional support from the organisation if workers are not to suffer 'burnout' and become unwell.

- Holding an 'efficiency credo' can enable a practitioner to meet the managerial demands of the agency and protect themselves from stress and emotional pressures. However, it can also mean that the practitioner's lack of emotional literacy means that they miss significant cues and messages from the offender about potential underlying reasons for their offending.
- Holding a 'punitive credo' can lead a criminal justice practitioner to impose negativity and potentially add to the punishment of the offender. Such practitioners need help in reflecting on the causes and implications of their own negativity to limit the impact on offenders.

Introduction

This chapter examines some of the definitions and meanings of 'emotion work' or 'emotional labour' within criminal justice organisations. It reflects on the degree to which organisations in the criminal justice system, through a combination of 'managerialism' (Raine 2007) and the operation of 'professional' rules of conduct, can inhibit the expression and validation of emotions within their working cultures. It will also examine the extent to which such organisations can, nevertheless, implicitly expect their staff to offer their 'emotional labour' in the pursuit of organisational objectives, exploiting this labour without necessarily providing the infrastructure to support or sustain it (Hochschild 1983). In addition to 'professional' rules, Hochschild's concept of 'feeling rules' within an organisation identify the potential for practitioners to be encouraged to maintain a form of 'emotional detachment' or 'neutrality' (Crawley 2004) in the pursuit of both technical efficiency and professionalism, thus denying or suppressing the emotions generated by the work, and the consequences of this for themselves and for the offenders with whom they work. Using Bolton's four typologies of emotion management in the workplace (Bolton 2005), this chapter explores the use and potential exploitation by the organisation of emotions in the workforce. An interrogation of the research data for this book and some of the wider literature offers an insight into what the probation service, as an example of a criminal justice organisation, might expect from its workforce and what unspoken 'rules', pressures or constraints may be impacting on staff as they employ their emotions as part and parcel of their practice repertoire. The context for this chapter is Layder's third domain of 'social settings' (Layder 2006) and illustrates how the organisational setting influences emotional literacy.

Emotion management or emotional labour?

In order to function effectively and smoothly, organisations are seen to need a calm and orderly workforce, where emotions are largely under control and subservient to the needs of the business (Du Gay 2003). Du Gay argues that such a culture is the means by which organisations achieve success and workers conduct themselves in ways that maximise their involvement in and contribution to the organisation (Du Gay 2003). Fineman argues, however, that it is naive to assume that emotions have been eliminated in this new organisational world and that in fact they are deeply woven into the fabric of all organisations and define and shape all manner of practices (Fineman 2001). Within the wider emotion theory literature the term used to identify the controlling of emotions in a working context is 'emotion management' and it is linked to the idea of individual emotional self-regulation. For example, Crawley's work in prisons highlights how when prison officers working in the emotionally painful environment of a prison express emotion, they need to do so in a structured way; she refers to this as the emotion management undertaken by them in order to perform their job in an 'appropriate manner' (Crawley 2009).

However, not only is emotion controlled, it can also be viewed as a resource to be *exploited* by the organisation (Hochschild 1983). This utilisation or exploitation of emotion in the workplace is generally defined as 'emotion work' or 'emotional labour', although these terms have tended to lack clarity and definition (Bolton 2005). Whilst the concept of emotional labour has some utility in explaining the use of emotion in, for example, service industries, where customer care is a valued commodity, it does not fully conceptualise the positive and freely offered 'gift' of emotion that occurs in organisations with a 'therapeutic' rather than a 'business' orientation (Bolton 2005).

In Chapter 4, with reference to Layder's continuum of interpersonal emotional control, there was discussion about the potential for criminal justice staff to use their emotional skills in positive or benign ways but also in negative or repressive ways in their work with offenders. It was suggested that some of the strategies of control employed by both police and prison officers could be viewed as falling legitimately into the 'repressive positional' in order to control violent or anti-social behaviour or recalcitrant prisoners (Layder 2004: 61). In contrast, the strategies employed by probation staff, given its history of care for offenders, might be viewed as falling within the normal/healthy range of Layder's continuum involving benign emotional control and 'soft' manipulation. However, it was also argued that the picture is rather more complex than this with both positive and negative emotional control occurring, in an unregulated manner, in all criminal justice settings.

Emotional labour

The difference between the private and public sphere of emotion regulation exposes differing ideas of how emotion might be managed (Hochschild 1983, Theodosius 2008). In the private realm, 'emotion work', defined as the work necessary to take care of the emotional lives of others, is considered to be 'personal' and 'individual', and takes place mostly in the home. It is seen as being largely undertaken by women (Bunting 2005). In contrast, 'emotional labour' is described as the display of expected emotions by service agents during service encounters and is seen to stimulate pressure for the person to identify with the service role (Ashforth and Humphrey 1993). A number of writers have engaged with the idea of 'emotion work' or 'emotional labour' in organisations (Hochschild 1983; Ashforth and Humphrey 1993; Bunting 2005; Theodosius 2008), in which employees are required to invest their personality and emotional skills in order to do a good job (Du Gay 2003). Du Gay suggests that there is emotional dissonance when service providers experience a conflict between the emotions they feel about the job and the required emotions the organisation has determined to be acceptable to display (Du Gay 2003: 291). Hochschild argues that when corporate expectations and pressures contradict worker's self-conceptions and emotions, workers are likely to experience a sense of inauthenticity, alienation and dissatisfaction (Hochschild 1983). Schaible and Gecas provide an example of this by looking at emotional labour and value dissonance within the police force in terms of its impact on subsequent 'burnout' (Schaible and Gecas 2010). They found that the greater the dissonance between the officer's own values and those of various reference groups, the greater their levels of burnout. Du Gay argues that not only have the emotional demands of the workplace increased significantly in recent years but also emotion work is remarkable for its sheer ordinariness, how it is frequently dismissed or belittled (Du Gay 2003: 61).

Hochschild defined emotional labour as occurring in organisations that involved frequent customer contact and in which emotion displays are controlled by the organisation (Hochschild 1983). She examined how flight attendants were trained to offer a quality service to passengers and referred to this as 'emotional labour'; staff had to learn how to project a certain image of themselves and of the organisation for which they worked (Hochschild 1983). Workers had to be taught how to do this rather than it being seen as something 'natural', and particular attributes and dispositions were seen to define a particular line of work. Crawley in her work on emotions in prisons demonstrates a blurring of the private/public sphere of emotion regulation and argues that prisons, in common with domestic settings, tend to be emotionally charged (Crawley 2004). She writes mostly about the emotional lives of prison officers rather than defining any of their work as 'emotional labour', although she acknowledges some of the caring that does take place in prison, particularly with regard to vulnerable prisoners, can amount to significant 'emotion work'. Prisons and probation hostels are both places where people have to live. Whether in fact any of the positive emotional work undertaken by staff with inmates or residents of these institutions can be defined as 'emotional labour' required by the organisation, or is actually more closely akin to emotions offered as a 'gift' by workers to offenders is explored in the rest of this chapter.

Feeling rules

Hochschild introduced the concept of 'feeling rules' which she argued guide emotions in organisations by establishing the sense of entitlement or obligations that govern emotional exchanges (Hochschild 1983: 56). Hochschild's feeling rules refer to socially shared (though often latent) understandings regarding emotions. They represent what emotions people should express and the degree of that expression according to social roles (Hochschild 1983). Fineman coins the term 'emotion engineers' and cites as an example the McDonalds enterprise which wants a 'smile industry' (Fineman 2001). Crawley's identification of the feeling rules within a prison as those of 'emotional detachment' provides a criminal justice example (Crawley 2004).

'Feeling rules' may include who does the emotional work in the organisation and may specify the range, duration, intensity and object of emotions that should be experienced (Hochschild 1983: 89). These feeling rules have also been referred to as 'display rules' that relate to behaviour rather than to internal states, and it is relatively easy for customers, managers and peers to observe the level of compliance with the rules (Goffman 1959/1990). Hochschild drew a distinction between surface acting and deep acting in the response to such rules. Surface acting is where the individual simulates or feigns emotions that are not actually felt. (This is accomplished by the careful presentation of verbal and non-verbal cues, by facial expressions, gestures and voice tone.) In contrast, deep acting is seen as the more genuine and felt responses to life events, in which the person attempts to actually experience or feel the emotions that they wish to display (Ashforth and Humphrey 1993). For example, criminal justice workers may not always feel like responding positively to every offender with whom they are working but will endeavour to 'put on' a positive front when commencing an interview and may well find that the resultant interaction begins to engage their more authentic feelings.

Whilst emotions are part and parcel of all human interaction, whether private or public, Goffman saw 'emotional labour' as performed at the direct or indirect behest of the organisation and operating as a performance or 'front stage' transaction, where the performance takes place, with its hidden aspects or outlet at 'back stage' (Goffman 1959/1990). For example, a nurse who is upset at a patient dying will manage her feelings and display an appropriate face when with the patient (front stage) but may cry when she comes to hand over to another colleague in a nurses-only area (back stage and 'deep acting')

(Theodosius 2008). A waitress may be required to be pleasant and polite to customers (surface acting) but may 'bad mouth' them to colleagues working behind the scenes (back stage) (Theodosius 2008). These two examples illustrate the expectations of emotional labour in different work contexts and the processes of emotion regulation as part and parcel of this labour (Theodosius 2008).

There are clear differences between emotions that are 'deep acting' and sincerely felt (the nursing example) and ones that are surface acting for the benefit of the organisation (the waitress example). Theodosius suggests that

> emotions must be understood within the structural relations of power and status that elicit them. (Theodosius 2008: 13)

Although both the nurse and the waitress in these examples are female, men too can be required to undertake emotional labour although they may find ways, through the power of their role, of sidestepping this (e.g. male hospital consultants can assume emotional detachment and expect nursing staff to undertake the emotional labour for them (Smith 1992, Theodosius 2008)).

Whilst 'emotion' is considered a feature and a resource of all organisations (Bolton 2005), it has also been viewed as a gendered concept, with women seen to undertake more of this emotional labour, particularly in the arena of nursing (Smith 1992, Ashforth and Humphrey 1993, Wellington and Bryson 2001, Theodosius 2008), and in the service sector (Du Gay 2003; Bunting 2005). Some have argued that in the public realm 'emotional labour' is sold for a wage as a commodity and takes place at work where, as a feminised commodity, it is largely undervalued (Hochschild 1983; Smith 1992; Du Gay 2003) and invisible. Whilst practical tasks, for example, those required within nursing to care for a patient, are visible and measurable, emotional responses may not be. Organisations also identified as 'high emotional labour jobs', including social services, teaching and other 'caring' professions (Brotheridge and Gradey 2005), have a preponderance of female staff at main grade level. This demographic is equally true of the modern probation service (see Chapter 3) (Knight 2007).

Hochschild considers that emotion work is not as important to men as to women and that there are reasons and consequences for this. She suggests that women traditionally have had less access to power, authority and financial resources than men and have lacked the status that men carry in society. She sees this as leading to four consequences for women:

1. Their lack of access to resources mean that women use feelings as a resource and offer them as a gift to men in return for more material resources that they do not have.

2. Boys and girls are taught differential ways of managing their feelings, for example, girls and women are taught to control their anger and aggression and 'be nice' whereas men are required to undertake 'aggressive' tasks against those who break the rules and that this requires them to control their feelings of fear and vulnerability.

3. The general subordination of women leaves them vulnerable to picking up the displaced feelings of others, what she describes as a weaker 'status shield' for verbal abuse from airline passengers (her study).

4. For both genders part of the 'managed heart' is used for commercial reasons. (Hochschild 1983: 163)

Emotional capital or emotional resource

The notion of 'emotional capital', which in itself is a metaphor, has also been deployed to capture the idea of emotions within a workplace, organisation or community. Drawing on Bourdieu's conceptual framework of social capital, ideas of emotional capital, as a subset of human capital, have been used to demonstrate how 'emotional resources' are circulated, accumulated and exchanged for other forms of capital (Zembylas 2007). Theodosius argues that in order for an exploitation of this emotional capital to occur for the benefit of the organisation, the organisation needs to impose its own set of rules and management (Theodosius 2008). However, if released from the potential for organisational exploitation, emotional capital could also represent a more equitable resource, a network of relationships and activities which may facilitate and enable people to maintain their mental and emotional health and well-being within their communities and at work (Adkins and Skeggs 2005). For example, Reay has used the term emotional capital to describe the emotional resources passed on from mother to child. She emphasises close relationships between emotional capital and well-being in the family and educational success (Reay 2004). Adverse conditions such as poverty are seen to diminish such capital. Zembylas refers to emotional capital in an educational setting being built over time within classrooms and schools and contributing to the formation of particular emotion norms and 'affective economies' (Zembylas 2007: 453).

In this book the term emotional 'resource' is favoured over that of 'capital' with its financial associations. The research participants identified that a degree of emotional resource accumulated for them through the pleasure that they took in building relationships with offenders and seeing them make positive changes in their lives. However, as illustrated in Chapter 5, there appeared to be a preponderance of negative emotions expressed by research participants about their work which to some extent impacted, and potentially diminished, the emotional resources built up within the probation service as a support to the workforce.

Emotion management in the probation service

The probation service has moved from the relatively non-hierarchical and laissez-faire culture of the 1970s to a performance management culture in which bureaucracy and managerialism have become the drivers through which the service aims to meet its targets of reducing offending and protecting the public (Whitehead 2010). These recent developments have focused on the measurable, 'hard' facts of processes and outcomes with a concomitant squeezing out of the 'softer' realm of feelings and emotions. Yet there continue to be significant emotional issues and trauma related to crime and offending behaviour that can challenge workers in the probation service in powerful, subtle and often contradictory ways, as explored in earlier chapters.

The research participants to the study identified concepts of 'professional rules' and organisational constraints as being significant in defining their occupational world and their personal regulation of emotion. They described how their sense of the correct 'professional' way to behave influenced how they controlled and used their feelings. 'Professionalism' as a concept is promoted by the organisation but also has a separate social reality; it is defined through membership of a 'profession' which imposes certain expectations and requirements on its members, as, for example, the profession of medicine expects its members to abide by the Hippocratic oath regardless of where they practice. It is suggested that with the changing ethos of the probation service, associated with its closer alignment with the prison service within the National Offender Management Service (NOMS), and the evolution of a 'managerial' culture, some unspoken 'professional' or 'feeling' rules have been created that expect emotional detachment in the workforce. In this instance the managerial, 'tough' and, often perceived as, 'male voice' is seen to be favoured over the softer, more emotional and, often perceived as, 'female voice'.

Bolton suggests that emotion work can be 'hard' and 'productive' as well as just something that people do (Bolton 2005). This form of analysis takes as its focus management efforts to control work undertaken by employees and shows how they are sometimes constrained to comply with managerial prescriptions (Bolton 2005: 8). She argues that some employers want more compliance from their employees including emotional commitment to the aims of the enterprise. Bolton argues that using one blanket term 'emotional labour' is insufficient to describe a complex phenomenon such as emotion management in organisations. She identifies four typologies of emotion work within organisations which she believes represents this greater complexity.

Bolton's four typologies of emotion work within organisations are:

1. 'Presentational' (emotion management according to general social rules)
2. 'Philanthropic' (emotion management given as a gift)
3. 'Prescriptive' (emotion management according to organisational/professional rules of conduct
4. 'Pecuniary' (emotion management for monetary gain) (Bolton 2005: 91)

Research findings

Evidence provided by research participants to the study suggests that their emotion management skills were largely illustrative of the first three of the above four typologies; presentational, philanthropic and prescriptive or professional.

i) Presentational

Presentational is the general and common type of emotion management in most organisations which require their staff to follow accepted social rules about emotions, such as to be polite, helpful, friendly at all times and to conceal expressions of negative emotion. This is fairly closely associated with Hochschild's concept of emotional labour (Hochschild 1983) although it does not necessarily include the 'pecuniary' element where emotional labour is specifically required to meet the objectives of the organisation. It also has a relationship with Goffman's 'display rules' (Goffman 1959/1990). There was some evidence in the data of research participants endeavouring to present an emotionally positive 'front'. For example, John demonstrates some ambivalence about the appropriateness of showing negative feelings in particular, which indicates a form of 'presentational' emotion work, albeit it is sincerely offered:

> The difference is that as a practitioner your role is much more to be a constant and be supportive and warm – you are not supposed to show you are frustrated with them or are feeling angry or frustrated – though some researchers would say that that's not necessarily a bad thing. (John)

Hannah is careful to choose which emotions to show, favouring the positive ones over the negative ones:

> I try never to forget and keep it there ... but I do not want to show my emotions ... to the offender how I feel about what they have done, but on the other hand I do show my emotions ... when I am really pleased with how they are working and I will tell them that and also show that in the way that I behave or, likewise when I am unhappy with the way things are going I will also say. There are different levels I suppose. (Hannah)

These research participants were working hard to present a positive emotional front to their service users, with the belief that expressing negative emotion would be counterproductive (Goffman 1959/1990).

ii) Philanthropic

'Philanthropic' emotion management describes the context in which the worker decides to give more of 'themselves' during a social exchange in the workplace (Bolton 2005). 'Philanthropy' is generally associated with organisations where staff (quite frequently women) engage in various forms of personal care work (Smith 1992; Theodosius 2008), and can occur in both paid and unpaid (voluntary) occupations. Emotion work in this context is seen as a 'gift' rather than an organisational requirement (Bolton 2005: 140). There were plenty of examples of the research participants' willingness to offer their emotional skills as a 'gift' to the offender, and a number of these are provided in Chapter 6 with reference to the use of empathy which is seen to provide the foundation of the relationship building process.

Nick's description highlights the presence in him, and absence in his prison officer colleague (both employed by NOMS), of philanthropic emotion management. Nick is describing his view of how some staff are unable to manage the emotional expressions of legitimately angry prisoners. In this example the male prison officer working with him is described as being in some discomfort:

> But sometimes they (prison staff or other probation colleagues) don't listen and are sometimes too quick to jump on that behaviour and the problem in terms of ... doing that, you set a precedent ... because next time they (prisoner) will feel ... that they can't ever express their emotions because that is a taboo thing to do with you and that it can't be had, and your reaction to it is so extreme that it will either result in you terminating the interview immediately or just not being willing to hear it. And I think sometimes it has been founded ... on negative experiences and ...a case in point, on Monday where a prison officer sat next to me and he was sort of dumbfounded by what this offender was saying and he clearly did not know how to deal with him and he was fidgeting and feeling uncomfortable sat next to me because his means of dealing with it would have been a far more 'right back to your cell'. (Nick)

This example demonstrates the emotion work being undertaken by Nick which is not understood by his colleague prison officer. As Bolton argues, this goes beyond any notion of emotional labour on behalf of an organisation for commercial gain (Bolton 2005). Nick is offering his emotional skills as a gift to the prisoner because he understands the reasons for his anger and feels the prisoner has a legitimate need to be heard. The emotion is 'subjective' – the prisoner experiencing anger and Nick's feelings of concern for him – 'external' in that it is being witnessed and judged differentially by Nick and the prison officer, 'situated' within the relationship between the three of them, and in a social context, that is, strongly influenced by the prison environment as the context for the prisoner's anger (Layder 2004).

iii) Prescriptive

Prescriptive emotion management refers to the ways in which an employee's emotion work can be controlled through the process of 'professionalisation' (Bolton 2005). In this typology emotions may be seen as risky, untrustworthy and unpredictable so a mantle of 'professionalism' is needed to keep them under control. This concept of professionalism may be closely prescribed; it is not necessarily for commercial gain, but it can be associated with issues of power and control (Lukes 2005), and linked to professional codes of conduct such as for doctors and lawyers. As introduced in Chapter 5, many of the research participants gave examples of how they endeavoured to manage their emotions in what they thought was the 'right' or 'correct' way within the workplace, and that this was influenced by their belief in the importance of being 'professional'. In becoming a teacher, GP, lawyer, psychiatrist, probation officer or social worker the staff member is inculcated into codes of conduct and ways of looking, sounding and 'being' professional when dealing with others. Fineman describes how this state of 'being' is often reached through a range of different and imitative learning experiences and reinforced in a variety of organisational settings, for example, through professional training establishments, fieldwork and consulting rooms. In many cases the expectations of the clients of these professionals adds to this process of emotion shaping and both are complicit in defining boundaries of each other's appropriate emotional display (Fineman 2001). For example, a patient's tears could be considered acceptable but a weeping doctor either in sympathy or in revealing his/her own anxieties is likely to compromise or strain the relationship (Fineman 2001: 226).

Lacey defines professionalism as responding to difficult issues without prejudice, and meriting the trust of the public (Lacey 1995). This conveys an image of confidence, fairness and trustworthiness. However, Mathiesen refers to a 'professionalisation' which silences dispute or contention (Mathiesen 2004). He argues that for individuals to become professionals in a particular setting they need to be inculcated with a particular way of thinking and introduced to a 'series of conceptualisations' within which they must operate if they are to be successful (Matheisen 2004: x). Crawley refers to the way in which prison officers engage in 'impression management' (Goffman 1959/1990), in order to appear authoritative and confident in their dealings with prisoners, whilst remaining emotionally detached (Crawley 2004: 147).

A number of research participants felt that being 'professional' meant keeping their own feelings and needs in check, not allowing their 'hearts to rule their heads' to coin a metaphor. They considered that whatever they might 'feel' about a particular issue or a particular piece of behaviour, they should not allow these feelings to influence their judgements or their responses.

> and actually having to be professional when you have got to handle and manage somebody else's emotions but keep your own ... tied down, without letting them know. (Mary)

Victoria felt that only certain people were able to exercise professionalism and she clearly views being professional as being about the concealment of feelings:

> I think it just takes a particular kind of person who can, keep their, in a professional way, can kind of keep those ... feelings ... under cover maybe ... definitely when we're with offenders, it's very professional. (Victoria)

This next respondent, Sandy, was clear about the need to operate within specific guidelines or 'feeling rules':

> I think, for me it always about professionalism because I came from a profession that if you squeaked in the wrong place you were rapped over the knuckles. (Sandy)

Hannah sees her professionalism as taking over from her emotional responses and enabling her to take charge of the situation in a positive manner. She is, however, also offering philanthropic emotion management:

> But if they are genuinely distressed and upset about ... the effect they've had on the other people and their family, then yes, I suppose it does upset me in some way but then again the professional side kicks in and you need to find a way to go forward and how you can change those emotions and turn them into something more positive. (Hannah)

What appears evident here in the manner in which the research participants embedded the 'rules' of professionalism and monitored themselves in terms of their own emotional behaviour. Alongside their need to control their feelings and remain professional, a large number of research participants held negative views about their perception of a culture of 'managerialism' within the organisation. Managerialism is defined as:

> The ascendancy of business management values and priorities within the public sector, and the corresponding decline in the influence and value base of the professions. (Raine 2007: 160)

New styles of management were imported from the private sector to the running of the probation service in the 1980s including greater emphasis on outputs rather than processes and the measurement of performance through the setting of specific targets and standards for practice; sometimes referred to as New Public Management (Canton 2011). In the probation context it was seen to place emphasis on a quantitative approach to the management of offenders in the community through the setting and monitoring of targets, and within a culture of control and public protection over and above a more qualitative process of helping and enabling change (Vanstone 2007). Whilst these aspirations may be aimed at improving the efficiency, effectiveness and economy of the service they can fail to capture the *quality* of practice and can sometimes lead to inappropriate practice in the pursuit of specific targets. Twenty-two of the 28 research participants made reference to what they perceived to be the 'managerialist' culture of the probation service which they considered was hampering their efforts to develop high-quality and emotionally literate practice. The following offer a flavour of the strength of feelings expressed by research participants on this subject:

Targets and throughput

The largest number of comments related to the imposition of targets that set particular goals and expectations that the research participants felt dominated their practice to the exclusion of any of the more creative or qualitative processes that they saw as essential.

That's what I don't like – this feeling of you have to perform – bums on seats – through put – that annoys me. (Michael)

It's targets, targets, targets, get this done, this needs to be done, you're not doing this quick enough, this is not ..., you know and so it's kind of a battle really in terms of that. (Damien)

I feel angry because I feel that ... I suppose angry at what they have done, what the men have done, but angry at the service for not allowing us to work more efficiently because it is all about tick boxes rather than allowing us to do the work, so that's what it elicits in me. (Sandy)

Having to cover your back all the time for safety, doing things just because in case it gets audited or it gets looked at ... the targets set by management hierarchy in Home Office that aren't necessarily related to the actual piece of work or actual job. (Mary)

'Jumping through hoops' – micromanagement

Associated with the target drive culture was the sense of being overly scrutinised about the detail, made to respond to quantitative demands at the expense of professional practice:

But I do have a problem with being so micro managed and scrutinised ... there's been a real narrowing ... What matters is programme completions, targets being met – running programmes is what matters. (Amy)
..The thing I least like the most which is management – politics – basically all the fucking about and the hoops that you have to jump through and the ill informed – in my opinion – changes, the pace of change in probation. (Howard)

Structures, rules and regulations

Some were concerned about the wider organisational frameworks for practice that inhibited their ability to be emotionally literate:

But sometimes it's the management, the organizational issues – the structures don't lend themselves to doing this kind of work. (Indira)
I think there is a lot of b'reaucracy ... in an organization like this, I think that ... the workers are not empowered to do... enough, I think they should have more power to do what they think is right ... there's a lot of rules and regulations and we are told to comply with certain things. (Robert)

Paperwork

There were also some very strong views about the overwhelming amount of paperwork needed to maintain the managerial ethos of the service, again at the expense of creative and emotionally literate practice:

What I don't like is ... the paperwork really ... I know what risks somebody poses but then having to spell it out to the point that it's almost ... covering my back almost, that's the bit I don't like. (Victoria)

The above extracts identify an anger and frustration at the managerialism and bureaucracy of the organisation that in the views of the research participants demonstrates a lack of interest by the organisation in emotional discourse and in some instances an actual blocking of their ability to work effectively. Whilst the need to abide by professional rules of conduct seemed to support a presentational typology of emotion management, to which the research participants largely subscribed, the impact of the managerialist culture seemed to be more of a 'deadening' or 'silencing' of emotional discourse and expression. Further examples of the research participants' frustrations about this perceived managerial culture are included in Chapter 10 when they acknowledge the lack of support from their organisation for emotional literacy and find their own strategies for surviving the 'silence' on emotional matters.

iv) Pecuniary

The fourth type, emotion management for pecuniary advantage, describes an exploitative use of emotion work more generally found in the commercial or service industries. Whilst this may be a less obvious form of emotion management within the probation service, there is a sense in which an organisation striving to meet targets and be 'efficient' and 'economic' does indeed exploit the emotional literacy of its workforce to meet these aims. It could also be argued that 'professionalism' can be motivated by pecuniary incentives such as higher salaries and recognition.

> It's very much performance, targets, you know, cases in through the door, are we meeting this, are we getting the money, is your high risk review done, you know I feel that we are very much on our own with the emotional literacy side. (Angela)

Maggie's frustration with the paperwork as associated with the constant setting of targets also implies a perception of an organisation that has instrumental rather than humanitarian ends:

> I don't like the amount of paperwork involved in the job because ... and the fact that we've got to meet targets, I don't like that ... I think they just see us as people who meet targets and that's that. (Maggie)

Amy sees the probation service as operating as a production line, which again implies the production of a commodity rather than a human process;

> The rise of managerialism, and target driven practice and office based practice – and practice that – looks at people, well it's a production line. Henry Ford would recognize the process. (Amy)

It could be argued that the lack of support to staff who offer their emotion literacy as a 'gift' to offenders is in itself a form of exploitation. Also, the exploitation of emotional labour may become increasingly evident with the drive towards the contracting out of significant areas of probation work to the private sector and the increasing emphasis on 'payment by results' (Ministry of Justice 2010).

Feeling rules for criminal justice organisations?

Unspoken, invisible but, nonetheless, powerful 'feeling rules' can identify the kind of emotions it is appropriate to express or conceal within the workplace. From the evidence presented above it seems that the research participants were affected both by 'professional' rules and by a managerialist culture in their management of emotions. Historically, the probation service was identified as a welfare-based service for offenders and the philosophy of the organisation, from the early days of the Police Court Missionaries, was grounded on the humanitarian principles of 'advise, assist and befriend' (Whitehead 2010). These principles gave staff a clear if tacit message that the unspoken 'feeling rules' of the organisation would support them in caring for offenders as a core requirement of the job. Such 'feelings rules' would seem to fit most closely with Bolton's typology of 'philanthropic' (Bolton 2005).

Some research participants demonstrated a sense of nostalgia for their recollection of a largely benevolent organisation that in previous years would have acknowledged a demonstration of care and concern for offenders and in which emotional difficulties for both offenders and staff would have been openly discussed:

> I know it's not that long ago but, when I first joined and you used supervision it was all about talking through your cases, reflecting about what happened, offloading, talking about practice, it was very much emotionally literate, it was very much about your emotions and how that reflected on you as an individual. Now it's like, 'how many Think First's have you had start', 'how many have you got in employment', you know, 'why was this review late?' ... do you know what I mean, it's almost like they're not really bothered anymore about how we feel. (Victoria)

In contrast, 'managerialism' and 'professionalism' both seem to define a culture of tight regulation and control of emotions. In looking for evidence for any 'feeling rules' determined for staff working in this modern, business-orientated and more punitive corrections agency (NOMS), Crawley's research provides some signposts. She was able to demonstrate how emotional detachment was prized amongst prison officers (Crawley 2004). She describes the way prison officers learn to conform to an occupational culture that expects them to disengage from their feelings and adopt the 'strategies of depersonalisation' and that this is a core part of their training (Crawley 2004). Crawley argues that it is imperative that prison officers learn these rules and that those who transgress these rules risk presenting themselves as unreliable and untrustworthy. Crawley refers to Goffman's ideas that those who transgress the rules or express the wrong emotions acquire a 'spoiled identity' and this is the price paid for ineffective impression management (Crawley 2004). Crawley describes how prison officers, within an occupational culture of 'machismo', engaged in degrees of humour, depersonalisation and detachment to avoid this spoiled identity.

Although employed primarily in the community, probation staff within NOMS work with the same offender group and are governed by the same organisational structures as these prison officers. Whilst probation staff are generally careful about their use of language, (Knight, Dominey et al. 2008), nevertheless, the common use of the word 'offender' across both services in itself has a strong depersonalising element. This term was widely used by research participants in the study although some made a conscious decision to use the word 'client' in defiance, it seemed, of the prevailing linguistic norm. This depersonalised approach is also sustained by a media that additionally uses terms such as 'feral', 'alien' and 'predator' in relation to offenders, which enhances this aura of detachment from the humanity of the offender (Hayles 2006).

Research participants had plenty to say about the lack of understanding of their managers of the significance of the emotional world of the job. They believed that their managers, to a large extent, saw the task of the probation officer to 'feed the computer' and 'meet the targets' (Sandy, Heather, Amy). The preoccupation with counting and data collection militated against the valuing of any of the more qualitative and emotional processes that they associated with good practice:

> There is no comprehension of whether I am a good facilitator, whether I am emotionally able to manage what comes round, I don't think they care as long as they've ticked all the boxes. (Sandy)

> I am saddened that .... at how (emotionally) illiterate an organization such as this is, where if we are not much at the forefront of how things are going to be I don't know who is going to be. (Heather)

> I don't think that they do invest in their staff at all. I don't think they particularly care how ... it impacts on staff as long as they hit their targets and they get their money, and there's no, the amount of SFO's is as low as possible, that's what they're bothered about, that's just my honest opinion about it. (Maggie)

> I'd put it a bit stronger, – I think not only are they buried and not valued I think there is hostility toward those (skills of emotional literacy) – that would be my feeling. (Amy)

The responses that research participants received from their line managers was perceived to be crucial to the way that they were then able to manage the emotional impact of the job. Some research participants expressed quite disparaging views about the ability of either their direct line manager or managers in general to understand the emotional context of their work or to recognise the level of stress that was being experienced:

> If you've got four child protection cases and three ICPC's to go to in one week and you expect us to go so that you hit your target, but if we don't go because we are too stressed out, then we get a bollocking for it, they don't look at the fact of 'why are they stressed out?' so I think they are just not interested at all. Not all managers, but specific ones, it has just been my experience of current managers. (Maggie)

> And I think that when you consider the emotional aspect of the work that we do, our supervision agenda that we have or not had for that long, you know, 'how are you feeling?' and 'how's your work load?' and that's it, it's almost straight back to work again, not you know, 'how are you feeling in yourself?' ... maybe if they spent more time looking at things on that kind of level then they might not have some of the problems with sickness that they have, because there are so many people who are struggling and who are stressed but it is almost like some of these people have to scream as loud as they can to management but they are not being listened to and then the only way they are going to get heard is to go off sick. (Gill)

> And sometimes I think that although you opt for it, I think that the work that we do is not always recognized by senior management in terms of the say, the stress, and the very nature of how a lot of these cases work is that they bring a lot of change, a lot of constant change and when you manage a case like this you understand the responsibilities that come with it. (Nick)

These research participants are reflecting the difficulties they find in communicating their concerns to senior colleagues. The organisation does not actually regulate the emotional and vulnerable underside of the working culture; it just succeeds in cutting off the channels through which it can be expressed. Tony expresses quite powerful negative feelings of mistrust of management but by contrast highlights the importance of peer support and help in working through the emotional impact:

> I have to concede that really it's not the work we do and it's not the guys we work with – they do have an impact on us, and we club together and share

that with each other, and its where we get our sustenance – but gnawing away at those highs and lows all the time is a distrust of management or a feeling that management don't trust us – we're not valued. That's all we want rather than just 'we've met the targets' – oh and 'by the way you just need to work a bit harder next year' – oh great. (Tony)

Linked to this lack of understanding from their managers was a concern that the quality of the work, which was equated with emotional processes, was of less importance to their line managers than the quantitative measurements:

It's ... people, managers who may make decisions without understanding what the work is about and not kind of like, keeping themselves informed about it, so ..., that I find frustrating ... one of the frustrations for me is when the quality of the work gets compromised for quantity. (Jai)

Everything is prescriptive ... the quality aspect is irrelevant really, it is how many people have you got through treatment?... not how effective treatment is, that really doesn't count for an awful lot ... so in terms of the manualised, prescriptive approach, the extra bits that we sort of put in ... aren't necessary. (Geoff)

I think the problem is that when you do actually come into practice, the offender becomes less of a focus if that makes sense. Because practice, targets, structures, policies become more important. (Nick)

These research participants are expressing considerable resentment at the target culture imposed by managerialism that they viewed as limiting and controlling their professional discretion. Heather sees the constraints of the Offender Assessment System (OASys) assessment scoring, which she sees as placing people in boxes as very depersonalising, a lack of a fit between the interpersonal processes and the scoring systems:

I find that the amount of time spent on recording and ..., the repetition of certain bits of recording which aren't about anything dynamically having changed, I think that is, is a waste of time ... I think that the whole way we are looking at probation now and objectifying people and giving them scores of nought to two, and I am not knocking the whole of OASys at all, I am really not, I am happy to have a focus on stuff, but this system of numerically scoring people, I find in some ways, very depersonalising and often we are in danger of boxing people and not allowing them to change as a system. (Heather)

Similarly, Lynn is concerned that not only are offenders being placed in boxes but so too are the workers, when they are judged according to some very specific criteria rather than to any of the worker's more emotionally literate skills:

> What you are judged on in your appraisals is as a group worker, is whether you are reaching the score level because the treatment manager will look at a video and then he will, he will score you against particular criteria. Which is group management skills, use of open questions and ... anti-discriminatory practice and ...whether you stuck to the time, timings of the session and the gender of the session. (Lynn)

These responses illustrate a perception by these research participants of an organisation that was not concerned about their 'feelings' or their emotional worlds. If 'feeling rules' apply to the probation service, or indeed other criminal justice organisations, they seem to be those of emotional detachment or disinterest; the organisation would prefer an absence rather than a presence of feeling.

Conclusion

As explored in Chapter 5 the research participants in the study acquired a degree of personal emotional regulation through the processes of 'growing up', 'learning on the job' and general maturation. However, as employees they have also been exposed to the 'professional rules' of practice and the emotion regulation required by an organisation of its staff, the 'feeling rules' which appear to be those of 'emotional detachment'. They demonstrated an acceptance of the former and some resistance to the latter. The probation service clearly benefits from the emotion work undertaken by its staff (Ministry of Justice 2010), but it is largely initiated by the staff themselves rather than being specifically required by the organisation. Not only did the research participants feel they must curb the expression of emotion in the workplace, they also felt silenced from talking about it. Unlike the research participants in Crawley's study of prisons, however, there was no evidence that they had been directly taught to be emotionally detached.

The combination or accumulation of these 'rules', some more acceptable to the workers than others, all seem to deny the significance of emotions in general and to expect a 'front' of only positive emotional expression (Goffman 1959/1990). The workers in this study have been left to find their own way through a turmoil of emotions, both those of the offenders they supervise and their own. The feeling rules of the organisation appear to be largely prescriptive; they determine what should not be expressed but do not offer any guidance or help in achieving this 'detachment' or in controlling the feelings when they do arise. Neither do they acknowledge the reality of the emotional content of much of the work undertaken, sometimes surreptitiously, by workers who understand very well the importance of philanthropy to their work, of offering their emotional skills as a gift. The discursive frameworks of managerialism and 'punishment in the community' have ordered reality in a certain way, a belief that the probation service can be seen to 'protect the community' and 'reduce the risk of reoffending, by the largely instrumental means of target setting, monitoring, surveillance and controlling of certain activities. These frameworks can influence who speaks, when and with what authority and who cannot.

9
Strategies for Sustaining Emotional Literacy in the Workplace

Practice examples

Anita has been working with a male offender, Alfie, who, in their last session, began to describe to her some of the abuse he experienced as a child from his mother. This included both emotional abuse and general neglect and as he talked about this Anita found herself getting upset at the awfulness of his early life. She kept her attention and focus on Alfie throughout the session and did not at any stage say to him that she was finding it hard to listen to him, but she did shed a few tears and recognised that Alfie had seen this.

After the session Anita called up her work-based mentor and asked for a session with her the following day. In the session Anita was able to express her true feelings of distress at what she had heard the previous day from Alfie and her concern that she had shown a little of this distress in a non-verbal way in the interview. The mentor listened for some time to Anita's account and asked her if it had stirred up any memories for her that she might want to talk about. Anita identified a time when her father had been very angry with her, and she could recall some of the fear and anxiety she had felt at the time. The mentor reassured Anita that her non-verbal demonstration of distress at Alfie's story had not appeared to disrupt his ability to talk to her about what had happened (he had thanked her at the end of the session for helping him describe his life to her) and had probably helped Alfie to feel that his pain and distress had been recognised and was being validated by Anita. Had Anita allowed her feelings to dominate the session this would have halted Alfie's attempts to disclose. Anita felt reassured that her feelings were congruent with the reality of Alfie's narrative and that as long as she was able to continue to prioritise and think about his needs and the right way forward for him, her feelings were a good resource and guide to her and were validated by her mentor.

Mike had been co-facilitating a group work programme on anger management. One offender in the group had been particularly provocative during the session and Mike had felt himself becoming increasingly 'wound up'. Towards the end of the session he shouted at the offender in question to shut up and keep his views to himself or he would be removed from the programme and taken back to court. All of the group members seemed startled at Mike's reactions and the session ended after a few further tense exchanges. During the debriefing at the end of the session Mike continued to justify his behaviour saying that the offender in question had had it coming to him – and he thought he should be breached. Mike's co-worker Anne suggested that Mike had overreacted and needed to reflect on what he had said and the impact on the group. Mike stormed out of the debriefing session slamming the door behind him. Anne knew that Mike was under a lot of stress at home and at work but felt that his behaviour in the group was unhelpful and modelled an inappropriate way of managing anger to the group members. She decided to give Mike time to calm down and then went and sought him out. She explained that she felt she had to raise what had happened with their line manager as it could have consequences for the continuing work on the group, but that what she most wanted to do was to help Mike reflect on his feelings and consider how he might have managed the situation differently. She suggested that they could meet with an experienced colleague who would be able to help Mike reflect and for both of them to work on improving their co-working relationship and consider the gender dynamics between them.

Key learning points

- Practitioners can demonstrate strong emotionally literate practice when they have opportunities for expressing and exploring their feelings in a safe environment.
- If practitioners lack opportunities for reflection and the development of self-awareness, their own feelings can dominate the agenda when working with offenders.
- Sometimes practitioners need time to 'let off steam' before they are able to reflect more calmly on the implications of their feelings and associated behaviour.

Introduction

It has been argued that emotionally literate practice requires a capacity to integrate and work with emotions in a manner congruent with the needs of both practitioners and offenders. However, this capacity needs to be developed and supported within the working environment if it is to be effective and if the mental health of staff is to be sustained and enhanced. This chapter considers the range of ways in which practitioners from the research study found support and validation for the emotions generated in them by their work with offenders and in their pursuit of emotionally literate practice.

Evidence from the preceding chapters illustrates the manner in which research participants have felt that their expression and articulation of feelings have been suppressed or silenced in a range of ways within the organisational context of their practice. Some of this is an internal process; the desire to be seen as 'professional' which they interpreted as requiring a calm and controlled outward appearance whatever feelings they might have under the surface (the 'paddling duck', Chapter 5). Some is related to the situation of their actual practice, in which they recognise that the emotional needs of the offender should take priority and precedence over their own feelings. However, significant elements of this suppression and silencing of feelings relates to the wider social setting and organisational domains within which they operate (Layder 2006). They related some of this 'silencing' of any significant discourse on emotions to the culture of managerialism within their organisation and the lack of permission or indeed interest from their managers to reveal their 'underground emotion work' (Layder 2006). The initial hesitancy of a number of them in talking about their feelings in the research interview appeared to reflect a level of unfamiliarity with such conversations in their normal working routine. However, they also felt 'silenced' by wider issues related to gender and to concepts of mental health and unwellness. For example, Karen talked of 'masking' her emotions to such an extent that no one realised how stressed she was until she went on sick leave. The data contains a great deal of evidence of research participants experiencing high levels of stress, which many related to an inability to express feelings in the workplace. Research participants gave examples of their fear that excess emotional expression would be interpreted by unspecified others as a sign of (often female) weakness, an excess of emotion that needed to be controlled or indeed of actual mental ill health.

This chapter examines the strategies that the research participants employed to deal with their feelings in the workplace to try and counteract the silence that the organisational feeling rules of 'emotional detachment' (see Chapter 8) imposed on them. These include both formal and informal strategies and a mixture of both:

Formal:

   i. Line or treatment manager supervision
  ii. Formal debriefing after group work programmes
 iii. Counselling – provided by the agency or undertaken on a private basis

Informal:

  iv. 'Letting off steam' with colleagues
   v. Support at home/with family

A mixture of formal and informal:

  vi. Team work
 vii. Reflective practice

The issue of training for emotionally literate practice is offered as a recommendation at the end of the chapter.

Research findings

Where do the feelings go?

If the feeling rules of the probation service, and other criminal justice organisations such as prisons, are 'emotional detachment' (Chapter 8) or 'silence' on the subject, how do workers learn to manage their emotions appropriately for the work that they do? Unlike counsellors and psychotherapists, who are trained to identify, understand and use their emotions in order to offer a constructive and empathic service to their clients, and who are offered clinical supervision in which their feelings are centre stage (Mearns 1997, Rogers 2004), probation staff have neither training nor formal supervision that relates specifically to their own emotions unless they choose to seek this out for themselves through external courses or counselling, or they happen to have an emotionally literate line manager. In the context of this study only two of the research participants, both employed as psychologists to work with a sex offender team, talked about formal, clinical supervision in which they identified opportunities to express and talk about the feelings generated by their work with offenders. For the remainder of the research participants, in the absence of any organisational or theoretical context for understanding their emotional lives, they described a variety of personal approaches and professional experiences that had aided this process.

i) Line or treatment management supervision

As Chapter 8 on organisations and emotions highlighted, a considerable number of research participants saw their line manager as actively blocking or disinterested in their emotional lives. However, approximately one-third of the research participants (nine in total) either had been or were currently able to use their line management supervision as a place to take some of their feelings about their work. This was clearly a significant emotional resource to them. Lynn, in her observation below, reflects the historical place of supervision in the probation service which was about personal development and casework practice and included a strong focus on the emotional well-being of the practitioner (Monger 1972):

> Yes ... I had some wonderful supervisors early on. Because ... you know, it was so important in those days, it was part of the job, you know, you must be having some uncomfortable feelings, how are you managing them, it seemed to be a regular part of the job. (Lynn)

These next quotes also demonstrate very positive examples of contemporary line management supervision that research participants found helpful:

> And then I went to see my manager and he is really nice and he put a smile back on my face and I went, (exhales ...) things are really better now, I sort of like reflected on it for a while because I thought I'm not going to get wound up about it and take it home with me. (Maggie)

> To be honest, my manager at the moment is absolutely fantastic ... the previous manager wasn't, but this one is absolutely brilliant, very supportive, I mean really good, ... I can go to him about anything. (Damien)

Pat and John similarly had very positive experiences but expressed some regret about the quantity of such available supervision and also a sense of the individual rather than institutional component of good supervision:

> There is supervision and X is the treatment manager ... we are certainly encouraged by X to consider ... and he is very very good ... how you managed that situation ... someone who is difficult. It probably doesn't happen as much as it should. (John)

> Y who unfortunately is leaving, she's brilliant, the senior, I know I can talk to her about anything anytime. (Pat)

However, some research participants highlighted the difficulties in talking in any depth in formal supervision about their feelings or the significance of particular cases because of the demands of the sheer volume of work and the priority afforded to the need to hit targets. They felt they would need to specifically request a session to talk about their feelings:

> Scheduled time is once a month with a senior probation officer in your supervision, but if I'm working between 30 and 40 cases, I've got an hour to talk through all their targets to make sure that I am hitting them and then ... right let's discuss your cases for the last twenty minutes so you have to pick which cases that you want to and it is normally your high risk cases that you monitor. (Mary)

The implication of Mary's statement is that she has to make prioritised choices about the 'riskiest' cases to discuss with her line manager, rather than those that are causing her the most emotional concern.

Hannah identified feelings of distress after a particular offender session. She recognised the importance of letting her line manager know of the severity of the impact on her, but had to wait a week, which is a long time to have to 'hold onto' such strong feelings. It appears that it would not have come up in supervision without her initiating it:

> Because I was still crying when I got home, and then I had supervision I think the following week, and I did bring it up again. Because I wanted my manager to be aware of the fact ... how much it had affected me and I wanted her to know how I had dealt with it and I had dealt with it fine, but they wouldn't normally routinely ask, how you are dealing with it? (Hannah)

Aruna identifies a difference between serious and less serious issues, seeing the outlet of feelings of frustrations best managed through colleagues. The 'boiler room' notion of emotions first proposed by Descartes (Evans 2003), in which steam has to be 'let out' in order to prevent the 'system' boiling over:

> But if it was something serious then I would arrange supervision and talk to my manager, if it was just generally ... letting go of frustrations so I could carry on for the rest of the day, that is something that colleagues would be best for. (Aruna)

As further illustrated in Chapter 8, there were a number who were not confident that their line managers could or would support them by listening to their expressions of emotion and so would not choose to go to them in times of emotional excess:

> (Managers) that have been replaced by senior probation officers that have no real knowledge or expertise of public protection work and therefore they are on a very steep learning curve and I think they are, I would be probably quite sort of reluctant to discuss that with them. (Nick)

This next comment relates to a worker newly involved in group work with sex offenders who felt unsupported and isolated in the work she was being expected to carry out:

> For both of us we didn't have anybody here that managed us so nobody actually said after the sessions 'how did that go?' ... I feel that we were both at sea with it. (Hannah)

For some, line management was the last place they looked for this level of emotional support:

> My immediate line management supervision ... is like out of a Kafka novel ... an instance of being elitist and arrogant and over intellectual. (Amy)

ii) Formal 'debriefing'

In addition to line or treatment management supervision as a potential place to take feelings some research participants referred to planned 'debriefing' after particular group work sessions with offenders. The term 'debriefing' refers to situations where staff have been exposed to particularly stressful or traumatic incidents at work and the debriefing is designed to enable them to talk through the incident and deal with feelings arising from it (Mackie 2009). This term has been transferred to the more routine, but, nevertheless, important role of talking through events arising from group work programmes with offenders. It implies a structured and timetabled space created for the purpose of allowing workers to express their views and feelings collectively or individually on a particular piece of work (usually, but not always, group work) and to reflect on their practice. This is different from the more routine allocation of time by the line manager to discuss targets, cases, progress, and so on. A significant proportion of the research participants (seven) looked for 'debriefing' particularly after group sessions. This was seen as an accepted part of their routine and a sign of good practice although it might not always involve talking about the worker's feelings:

> After the groups we try and debrief and talk about the challenging cases together. Sometimes in terms of the focus of the work must be about the man and managing the risk of the man. You will have feelings and biases in terms of some men. (Indira)

Kim articulates this as a slightly more random, although, nevertheless, important process:

> Yes ... we always have an opportunity to talk ... we work to the very last minute ... we get thrown out of the building at 9.30 p.m. ... or in the break if something is relevant ... we could talk about it as appropriate. Always an opportunity ... in supervision also.(Kim)

However, a number articulated the time pressures and constraints on this, and how it could fall by the wayside in the light of other external pressures on them.

> We used to have a sex offenders support group because it was acknowledged that obviously we have all these feelings to deal with, we may have to go home and have small children that we have to bath, and ... I found it quite useful particularly when I was a fairly new officer, but however, the will to keep that going went, I mean, I was ... I'm not boasting but I was a bit of a leading light to keep that going, but in the end I thought crikey, that if nobody else wants it then ... we don't have that. (Sophie)

iii)   Counselling

Most probation trusts offer access to counselling services to their staff and some make specific provision for staff working with high-risk offenders which may be referred to as 'counselling' or as 'clinical supervision'.[1] Some research participants had had experience of counselling external to the service either through choosing to go into therapy for themselves or by learning how to become counsellors:

> I started doing a counselling course in college to try and understand more about that ... and I've been to see counsellors myself, for my own kind of stuff ... To look at ... my kind of thoughts, feelings and behaviours ... it helped me ... move on and, it was good, it was such a big change in my life ... Massive. (Damien)

Damien was also able to benefit from supervision by a psychologist external to the probation service in increasing his understanding and subsequent management of his feelings provoked by the process of transference and countertransference between himself and an offender who reminded him of his brother:

> I was being supervised by a psychologist at the time as well and we kind of talked about transference and that kind of stuff ... and again, I didn't realise at the time what was going on, ... and I saw this person as kind of like my brother ... and I think he reflected that back and ... I think ... that was the disappointing bit, this was my brother that had let me down rather than this was an offender, ... I am much more aware of that now. (Damien)

However, of the research participants who made reference to the availability of some form of formal counselling within the service, none was particularly impressed either through direct experience of such a service or because they perceived it to be aimed at dealing with problems when a staff member was not coping. Tony saw the provision of counselling as patronising and something of a sticking plaster being offered by management in the absence of any real understanding of what the practitioners had to deal with. Whilst he acknowledged that some of this may reflect his own resistance, as a man, to exploring his feelings, he felt that genuine support came from other colleagues who were around when he most needed an outlet:

> Fundamentally most of the support or acknowledgement would come from other members of the team and still does. I don't think that is acknowledged really, except in the formal sense that 'yes we understand that that is happening and therefore you need counselling twice a year' ... it's that sort of thing, but actually you don't understand and actually I'm not always sure

that I do want that counselling ... sometimes I feel that I'm being patronised to some extent and there's a paternalistic view that because I'm doing this hard work ... go away and have a good cry and you'll feel a lot better. I try to examine that in myself and try to see whether it's me being ... whether it's a really masculine trait in me ... gender learned, or whatever, and there may be some of that there. But at the same time I do actually I do feel ... I don't really need ... there are times when I want to offload but it won't be to order ... you can only offload on the 23rd July ... (laugh ...) (feelings don't work like that ... book an appointment to have a feeling). (Tony)

Lynn also identified a negative association with counselling that implied the problem lay within the worker rather than within the nature of the work:

Oh yes, yes, and it's you know, you've got to say to yourself, 'oh I've got a problem' first and ... Yes. (Lynn)

Geoff saw counselling as relevant to him when he was new in the role, but no longer necessary, and for him the support came from his colleagues, debriefing opportunities and supervision:

Early on in the process ... because there is an opportunity for counselling services ... then I would have sought that ... but it has been years since anybody at this team has had any kind of formal counselling and that's not because we are unhealthy in that respect or keeping all this sort of stuff under the surface because this stuff is not an issue, but on the rare occasions when it does ... we've got peer supervision, debriefing after the end of every session, we've got treatment manager supervision, which is also part of my role, for the other treatment managers ... and then we've got sort of line-manager supervision from the programme manager and that really does seem to cover all bases. (Geoff)

iv) Team work
The largest group (Michael, Amy, John, Lynn, Heather, Tess, Nick, Janet, Damien, Jai, Aruna, Maggie, Sandy and Robert) looked to their team colleagues for peer support, to discuss their work and give vent to feelings arising from the work as this was available more spontaneously than the formal avenues of line management supervision, debriefing or counselling and was also more 'trusted' to meet the need. Team work offered intellectual stimulation, support, advice and encouragement. It was also in the context of supportive team colleagues that they felt able to be themselves, expressing feelings without feeling judged. These research participants saw their colleagues as providing a constant source of support, stimulation and resource.

The other thing I like about this specific job ... because it's a specialist job. I've never ever been so close to a team ever ... it's really like a marriage if you like. I've discussed it with members of the team... (Michael)

Tremendous feelings of sort of comradeship and companionship in teams when you were working well. (Lynn)

And I like working as part of a team, I really enjoy it ... I mean whatever role I am in, whether it is offender management, but in a programmes team you really do have to work together because you know, you've got co-worker responsibility. (Karen)

The team, again are fantastic, I am able to talk to them. (Damien)

I think there is something really powerful about being part of a team, I mean we are seen as experts a bit because we are in a small team, but actually within a team we all have different skills and what I like is when I feel vulnerable, I can go to one of my colleagues and say, this is how I feel, or X and Y is going on and I can tell them ... and it feels much more therapeutic so I suppose I have a sense of being more valued [by the team] yes and I probably value my colleagues more in this team than I might if I was in another team. (Sandy)

The team are part of my sanity ... I value my colleagues enormously. Team work is great. (Amy)

v) 'Letting off steam'

Although it has been proposed in Chapter 8 that there are unspoken feeling rules of emotional detachment within the modern probation service, Hochschild suggests that in all organisational settings there are circumstances or physical zones where different emotion rules may prevail (Hochschild 1983). These may be places where the organisation's direct control and surveillance is less obvious but where informal norms of what feelings can (and cannot) be expressed will come to the surface. Hochschild believes that the physical architecture shapes, to an extent, the emotional architecture where meanings of privacy, confidentiality, secrecy and honesty are differentially shaped and defined. For example, in the relative privacy of the galley area of an aircraft she suggests that the niceties of customer care can be suspended and 'real' feelings expressed, including the derision or mocking of certain passengers (Hochschild 1983). In a different context Crawley identifies 'emotional zones' within a prison which she argues constitute places and settings with which particular emotions are associated and legitimated, and she links this with the feeling rules of the organisation (Crawley 2004). There are certain zones in which 'blowing off steam' may be legitimate, (e.g. the gym) and others (e.g. the chapel or probation office), where it is acceptable for a prisoner to express sadness or grief. In other, more formal places in the prison, for example, the gatehouse, emotional reticence is the norm (Crawley 2004:148). The metaphor 'letting off steam' seems an appropriate one as it captures the immediacy of the feeling and the need for a safe place to discharge it, without the fear of negative judgement or misunderstanding.

> Debriefing ... letting off steam ... I do it in the office and I do it at home as well. (Howard)

In the following exchange I asked Aruna to say a bit more about the metaphor she had used earlier:

C. 'And you mentioned about, you didn't call it debriefing, you called it 'letting off steam' ... you can do that in this setting? You can go to someone who will listen to you?'

A. 'In probation it happens often, I don't know anyone who doesn't do it, I think you have to really, you will get frustrated, especially if you have put a lot of time and effort into a piece of work and it isn't making any difference or you've spent a lot of time with an agency and they've not done what they're supposed to do, I mean we all do it, we all sit there and have a moan'

This form of support, whilst sometimes referred to as 'debriefing', was more generally expressed as a place to take feelings when they arose unexpectedly in relation to the work. They described the relief at being able to give vent to feelings and that what they were seeking was not necessarily advice or guidance on what to do next but a sympathetic ear:

> You can go to your SPO, but I find I go to my work colleagues more than anything else because they are the ones more likely to have had the same experience and I know SPO's would have done but they are a bit more removed from it because they're not case managers anymore, but I do tend to go to colleagues about it. (Maggie)

Victoria considered her colleagues to be sufficiently tuned in to her emotional state to actually check her out when she had had a particularly difficult interview:

> When you say about reading peoples feeling and because if someone comes back up stairs, you kind of know if there's something wrong ... I've come up the stairs several times when I've had quite a heavy session with somebody and

straight away somebody'll say, 'oh are you okay?', 'how was it?', 'what went on?' and you kind of use your colleagues in that way for support. (Victoria)

Angela provided a good example of her need for attention and recognition when distressed, and how when this was made available it helped her to regain her thinking capacities:

Yes because I find both professional and personally in my head it gets like muddy ... do you know what I mean and then I like to, this is where the talking comes in, just sit and listen, then I splurge it all out and I can see the wood for trees again, if that makes sense and it clears and I can think more rationally about it. (Angela)

Research participants also expressed views about emotional zones or the emotional architecture (Hochschild 1983), where feelings could be safely discharged or ventilated and through which research participants could manage the sometimes confusing and muddled feelings generated by the work. For Mary the safe place was created both physically, by the door shutting thus creating a barrier between her and others who might judge her, and by empathic colleagues:

I'll ... walk through and ..., if it has been very stressful or very emotional I'll quite often be quiet for about a minute and then one of my colleagues will say 'what's been happening', 'what's gone on?' I suppose you would call it debriefing ... and I would, apart from just talk about what has just happened, they'll give feedback and I'll give feedback and I'll go out for a cigarette and get some fresh air ... I think I feel safe to go back into the office and swear and not have somebody say 'what's the matter with you?', 'don't say those words' or something, they'll shut the door so no one else hears, (laughs) and go 'what's the matter?' and I feel able and I don't feel closeted to keep my mouth shut or 'behave professionally, that's not very good'... or ...(Mary)

Gill described herself as someone able to keep her feelings on hold while with an offender, but needing to let them out as soon as possible afterwards:

I'm one of these people whereby I don't keep things to themselves, you know, straight out of an interview room and go into another room and go 'aaarrrggghhh' I do that, I'm quite an expressive person and I go 'oh my god he's just done my head in'. (Mary)

One of the most valued aspects of this informal support was the sense that they would not be judged by the language or expressions they might use in this process of 'letting off steam'. This might be emotional distress that they would not want others to witness or it might come out in the form of 'risky' humour. Some commented specifically on the use of humour and occasionally 'disrespectful language' in the process of letting off steam. This was seen as a necessary safety valve after a difficult session, and as a coping mechanism. However, it was feared that this could be judged negatively if overheard by the 'wrong' people. This was similar to the experience of airline staff in Hochschild's study who let off steam about passengers in the galley area (Hochschild 1983). Pat offers an illustration of the use of illicit humour and also describes how she is able to continue to work with an offender she dislikes, by using this humour in a 'safe' place, that is, the staff room which offenders are not allowed to enter:

> I've shared an office with three different people now and you can say anything, you know you can talk to them, you sound off them, if you listen to people, you know like we often joke, like if you've got a Daily Mail journalist in there if you know what I mean, because you're in the staff room, and you are laughing because you're allowed to laugh at certain things. (Pat)

Hannah gives another example of risky humour, and whilst expressing some shame at the need for it sees it as a necessary release:

> We do debrief but it is really tempting to be really ... un-PC and just ... and I think we do sometimes do that or when I am reading something and I go, 'Oh My God!' or I say to someone, 'Look at that', it is actually but sometimes I am embarrassed, a bit ashamed at how we talk about the men afterwards, because if they heard us they would be mortified ... yes, it is, and it does help because we laugh about it ... yes I suppose it is necessary because if I didn't have it would be fairly difficult. (Hannah)

Sophie also sees it as a coping mechanism and as a way of discharging feelings at work, in order not to take them home with her:

> I work in an open plan office and we talk to each other about our cases and ... I think sometimes ... some of the words that we use are very disrespectful and very non-P.C. and you know ... but that is a coping mechanism ... I always try to ..., have ... if I can, to have talked about stuff like that before I go home. (Sophie)

This 'offloading' of feelings is clearly a very important release mechanism for workers but it does not necessarily provide them with sufficient opportunity to also engage in reflection and appraisal of the feelings.

vi) Being selective about who to talk to

Of the 12 research participants who looked for support mainly from their colleagues, 3 felt they needed to be careful about who they chose to talk to about their feelings.

> And also you talk to your colleagues and you've got the colleagues you talk to about certain things because there's a girl here who won't do anything with sex offenders at all, won't even go on the training, so I just assume something has happened to her ... in her life, because you have to do this training and I've noticed that she doesn't go, so I wouldn't talk to her. (Pat)

Pat is acknowledging her understanding that one of her colleagues must have difficulties in dealing with sex offenders, and therefore would be unlikely to be able to hear any revelations from Pat about how they made her feel. Whereas for Jai, it's a combination of pragmatism (sharing a car) and choice:

> Yes, if I do evening groups then I generally, a colleague drops me off because she lives near me and ..., we'll talk in the car, if there is a daytime group there is room to talk about it, there is one colleague that I work with who is, usually zooms off after it is finished, but ... I, wouldn't choose to talk with her necessarily because I, ... I think, that there would be other colleagues that would understand it at a deeper level, so ... it is not that I am left stranded. (Jai)

vii) Support at home

Research participants were mixed in their views about taking their feelings home with them. Some made reference to the importance of having a stable home life as prerequisite for doing the job:

> My private life is very stable and supportive a real biggy for me – I'm fairly impervious because of the strength from that ... I don't know how it would be if I didn't have a happy and contented and secure home life. (Michael)

Tess and Heather used, or had used, their partners to help her with this process:

> Speaking out about things does help to clarify my thinking (particularly with my partner). (Tess)

> I suppose I was lucky for years ... you know, my partner did the same job and he was the one who got it actually and because he had a different way of dealing with ... (Heather)

Janet actively held onto her feelings until she got home, where her partner or friends would help her:

> No, mine come out when I get home, with my partner, if anything has happened, I can tend to turn to my friends or I turn to my partner, he is very, very supportive, I am very lucky really. (Janet)

Whilst for others this was more problematic. Sophie was keen not to take her work home with her and had a particular reason for wishing to separate out her professional work with domestic violence abusers from her family life:

> I think I find it more difficult in terms of working with my cases of domestic violence that I work with that I show how I feel, because ... and it doesn't just apply if you've got children of your own at all, you might know children, but because I have children ... I have to separate myself and ... I do separate myself from my offenders and my offenders don't know anything about my personal life and that's how, that's how I want it. (Sophie)

Some research participants found alternative ways of letting go of their feelings:

> I was conscious that I found my own ways of ... I didn't often express them to the person concerned, wouldn't often express anything otherwise, but that it was sort of through other things, through things like sport. (Lynn)

Building emotional resources

Research within the field of psychotherapy identifies the suppression of overwhelming feelings arising from abusive and damaging behaviour, particularly in young children, as a survival strategy in adulthood (Diamant 2001, McLeod 2001). The process of psychotherapy is focused on the task of uncovering and re-examining these feelings in a safe environment. Probation workers may or may not have had similar early experiences. However, if they have to suppress feelings that are triggered by a combination of their earlier life experiences and their current work they may find themselves ambushed by these feelings in present situations. Issues of transference and countertransference, between counsellor and client (offender and worker), as explained in the psychotherapeutic literature, can have significant implications for staff who are unaware of the potential for these processes to occur (Murdin 2010). The strategies employed by these research participants suggest the potential for the building of emotional 'capital' or resource, as identified by a number of writers (Reay 2004, Gillies 2006, Zembylas 2007). The joint efforts of family, people in the past, social support networks, team networks and sometimes line managers may produce a resource that is sustaining for these staff. It is identified as a collective activity that forms a supportive network from which the skills of emotional literacy can be fostered and sustained. For the research participants a degree of emotional resource was built up through the pleasure that they took in building relationships with offenders and seeing them make positive changes in their lives. However, as illustrated in Chapter 5, there appears to be a preponderance of negative emotions expressed by research participants about their work which may impact, and potentially diminish, the emotional resources built up within the probation service as a support to the workforce.

Training

None of the participants interviewed for the study had received any probation-specific training on emotions and emotional literacy. Some had learnt about this via the training manuals for accredited programmes, in relation to the emotions of offenders. Some had chosen to pursue external counselling courses. Most, when asked, indicated a wish to see more probation-specific training in this area.

Pre- and post-qualifying training could be adapted to include opportunities for staff to 'rehearse' their emotional literacy in a range of different settings and be offered guidance and opportunities for reflection on this. As highlighted in the literature, drama or role play can provide a context in which feelings and language can be rehearsed and experienced at a safe distance (Evans 2003). However, often the best learning about emotions comes from an opportunity to 'catch' the feelings as they occur and then have an opportunity to reflect on them through discussion or mentoring before their significance fades or is dismissed. Well-qualified practice assessors or tutors are often ideally placed to help new staff to reflect constructively on the emotions engendered in them by the work.

Further input on the emotional component of offending behaviour and penal policy (Karstedt et al. 2011) should be incorporated in training curricula, and with particular reference to attachment theory (Bowlby 1978), and to principles informed by the counselling and psychotherapy literature (Gerhardt 2004, Rogers 2004). Staff who, as students, are introduced to these ideas and given opportunities to rehearse them by role play, and reflect on their feelings as they arise, are more likely to then expect these opportunities to be available to them in the workplace.

Conclusion

The provision of counselling, 'keeping staff healthy' and peer mentorship schemes within organisations, can offer practitioners a confidential and safe space for emotional expression and for reflection on these emotions. However, there is also the need for other avenues for emotional expression and discussion. Research participants used a range of strategies to manage and express the feelings that arose from work. What seemed to help them the most was the opportunity to 'let off steam', that is, to express their feelings in an immediate and uncensored way with colleagues that they trusted and in places in which they felt safe and unjudged. Whilst there was an appreciation of good line management supervision this was not routinely available and some were actively cautious about revealing too much vulnerability in front of a line manager for fear of being negatively judged. It was clear that research participants were making decisions about 'safety' and 'appropriate places' in which to be 'emotional' and that the agency as a whole did not routinely provide these emotional places for letting off steam; they arose through informal networks and most significantly 'team work' in which strong and mutually beneficial relationships were built. Some of them appeared to be able to develop a 'helping relationship with themselves' (Rogers 2004), and had learnt to 'self-soothe' (Gerhardt 2004), by understanding where their feelings came from, taking care of themselves and seeking the support of family and friends to sustain them (Herman 1997).

Whilst all of this is an important resource to workers it does not necessarily provide them with the additional guidance and support needed to reflect on and appraise their emotional expressions and to move on to consider the best way forward with a particular offender or work situation. Also, given the evidence of impact issues on staff working with high-risk offenders, from both the literature (Schauben and Frazier 1995, Dwyer 2007, Knight and Clow 2010, Schaible and Gecas 2010) and the data in this research project, it is all the more surprising that the systems in place to offer support, debriefing and advice seem to be piecemeal and arbitrary. The support of emotional literacy in the workforce offers the opportunity for practitioners to make 'embodied' decisions that reflect both cognitive and emotional processes (Lakoff 1987), which is a crucial capacity in complex work with offenders (Munro 2011).

10
Conclusion

Introduction

The research for this book has evolved from many years of probation practice experience and of teaching probation students. The themes are drawn from the experiences of current probation practitioners and illustrate the phenomenon of emotion and emotional experiences in practice with offenders. What has always interested me has been this 'underground' and largely invisible world of emotion that can exert such a powerful influence on the behaviour and inter- actions of practitioners in their work with offenders, and yet remains largely unarticulated and hidden within organisational structures. This book has been an attempt to draw out some of these emotional processes, exposing them to the light in such a way that their influences, both positive and negative, can be identified and examined. The core theme is the positive use of emotions in practice with offenders, what has been termed 'emotional literacy', but there has also been reflection on the alternative use of emotions to exercise more repressive and manipulative control of offenders. The single most important factor is the ability to think reflectively and carefully about the emotions gen- erated in us, as workers, and in service users.

The research provided illustration of the core components of emotional literacy as described by research participants, including motivation, self- awareness, self-regulation, building relationships and expressing empathy, as well as examining a number of additional factors relevant to the exercis- ing of emotional literacy in a criminal justice context. Research participants formulated their interventions with offenders as a learning process rather than a coercive and didactic process. There were some accounts offered by research participants of colleagues who appeared to exercise more manipu- lative or aggressive forms of emotional control, but this is clearly 'hearsay' evidence and would require a much wider study involving a random sample of staff, rather than volunteers with an interest in the subject area, to examine this. Practice with offenders is seen to involve the 'soft' terrain of feelings, thoughts, fantasies and interpersonal perceptions as opposed to the hard-edged business of surveillance, monitoring and external regulation of behaviour that is the public face of criminal justice. In the current punitive climate of criminal justice, certain different forms of knowledge production are favoured over others; there is a favouring of 'hard' facts or statistics over 'soft' emotions. This applies equally to the favouring of 'hard' practices, for example, community payback and electronic monitoring, over 'softer' interpersonal relationships.

The research findings highlight the preponderance of negative emotions in probation staff, their individual and subjective attempts to control and manage this in the interests of 'professionalism'. The findings illustrated their efforts to be 'non-judgemental', of doing the best for the offender, in a climate of 'emotional detachment' encouraged by the managerial ethos of the service. This ethos was seen to inhibit and suppress both the expression and the discourse of emotions in a practice arena suffused with emotion. The gender associations of emotions as 'soft' and 'irrational' in the context of a criminal justice system needing to be viewed as 'tough', and 'rational', continue to hold this silencing and suppression in place. The discourse of being 'tough' on crime restricts the space for more subtle and nuanced explorations of the 'soft' emotional skills that actively engage with, motivate and provide positive learning experiences for enabling offenders to make changes in their lives. It also creates space for the potential misuse of emotional control through coercive, manipulative or repressive means in staff who may have less emotional awareness, less skill in emotion regulation and/or lacking the values to support the therapeutic and 'legitimate' exercise of controls.

The resistance of some research participants to identifying the potential 'victim' status of offenders is a cause of concern, restricting as it does the opportunities for such offenders to benefit fully from the learning opportunities provided. The building of emotional resources for staff within the organisation, offering support, a space for the expressions of emotions and the subsequent appraisal and reflections on emotions, like emotional literacy itself, remains a largely invisible quality. Its characteristics seem to include positive emotions generated within individual staff members by rewarding and productive encounters with offenders, a positive set of peer relationships in which there is a commitment to mutual sharing of feelings and ideas and managers who understand the significance of the emotional components of the work and can either offer empathy themselves or provide the space and resources where this can be provided.

What is emotional literacy?

The earlier chapters of the book illustrate the way in which some probation practitioners have learnt to identify, regulate and use their emotions in their practice with offenders. A framework for understanding emotional literacy summarised from some of the key thinking of authors in the field of emotional intelligence and emotional literacy has identified five criteria of 'motivation, self-awareness, self-regulation, social competence and empathy' (Killick 2006). Evidence from the research data for this book extended these criteria and additionally highlighted the impact of the organisational context in which emotional literacy can be exercised and its gendered implications. These are outlined in the next sections.

Motivation

Probation workers are significantly motivated to work with offenders from the pleasure they gain in building relationships with them and seeing them work towards positive change in their lives. They are also motivated by strong peer and team relationships and by supportive managers. However, they also, like other criminal justice workers, deal with a predominance of 'negative' emotions, both in themselves and in the offenders they work with. In order to manage and contain this in offenders and in themselves they need sufficient levels of positive emotional resource to offset and balance this negativity. The ability to work with offenders in an emotionally literate manner is motivated and enhanced by the emotional resources that build as a result of positive relationships with offenders, with contemporaries in the workplace and with an organisation that offers appropriate and safe outlets for emotional expression and opportunities for reflection and appraisal. Workers in other criminal justice settings may have similar or different motivations for their practice, but all will benefit from a positive environment in which emotional support is available and emotional connections valued.

Self-awareness

Self-awareness in the emotional literacy literature refers to

> being aware of one's own emotional state, to be able to recognize what feelings are being experienced at any one time and being aware of the thoughts that are involved in this. (Killick 2006: 10)

Additionally, and particularly with reference to a probation context, it can include the concept of 'use of self', which combines an understanding of one's own emotions and what triggers them, with an offering of one's 'emotional' self to the offender as a 'gift'. This concept accords with Bolton's category of emotion management as 'philanthropic' (Bolton 2005). This 'use of self' differs from Hochschild's concept of 'emotional labour' (Hochschild 1984), in that while such emotion management benefits the work of the service it is not (yet) deliberately taught or exploited for commercial gain. The use of metaphor was significant in how the research participants explained their feelings. An understanding of the significance of metaphor in the articulation of feelings could enhance sensitivity towards and awareness of another's feelings.

Self-regulation

Controlling emotions in the interests of 'professionalism' is seen as necessary in order to maintain the focus on the needs of the offender. This involves the holding back of one's own emotions and enabling the emotional needs of the offender to take priority. This is of considerable importance in all criminal justice settings where strong feelings can be to the fore. Police officers dealing with violent behaviour or prison officers managing unruly or angry prisoners need to be able to contain their own feelings about this behaviour if they are to judge how best to manage a volatile situation. In addition to the need to remain professional and control feelings for the benefit, or management of the offender, workers also feel constrained by the 'feeling rules' of the organisation which expect emotional neutrality or detachment. This can result in workers adopting strategies of excessive control of, or detachment from, their emotions, which can have negative consequences for both the worker and the offender. Repression of emotion may cause the worker to have a reduced capacity to deal with stress and face the risk of mental ill health; they may be less aware of, and able to respond to, the emotional issues impacting on the offender and/or they may portray a degree of inauthenticity or insincerity in their work.

Empathy

Demonstrating empathy, referred to as 'standing in their shoes', even and particularly with offenders who have committed very serious and unpleasant crimes, is seen as crucial in building their motivation to engage and change. The research data highlights the significance of a value base of respect, positive regard and a non-judgemental approach to offenders/service users in the exercising of emotional literacy. These values inform an understanding of the potential for making judgements based solely on emotions, and the need to withhold such judgements in face-to-face work with offenders. It recognises that a benign and 'soft' approach to interpersonal emotional control rather than a repressive, manipulative or punitive emotional control is more conducive to offender learning and development (Layder 2004). Also explored is the concept of 'ambivalent investment', the struggle that workers are likely to have in holding or containing the tensions between potentially conflicting emotional states in themselves as well as in others, without being rejecting of, or collusive with, any of these states. For example, building positive relationships with offenders whilst also having to carry out enforcement procedures and liking offenders whilst also being cross with them about failures to comply or continuing offending.

Social competence

Social competence includes a number of related skills but is broadly centred on the building of relationships with offenders. It includes the use of empathy, the use of intuition and the reading and interpretation of non-verbal signs. In particular the issue of building trust within the relationship, from which disclosures that inform risk assessments, and the motivation to change, can potentially emerge, was seen to be significant. This building of trust can lead to levels of emotional closeness between worker and offender which are generally conducive to positive work but also require the holding of emotional boundaries between worker and offender. These boundaries are needed to protect the worker and to ensure that awareness of 'risk' and of enforcement procedures is not lost. It is also important that workers have an awareness of, and transparency about, the potentially negative consequences for the offender of any significant disclosures they may make (e.g. potentially leading to an increased risk assessment and greater levels of surveillance and control). Emotionally supportive supervision can help a worker identify how and where to set the boundaries and demonstrate transparency, but this is often not available to staff. Whilst these issues impact directly on probation officers working to achieve a reduction in offending behaving, they can equally apply to other criminal justice staff who build significant relationships with offenders.

There is a need to recognise that offenders may also be victims and that in order to enhance their ability to learn from any programmes of intervention some attention and validation should be afforded to this aspect of their identity. The ability to learn is significantly affected by emotions. In order to take responsibility for their own learning and development, offenders gain most from an environment in which they feel valued and encouraged rather than negatively challenged or humiliated.

The organisational context

Many of the research participants struggled to articulate their emotions, which indicated a lack of practice in this in the work setting. Some of them felt 'silenced' by their organisation on issues of emotion and emotional literacy. Some of them illustrated how this could also add to the risk of negative emotional impact, and result in stress for the worker who has no release for their feelings, and whose mental health may suffer as a result. The organisation can assume that staff working with sex offenders, in particular, should somehow be immune to any strong reactions to these offenders and that if they are affected this renders them less objective and professional (Moulden and Firestone 2010). It is suggested that an active building of emotional resource within the organisation would legitimise the expression and discussion of feelings and help to maintain a healthy workforce. The building of emotional resources would help to change the 'feeling rules' of a organisation from 'emotional detachment' to 'emotional engagement'. This includes the recognition of the need for safe 'emotional spaces' and opportunities in which staff can express their feelings, and be enabled to subsequently appraise and reflect on the implications of these feelings for their practice.

Criminal justice organisations should recognise the need to offer training and education in the role of emotions in practice, in particular help in building emotion vocabularies and fostering a climate in which articulating feelings and thinking about feelings is valued, facilitated and included on policy agendas.

Gender

Gender is a significant 'identity' factor in the expression of emotional literacy. Women are more likely than men to evolve these skills but both genders can become emotionally literate. Female workers can feel unsupported by unaware male colleagues, particularly in the context of group work programmes with male offenders. If men and women value the skills of emotional literacy equally, the opportunities for both to develop these skills, and be supportive of colleagues, will be enhanced. Within the wider criminal justice arena the (predominately male) ideology of 'tough', 'hard', 'punitive' and measurable strategies seen as appropriate for work with offenders needs to be challenged by the (predominately female) 'softer', emotional realities of social life and the evidence that ultimately, whilst the control of dangerous and undesirable behaviour has to be managed, the process of 'change' in offenders is only likely to occur when emotions as well as cognitions are recognised, valued and engaged.

A new definition

A new definition of emotional literacy is proposed for work within the criminal justice system which takes account of the interactive nature of relationships built between workers and offenders and includes an ethical base for practice:

> Emotional literacy as a skill in criminal justice practice requires knowledge of our own emotions and the ability to recognize and respond empathically to the emotions of others. It includes an awareness of the causes, triggers and expression of emotions in ourselves and in others, and requires an underpinning value base of respect, positive regard and a non-judgemental approach towards offenders.

Summary

Practice

1. The use of emotional literacy can aid disclosure of sensitive and personal information that may lead to an increased level of risk assessment and subsequently more controlling risk management strategies. The worker may be able to contain the tensions generated by this process or may resort to cutting off from the emotional discomfort and anxiety generated (Menzies 1959), and fail to support the offender sufficiently well, particularly in their need for transparency and honesty. This remains a largely invisible process that falls below the radar of the organisation.
2. The different strategies that workers use to manage their emotions in the workplace – controlling, detaching and integrating – have implications for their practice with offenders and for their own mental health.
3. The creation of a 'learning' environment in which offenders are encouraged to develop their own self-regulation and understanding through supportive emotional relationships with workers is different from an 'instructional' and potentially manipulative or coercive programme of interventions. Which environment is created seems to be based more on the subjectivity of the workers than directed through organisational policy.
4. An understanding of the potential 'victim' status of offenders in order to help them progress, and the use of attachment theory to aid knowledge of deficient attachment styles caused by early abuse and disadvantage, is currently under-valued in practice. This has implications for building relationships with offenders and in victim empathy work, which should model this awareness.

Management

1. The enhancement and development of sufficient emotional resources within the organisation to enable staff to safely express, process and appraise

their emotional reactions to a range of offender behaviour and situations. Enabling staff to learn how to develop a 'helping relationship with self' (Rogers 2004), and to 'self-soothe' (Gerhardt 2004), may be an important component in reducing the levels of mental ill health and sickness absence in the service.

2. Emotional literacy deployed for the benefit of the offender may cease to be a 'gift' offered by the worker and become a 'pecuniary' advantage to the organisation (Bolton 2005). The expansion of contracting out of areas of probation practice to the private sector for profit may see the use of the skills of emotional literacy to secure the contracts and bring in the 'clientele'. Most writers seem to share Hochschild's pessimistic concerns about the negative consequences of an organisation that aims to shape and control the feelings of its employees (Bolton 2005).

3. Criminal justice organisations should identify the sources of building and maintaining emotional resource within their organisation and provide a commitment to its enhancement. In her review of child protection procedures, Munro suggests that in order to fully assess risk and protect children staff need skills to 'explore the deeper reaches and inner lives of service users' (Munro 2011:105). There are similarities for staff working with sex offenders in particular. Munro states that:

> They (workers) can only really take risks if they feel they will be emotionally held and supported on returning to the office, that their feelings and struggles will be listened to. Workers' state of mind and the quality of attention they can give to children is directly related to the quality of support, care and attention they themselves receive from supervisors, managers and peers. (Munro 2011: 163)

4. Many of the organisations within the criminal justice system become enmeshed in a culture of managerialism and performance management. A change in emphasis with targets set to raise the profile of emotional literacy, and an increase in the provision of emotional support to practitioners, would aid the process of building of emotional resources within the agency and the inclusion of all these factors on policy and practice agendas. A number of issues need to be considered that relate to the building and sustaining of emotional resources:
   o Debriefing opportunities that include space for sharing of emotional experiences; provided and monitored for all group work programmes
   o Provision of a mentoring or 'keeping staff healthy' scheme
   o Routine availability of counselling opportunities
   o Recruitment and selection of staff with the appropriate potential to learn or enhance these skills
   o Inclusion of 'emotion' issues on a wide range of agendas

Debriefing

Research participants referred to debriefing opportunities after group work programmes and had generally found them to be helpful. However, there was an indication that sometimes these were rushed or squeezed out by other work priorities. It is suggested that adequate time for debriefing should be automatically built into programme schedules and that these should be facilitated in a manner that allows for the expression, sharing and reflection on emotions generated by the work.

Mentoring/'keeping staff healthy'

Whilst line managers continue to hold responsibility for the overall performance of their teams and the meeting of targets and standards, it is unlikely that they can routinely be expected to additionally offer emotional support and supervision to their team members. Also it may not always be appropriate for staff to go to their line manager with difficult feelings that they have not yet had the opportunity to process. As research has indicated (Aiyegbusi and Clarke-Moore 2009), staff may well have negative feelings about some of the offenders they work with. They may feel degrees of embarrassment, disgust or even shame at some disclosures by offenders, and fear censure or negative judgement if they admit these feelings to a line manager. The provision of mentoring or 'clinical supervision' such as the scheme described in Chapter 9 offers support and debriefing that sits somewhere between informal networks of colleagues and the more formal counselling or debriefing sessions. There are resource implications for providing such mentoring. If it is 'in-house' then experienced staff need to be given workload relief to offer time to colleagues. If it is provided by an external consultant, it needs to be adequately resourced.

Counselling

The formal provision of counselling may not always be what workers need to 'let off steam' immediately after a challenging event, which is why mentoring or 'clinical supervision' may be a more flexible and available resource. Although many services do already offer a counselling service it may not be highly visible, and as some research participants indicated, carries with it the stigma of emotional 'problems' or difficulties lying within the worker rather than in the nature of the work. However, a routine and visible provision of counselling opportunities, offered regularly and supportively to staff, may help to create an organisational atmosphere in which the expression and discussion of emotions is seen as appropriate and indeed welcomed. If such counselling opportunities were referred to as 'clinical supervision' or 'mentoring' as above, and a minimum attendance required by staff, if may be used more regularly.

Recruitment, selection and promotion of staff

If, as suggested, female staff are more likely to have or to develop the skills of emotional literacy, then the continuing preponderance of female staff at practice level is to be welcomed. However, the encouragement and support of male staff to develop these skills should also be part of this process, and an inclusion in the promotional literature for the organisation of the importance of these skills might help to legitimise the skill in both genders. The slow progress of women into leadership and management roles may also help with this process although a major shift in the masculine ethos of the criminal justice system is unlikely to happen in the near future.

Emotion on agendas

The aim of building emotional resources in an organisation from which staff can take sustenance and support would be enhanced by the provision of routine mentoring or clinical supervision, but overall building emotional resource is a nebulous and diffuse process. As has been identified from this project, emotional resource is built through positive experiences of developing relationships with offenders, through positive experiences of team work and through strong peer relationships. It can be damaged and eroded by a preponderance of negative experiences with offenders, with a lack of opportunity to process and manage the feelings generated, and with workloads that pay no heed to the inherent and variable emotional demands of the job. Staff feeling silenced or restricted in how they share feelings and are acknowledged and validated also erodes emotional resource. For criminal justice organisations to begin to move towards a 'softer' ambience will not be an easy task. Nevertheless, it is not incompatible with work already being undertaken and the examples set by some of the empathic line managers described by research participants (Chapter 9). For example, a more routine inclusion of 'emotional' issues and processes on a wide range of agendas may help to enhance this process.

Contribution to training

Pre- and post-qualifying training should be adapted to include opportunities for staff to 'rehearse' their emotional literacy in a range of different settings and be offered guidance and opportunities for reflection on this. As highlighted in the literature, drama or role play can provide a context in which feelings and language can be rehearsed and experienced at a safe distance (Evans 2003). Further input on the emotional component of offending behaviour and penal policy (Karstedt et al 2011), and with particular reference to attachment theory (Bowlby 1978), and to principles informed by the counselling and psychotherapy literature (Rogers 2004; Gerhardt 2004 etc), should be included in the training curricula. Staff who are introduced to these ideas and given opportunities to rehearse them by role play are more likely to then expect these opportunities to be available to them in the workplace.

Notes

1 Introduction: The Challenge of Uncovering and Using Emotions in Criminal Justice

1. Victim Personal Statements: www.justice.gov.uk/downloads/victims-and-witnesses/working-with-witnesses/making-victim-personal-statement-leaflet.pdf

2 Emotions and Criminal Justice

1. The classical school of criminology saw individuals as exercising rational choice and 'free will'. An offender is someone who is free to choose their behaviour but lacks the self-discipline of which we are all capable or who chooses to break the law (Crowther, C., 2007). *An Introduction to Criminology and Criminal Justice*. Basingstoke, Palgrave Macmillan.

3 Diversity, Power and Emotion

1. Personal, cultural and social.

9 Strategies for Sustaining Emotional Literacy in the Workplace

1. For example, Lavender Psychotherapy offers 'clinical supervision' to staff in three Probation Trusts. This scheme is referred to as 'keeping staff well'.

Bibliography

Adams, G. A. and B. J. (2010). "Social stressors and strain among police officers. Its not just the bad guys." *Criminal Justice and Behaviour* **37**(9): 1030–1040.

Adkins, L. and B. Skeggs (2005). *Feminism after Bourdieu: International Perspectives,* Blackwell.

Aiyegbusi, A. and J. Clarke-Moore (2009). *Therapeutic Relationships with Offenders. An Introduction to the Psychodynamics of Forensic Mental Health Nursing.* London, Jessica Kingsley.

Akerjordet, K. and E. Severinsson (2004). "Emotional Intelligence in mental health nurses talking about practice." *International Journal of Mental Health Nursing* **13**: 164–170.

Alcott, C. (2012). "Reforming the Force: An Examination of the Impact of the Operational Sub-Culture on Reform and Modernisation Within the Police Service." *British Journal of Community Justice* **10**(1): 5–14.

Andrade, E. B. and J. B. Cohen (2007). "On the consumption of negative feelings." *Journal of Consumer Research* **34 (October)**: 283–300.

Andrews, D. A. and J. Bonta (2010). "Rehabilitating Criminal Justice Policy and Practice." *American Psychological Association* **16**(1): 39–55.

Annison, J. (2007). "A gendered review of change within the probation service." *Howard Journal of Criminal Justice* **46**(2): 145–161.

Annison, J., et al. (2008). People First: Probation Officer Perspectives on Probation Work. *Probation Journal.* **55**: 259–271.

Ansbro, M. (2008). "Using attachment theory with offenders." *Probation Journal* **55**(3): 231–233.

Ashforth, B. E. and R. H. Humphrey (1993). "Emotional labor in service roles: The influence of identity." *The Academy Management Review* **18**(1): 88–115.

Austin, E. J. (2010). "Measurement of ability emotional intelligence: Results from two new tests." *British Journal of Psychology* **101**: 563–578.

Bachmann, J., et al. (2000). "Emotional intelligence in the collection of debt." *International Journal of Selection and Assessment* **8**(3): 1–7.

Bagihole, B. (2009). *Understanding Equal Opportunities and Diversity. The Social Differentiations and Intersections of Inequality.* Bristol, The Policy Press.

Bar-On, R. and J. D. A. Parker (2000). *Handbook of Emotional Intelligence: Theory, Development, Assessment and Application at Home, School and in the Workplace.* San Francisco, Jossey-Bass.

Barbalet, J. (2002). *Emotions and Sociology.* Oxford, Blackwell Publishing.

Barbalet, J. (2011). "Emotions beyond regulation: backgrounded emotions in science and trust." *Emotion Review* **3**(1): 36–43.

Baron-Cohen, S. (2003). *Mind reading – The Interactive Guide to Emotions.,* Jessica Kingsley.

Barrett, L. F. and J. J. Gross (2001). Emotional Intelligence; A Process Model of Emotion Representation and Regulation. *Emotion; Current Issues and Future Directions.* T. J. Mayne and G. A. Bonanno. London, The Guildford Press.

Batson, C. D. (2011). "What's wrong with morality?" *Emotion Review* **3**: 3.

Bendelow, G. and S. J. Williams (1998). *Emotions in Social Life.* London, Routledge.

Berking, M., et al. (2010). "Enhancing Emotion – Regulation Skills in Police Officers: Results of a Pilot Controlled Study." *Behaviour Therapy* **41**: 329–339.

Berkowitz, L. (2000). *Causes and Consequences of Feelings*. Cambridge, Cambridge University Press.

Biestek, R. (1961). *The Casework Relationship*. London, George, Allen and Unwin.

Bolton, S. C. (2005). *Emotion Management in the Workplace*. Basingstoke, Palgrave Macmillan.

Bondi, L. (2005). The place of emotions in research: From partitioning emotion and reason to the emotional dynamics of research relationships. *Emotional Geographies*. J. Davidson, L. Bondi and M. Smith. Aldershot, Ashgate.

Boswell, G. (1996). *Young and Dangerous: The Backgrounds and Careers of Section 53 Offenders*. Aldershot, Avebury.

Boswell, G. (2000). *Violent Children and Adolescents. Asking the Question Why*. London, Whurr Publishers.

Bottoms, A. (1995). The Philosophy and Politics of Punishment and Sentencing'. *The Politics Sentencing Reform*. C. Clarkson and R. Morgan. Oxford, Clarendon Press.

Bottoms, A. and J. Tankebe (2012). "Criminology: Beyond Procedural Justice: A Dialogic Approach to Legitimacy in Criminal Justice." *The Journal of Criminal Law and Criminology* **102**(1): 119–170.

Bowlby, J. (1969). *Attachment and Loss. – Vol 1: Attachment*. London, Pimlico.

Bowlby, J. (1978). *Attachment and Loss.– Vol 2: Separation: Anxiety and Anger*. London, Pimlico.

Bowlby, J. (1980). *Attachment and Loss, Vol 3 Loss: Sadness and Depression*. New York, Basic Books.

Braithwaite, J. (1989). *Crime, Shame and Reintegration*. Cambridge, Cambridge University Press.

Brotheridge, C. M. and A. A. Gradey (2005). "Emotional labour and burnout: Comparing two perspectives of 'people work'." *Journal of Vocational Behaviour* **60**(1): 17–39.

Brownmiller, S. (1975). *Against Our Will. Men, Women and Rape*. New York, Ballantine Books.

Bryant, M., et al. (1978). "Sentenced to social work?" *Probation Journal* **25**(4): 110–114.

Buckley, K. (1999). Managing violence; managing masculinity. *Good Practice in Working with Violence*. H. Kemshall and J. Pritchard. London, Jessica Kingsley.

Bunting, M. (2005). *Willing Slaves*, Harper Perennial.

Burke, L. (2013). "The rise of the shadow state?" *Probation Journal* **60**(1): 3–8.

Burnett, R. and F. McNeill (2005). "The place of the officer–offender relationship in assisting offenders from desisting from crime." *Probation Journal* **52**(3): 247–268.

Cameron, L. (2011). Introduction to metaphor analysis: Post-conflict reconciliation. *Realities Training Workshop – Metaphor Analysis*. The Morgan Centre, University of Manchester.

Cameron, L. and G. Low (1999). *Researching and Applying Metaphor*. Cambridge, Cambridge University Press.

Cameron, L., et al. (2009). "The discourse dynamics approach to metaphor and metaphor led discourse analysis." *Metaphor and Symbol* **24**(2): 63–89.

Campos, J. J., et al. (2011). "Reconceptualising Emotion Regulation." *Emotion Review* **3**(1): 26–35.

Canton, R. (2009). "Nonsense upon stilts? Human rights, the ethics of punishment and the values of probation." *British Journal of Community Justice* **7**(1): 5–22.

Canton, R. (2011). *Probation Working with Offenders*. Abingdon, Routledge.

Cavadino, M. and J. Dignan (2006). *Penal Systems. A Comparative Approach*. London, Sage.

Chakraborti, N. and J. Garland (2009). *Hate Crime: Impact, Causes and Responses*. London, Sage.

Chamberlayne, P. (2004). "Emotional retreat and social exclusion: Towards biographical methods in professional training." *Journal of Social Work Practice* 18(3): 337–350.

Chapman, H. A. and A. K. Anderson (2011). "Varieties of moral emotional experience." *Emotion Review* 3(3): 255–257.

Chapman, T. and M. Hough (1998). *Evidence Based Practice: A Guide to Effective Practice*. London, Her Majesty's Inspectorate of Probation.

Charland, L. C. (2011). "Moral undertow and the passions: Two challenges for contemporary emotion regulation." *Emotion Review* 3: 83–91.

Cherniss, C. and D. Goleman (2001). *The Emotionally Intelligent Workplace*, Jossey-Bass.

Cherry, S. (2010). *Transforming Behaviour: Pro-social Modelling in Practice*. Cullompton, Willan.

Ciarrochi, J., et al. (2001). *Emotional Intelligence in Everyday Life. A Scientific Enquiry*. Hove, Psychology Press. Taylor and Francis Group.

Ciarrochi, J., et al. (2005). "Can men do better if they try harder: Sex and motivational effects on emotional awareness." *Cognition and Emotion* 19(1): 133–141.

Clarke, N. (2006). "Developing emotional intelligence through workplace learning: Findings from a case study in healthcare." *Human Resource Development International* 9(4): 447–465.

Cohen, S. (1972). *Folk Devils and Moral Panics*. London, MacGibbon and Kee.

Collins, S., et al. (2009). "Stress, support and wellbeing as percieved by probation trainees." *Probation Journal* 56(3): 238–256.

Council of Europe (2010). "Recommendation of the Committee of Miniters to Member States on the Council of Europe Probation Rules."

Coupland, C., et al. (2009). "Saying it with feeling: Analysing speakable emotions." *Human Relations* 61: 327–353.

Cowburn, M. (2005). "Hegemony and discourse: Reconstructing the male offender and sexual coercion by men." *Sexualities, Evolution and Gender* 7(3): 215–231.

Crawford, L. E. (2009). "Conceptual metaphors of affect." *Emotion Review* 1: 129–139.

Crawley, E. (2004). *Doing Prison Work: The Public and Private Lives of Prison Officers*. Cullompton, Willan.

Crawley, E. M. (2009). "Emotion and performance: Prison officers and the presentation of self in prisons." *Punishment and Society* 6: 411–427.

Crewe, B. (2011). "Soft power in prison: Implications for staff-prisoner relationships, liberty and legitimacy." *European Journal of Criminology* 8(6): 455–468.

Crittenden, P. M. and A. H. Claussen (2000). *The Organisation of Attachment Relationships: Maturation, Culture and Context*. Cambridge, Cambridge University Press.

Crowther, C. (2007). *An Introduction to Criminology and Criminal Justice*. Basingstoke, Palgrave Macmillan.

Damasio, A. R. (1996). *Descartes' Error: Emotion, Reason and the Human Brain*. London, Papermac.

Darwin (1998). *The Expression of the Emotions in Man and Animals*.

Darwin and P. Ekman (1872/1998). *The Expression of Emotions in Man and Animals*.

Davidson, M. J. and C. L. Cooper (1992). *Shattering the Glass Ceiling: The Woman Manager*. London, Paul Chapman Publishing Ltd.

Day, A., et al. (2010). *Transitions to Better Lives: Offender Readiness and Rehabilitation*. Cullompton, Willan.

Dayton, T. (2000). *Trauma and Addiction: Ending the Cycle of Pain Through Emotional Literacy*. Florida, Health Communications, Inc.

De Coster, S. and C. Z. Zito (2010). "Gender and general strain theory: The gendering of emotional experiences and expressions." *Journal of Contemporary Criminal Justice* 26(2): 224–245.

De Haan, W. and I. Loader (2002). "On the emotions of crime, punishment and social control." *Theoretical Criminology* 6: 243–253.

Department of Health (2012). Transforming Care: a national response to Winterbourne View Hospital Department of Health Review. DH. London, DH.

Diamant, I. (2001). "On not being able to know others' minds: The debate on recovered memories of abuse from a relational perspective." *British Journal of Psychotherapy* 17(3): 344–352.

Dobash, R. E., et al. (2000). *Changing Violent Men*. London, Sage.

Dowden, C. and D. Andrews (2004). "The importance of staff practice in delivering correctional treatment: A meta-analysis." *International Journal of Offender Therapy and Comparative Criminology* 48(2): 203–214.

Du Gay, P. (2003). *Production of Culture/Cultures of Production*. London, Sage.

Duff, A. (2007). Punishment as Communication. *Dictionary of Probation and Offender Management*. C. Canton and D. Hancock. Cullompton, Willan.

Dworkin, A. (1981). *Pornography – Men Possessing Women*. London, Women's Press.

Dwyer, S. (2007). "The emotional impact of social work practice." *Journal of Social Work Practice* 21(1): 49–60.

Dyson, S. and B. Brown (2006). *Social Theory and Applied Health Research*. Maidenhead, Open University Press.

Ekman, P. (2004). *Emotions Revealed. Understanding Faces and Feelings*. London, Phoenix.

Ekman, P. (2008). *Emotional Awareness. A Conversation between The Dalai Lama and Paul Ekman*. New York, Holt Paperbacks.

Ekman, P. and F. Wallace (1975). *Unmasking the Face: A Guide to Recognising Emotions from Facial Clues*. Englewood Cliffs, NJ, Prentice-Hall.

Ekman, P. and F. Wallace (2002). Facial Action Coding System. *A Research Nexus Ebook*, Salt Lake City, Utah: A Human Face.

Equality and Human Rights Commission (2010). How Fair is Britain? Equality, Human Rights and Good Relations in 2010. The First Triennial Review. London, Equality and Human Rights Commission.

Equality and Human Rights Commission (2011). Sex and Power 2011 http://www.equalityhumanrights.com.

European Council of Human Rights (1950). "European Convention on Human Rights." Retrieved 20/05/13, 2013.

Evans, D. (2003). *Emotion. A Very Short Introduction*. Oxford, Oxford University Press.

Fargason, C. A. (1995). "The influence of feelings on professional judgment." *Journal of Child Sex Abuse* 4(1): 99–102.

Farrall, S. (2002). *Rethinking What Works with Offenders: Probation, Social Context and Desistance from Crime*. Cullompton, Willan.

Farrall, S. and A. Calverley (2006). *Understanding Desistance from Crime*. Maidenhead, Open University Press.

Farrow, K., et al. (2007). *Offenders in Focus. Risk, Responsivity and Diversity*. Bristol, Policy Press.

Fineman, D. (2003). *Emotion in Organisations*. London, Sage.

Fineman, D. (2004). "Getting the measure of emotion – and the cautionary tale of emotional intelligence." *Human Relations* 57(6): 719–740.

Fineman, S. (2001). Emotions and organizational control. *Emotions at Work. Theory, Research and Applications for Management.* R. L. Payne and C. L. Cooper. Chichester, John Wiley.

Fischer, A. H. (2000). *Gender and Emotion. Social Psychological Perspectives.* Cambridge, Cambridge University Press.

Fitzgibbon, W. (2011). *Probation and Social Work on Trial. Violent Offenders and Child Abusers.* Basingstoke, Palgrave Macmillan.

Fitzmaurice, C. and K. Pease (1986). *The Psychology of Judicial Sentencing.* Manchester, Manchester University Press.

Foren, R. and R. Bailey (1968). *Authority in Social Casework.* Oxford, Pergamon Press.

Franks, D. D. (2010). "Emotions on a continuum." *Emotion Review* 2: 105–106.

Freshwater, D. and C. Robertson (2002). *Emotions and Needs.* Buckingham, Open University Press.

Freud, S. and A. Freud (2005). *The Essentials of Psychoanalysis.* Harmondsworth, Penguin.

Frijda, N. H. (1986). *The Emotions.* London, Cambridge University Press.

Frijda, N. H., et al. (2000). *Emotions and Beliefs: How Feelings Influence Thoughts.* Cambridge, Cambridge University Press.

Fuller, C. and P. Taylor (2003). Toolkit of Motivational Skills. A Practice Handbook for using Motivational Skills in the Work of the Probation Service. London, National Probation Directorate.

Gardener, H. (1984). *Frames of Mind. The Theory of Multiple Intelligences.* London, Basic Books.

Gardener, H. (1993). *Frames of Mind. The Theory of Multiple Intelligences.* London, Fontana Press.

Garey, A. I. and K. V. Hansen (2011). *At the Heart of Work and Family. Engaging the Ideas of Arlie Hochschild.* London, Rutgers University Press.

Garland, D. (1990). *Punishment and Modern Society: A Study in Social Theory.* Oxford, Oxford University Press.

Garland, D. (2002). Of Crimes and Criminals. The Development of Criminology in Britain. *The Oxford Handbook of Criminology.* M. Maguire, R. Morgan and R. Reiner. Oxford, Oxford University Press.

Gelsthorpe, L. (1989). *Sexism and the Female Offender.* Aldershott, Gower.

Gelsthorpe, L. (2002). Feminism and Criminology. *The Oxford Handbook of Criminology.* M. Maguire, R. Morgan and R. Reiner. Oxford, Oxford University Press.

Gelsthorpe, L. (2009). Emotions and Contemporary Developments in Criminology. *Emotion. New Psychosocial Perspectives.* S. D. Sclater, D. W. Jones, H. Price and C. Yates. Basingstoke, Palgrave Macmillan.

Gelsthorpe, L. and G. McIvor (2007). Difference and Diversity in Probation. *Handbook of Probation.* L. Gelsthorpe and R. Morgan, H. Cullompton, Willan.

Gendron, M. (2010). "Defining emotion: A brief history." *Emotion Review* 2(4): 371–372.

Gendron, M. and L. F. Barrett (2009). "Reconstructing the past: A century of ideas about emotion in psychology." *Emotion Review* 1: 316–339.

Gerhardt, S. (2004). *Why Love Matters; How Affection Shapes a Baby's Brain.* London, Routledge.

Gillies, V. (2006). "Working class mothers and school life: Exploring the role of emotional capital." *Gender and Education* 18(3): 281–293.

Gladwell, M. (2005). *Blink. The Power of Thinking without Thinking.* London, Allen Lane.

Glenberg, A. M., et al. (2009). "Gender, emotion, and the embodiment of language comprehensions." *Emotion Review* **1**(2): 151–161.

Goffman, E. (1959/1990). *The Presentation of Self in Everyday Life*. London, Penguin Books.

Goldacre, B. (2010). Why Two Little Boys Can make Me Cry. *The Guardian*. Manchester.

Goldie, P. (2009). "Narrative thinking, emotion and planning." *The Journal of Aesthetics and Art Criticism* **67**(1): 99–106.

Goleman, D. (1995). *Emotional Intelligence*. New York, Bantam.

Goleman, D. (1996). *Emotional Intelligence: Why it Can Matter More than IQ*. London, Bloomsbury.

Goleman, D. (1998). *Working with Emotional Intelligence*. London, Bloomsbury.

Goleman, D., Boyatzis, R. and McKee, A. (2002). *The New Leaders. Transforming the Art of Leadership into the Science of Results*. London, Time Warner Paperbacks.

Greene, J. D. (2011). "Emotion and morality: A tasting menu." *Emotion Review* **3**(3): 227–229.

Griffin, M. L., Hogan, N.L., Lambert, E.G., Tucker-Gail, K.A. and Baker, D.N. (2009). "Job involvement, job stress, job satisfaction, and organisational commitment and the burnout of correctional staff." *Criminal Justice and Behaviour Online* XX(X): 1–17.

Groombridge, N. (2006). Queer Theory. *The Sage Dictionary of Criminology*. E. McLaughlin and J. Muncie. London, Sage.

Gross, J. J. and L. F. Barrett (2011). "Emotion generation and emotion regulation: One or two depends on your point of view." *Emotion Review* **3**(1): 8–16.

Haidt, J. (2001). "The emotional dog and its rational tale: A social intuitionist approach to moral judgment." *Psychological Review* **108**(4): 814–834.

Harré, R. and W. G. Parrott (1996). *The Emotions: Social, Cultural and Biological Dimensions*. London, Sage.

Harrison, K. (2010). *Managing High Risk Sex Offenders in the Community*. Cullompton, Willan.

Harvey, J. and K. Smedley (2010). *Psychological Therapy in Prisons and Other Secure Settings*. Abingdon, Willan.

Hayles, M. (2006). Constructing safety: a collaborative approach to managing risk and building responsibility. *Constructive Work with Offenders*. K. Gorman, M. Gregory, M. Hayles and N. Parton. London, Jessica Kingsley Publishers.

Heidensohn, F. (1985). *Women and Crime*. Basingstoke, Macmillan.

Heidensohn, F. (2002). Gender and Crime. *The Oxford Handbook of Criminology*. M. Maguire, R. Morgan and R. Reiner. Oxford, Oxford University Press.

Heidensohn, F. (2006). *Gender and Justice: New Concepts and Approaches*. Cullompton, Willan.

Hennessey, R. (2011). *Relationship Skills in Social Work*. London, Sage.

Herman, J. (1997). *Trauma and Recovery. The Aftermath of Violence – From Domestic Abuse to Political Terror*. New York, A Member of the Perseus Books Group.

Higgs, M. J. and V. Dulewicz (1999). *Making Sense of Emotional Intelligence*. NFER-Nelson, Windsor.

Hochschild, A. R. (1983). *The Managed Heart*. London, University of California Press.

Home Office (1992). National Standards for the Supervision of Offenders in the Community. London, Home Office.

Home Office (2010). Equality Act 2010. H. Office. London: http://www.legislation.gov.uk, Home Office.

Howard, M. (1993). Speech to the Conservative Party Conference. *Conservative Party Annual Conference 1993*. Brighton.

Howe, D. (2008). *The Emotionally Intelligent Social Worker*, Palgrave Macmillan.

Hubbard, G., et al. (2001). "Working with emotion: Issues for the researcher in fieldwork and teamwork." *Social Research Methodology* 4(2): 119–137.

Hughes, M. and J. Bradford Terrell (2012). *Emotional Intelligence in Action. Training and Coaching Activities for Leaders, Managers and Teams*. San Francisco, Pfieffer.

Independent Police Complaints Commission (2009). IPCC Report into contact between Fiona Pilkington and Leicestershire Constabulary 2004–2007. London, Independent Police Complaints Commission.

IPCC (2011). "Pilkington Inquiry." 2013.

Itzin, C. and J. Newman (1995). *Gender, Culture and Organizational Change: Putting Theory into Practice*. London, Routledge.

Izard, C. (2010). "More meanings and more questions for the term 'Emotion'." *Emotion Review* 2(4): 383–385.

Jack, D. and R. Jack (1996). Women Lawyers: Archetype and Alternatives. *Mapping the Moral Domain*. C. Gilligan, J. C. Ward and J. McLean Taylor. Harvard, Harvard University Press.

Jordan, W. (1970). *Client–Worker Transactions*. London, Routledge and Kegan Paul.

Kagan, J. (2010). "Some plain words on emotion." *Emotion Review* 2(221–224).

Kaplan, K. (1972). "On the ambivalence–indifference problem in attitude theory and measurement: A suggested modification of the semantic differential techniques." *Psychological Bulletin* 77: 351–372.

Karstedt, S. (2002). "Emotions and criminal justice." *Theoretical Criminology* 6(3): 299–317.

Karstedt, S. et al. (2011). *Emotions, Crime and Justice*. Oxford, Hart Publishing Ltd.

Katz, J. (1999). *How Emotions Work*. Chicago, University of Chicago Press.

Keith, B. (2006). Report of the Zahid Mubarek Inquiry Volumes 1 and 2. London, The Stationery Office.

Kemshall, H. (2003). *Understanding Risk in Criminal Justice*. Maidenhead, Open University Press.

Kemshall, H. (2008). *Understanding the Community Management of High Risk Offenders*. Maidenhead, McGraw-Hill Open University Press.

Kemshall, H. (2010). The role of risk, needs and strengths assessment in improving the supervision of offenders. *Offender Supervision: New Directions in Theory, Research and Practice*. F. McNeill, P. Raynor and C. Trotter. Abingdon, Willan.

Killick, S. (2006). *Emotional Literacy at the Heart of the School Ethos*. London, Paul Chapman Publishing.

King, A. (2008). "Keeping a safe distance: Individualism and the less punitive public." *British Journal of Criminology* 48(2): 190–208.

Klug, F. (2000). *Values for a Godless Age. The Story of the United Kingdom's New Bill of Rights*. London, Penguin Books.

Knight, C. (2007). "Why choose the probation service?" *British Journal of Community Justice* 5(2): 55–69.

Knight, C. (2012). Soft Skills for Hard Work: An Exploration of the Efficacy of the Emotional Literacy of Practitioners Working Within the National Offender Management Service (NOMS) With High Risk Offenders. *Division of Community and Criminal Justice*. Leicester, De Montfort University. PhD: 449.

Knight, C. and D. Clow (2010). Supporting Practitioners in Dealing with the Emotional Impact of their work. *Offender Engagement Research Bulletin*. Ministry of Justice. London, Ministry of Justice. **Issue 1.**

Knight, C. et al. (2008). Diversity: Contested Meanings and Differential Consequences. *Applied Criminology*. B. Stout, Yates, J. and Williams, B. London, Sage

Knight, C. and K. White (2001). "The integration of theory and practice within the diploma in probation studies: How is it achieved?" *Probation Journal* 48(3): 203–210.

Kram, K. E. and M. McCullom (1998). When Women Lead: The Visibility–Vulnerability Spiral. *The Psychodynamics of Leadership*. B. Klein, F. Gabelnick and P. Herr. Madison, CT:Psychosocial Press.

Kuppens, P. (2010). "From appraisal to emotion." *Emotion Review* 2: 157–158.

Lacey, M. (1995). Working for justice: fairness. *Probation Working for Justice*. D. Ward and M. Lacey. London, Whiting and Birch.

Lakoff, G. (1987). *Women, Fire and Dangerous Things: What Categories Reveal about the Mind*. Chicago and London, University of Chicago Press.

Lane, R. D. and L. Nadel (2000). *Cognitive Neuroscience of Emotion*. Oxford, Oxford University Press.

Langford, W. (1997). "'You make me sick': Women, health and romantic love." *Journal of Contemporary Health* 5: 52–55.

Laster, K. and P. O'Malley (1996). "Sensitive new-age law: The reassertion of emotionality in law." *International Journal of the Sociology of Law* 24(1): 21–40.

Layder, D. (2004). *Emotion in Social Life: The Lost Heart of Society*. London, Sage.

Layder, D. (2006). *Understanding Social Theory*. London, Sage.

LeDoux, J. (2003). *The Emotional Brain*. London, Phoenix.

Lipscombe, S. (2012). Sarah's Law; the child sex offender disclosure scheme. H. Affairs. London, House of Commons Library.

Loader, I. (2005). "The affects of punishment: Emotions, democracy and penal politics." *Criminal Justice Matters* 60(1): 12–13.

Locke, E. A. (2005). "Why emotional intelligence is an invalid concept." *Journal of Organisational Behaviour* 26: 425–431.

Loewenstein, G. (2010). "Insufficient emotion: Soul-searching by a former indicter of strong emotions." *Emotion Review* 2: 234–239.

Lowdell, A. and G. Adshead (2009). The Best Defence: Institutional Defences Against Anxiety in Forensic Services. *Therapeutic Relationships with Offenders*. A. Aiyegbusi and J. Clarke-Moore. London, Jessica Kingsley.

Lukes, S. (2005). *Power: A Radical View*. Basingstoke, Palgrave Macmillan.

Mackie, S. (2009). Reflecting on Murderousness: Reflective Practice in Secure Forensic Settings. *Therapeutic Relationships with Offenders. An Introduction to the Psychodynamics of Forensic Mental Health Nursing*. A. Aiyegbusi and J. Clarke-Moore. London, Jessica Kingsley.

Macpherson, W. (1999). The Stephen Lawrence Inquiry Report. London, Stationery Office.

Mair, G. (2004). *What Matters in Probation*. Collumpton, Willan.

Marmot, R. (2010). Fair Society, Healthy Lives. Strategic Review of Health Inequalities in England post 2000. London, Department of Health.

Marshall, W. L. (1989). "Invited essay: Intimacy, loneliness and sex offenders." *Behaviour, Research and Therapy* 27: 491–503.

Marshall, W. L. and H. E. Barbaree (1990). An Integrated Theory of the Etiology of Sex Offending. *Handbook of Sex Assault – Issues, Theories and Treatment of the Offender*. W. L. e. a. Marshall, D. R. Laws and H. E. Barbaree. New York, Plenum Press: 257–275.

Marshall, W. L. and G. A. Serran (2004). "The role of the therapist in offender treatment." *Psychology, Crime and Law* 10(3): 309–321.

Maruna, S. et al. (2004). Ex-offender Reintegration: Theory and Practice. *After Crime and Punishment: Pathways to Offender Reintegration.* S. Maruna and R. Immarigeon. Cullompton, Willan.

Maruna, S. and T. P. LeBel (2010). The desistance paradigm in correctional practice: from programmes to lives. *Offender Supervision: New Directions in Theory, Research and Practice.* F. McNeill, P. Raynor and C. Trotter. Abingdon, Willan.

Mathiesen, T. (2004). *Silently Silenced. Essays on the Creation of Acquiescence in Modern Society.* Winchester, Waterside Press.

Mawby, R. C. and A. Worrall (2011). Probation workers and their occupational cultures. Leicester and Keele, ESRC.

Mayer, J. D. and P. Salovey (1997). What is Emotional Intelligence. *Emotional Development and Emotional Intelligence: Educational Implications.* P. Salovey and D. Slayter. New York, Basic Books.

McCann, L. and L. A. Pearlman (1990). "Vicarious traumatisation: A framework for understanding the psychological effects of working with victims." *Journal of traumatic stress* 3(1): 131–149.

McLeod, J. (2001). *Qualitative Research in Counselling and Psychotherapy.* London, Sage.

McNeill, F. (2004). "Supporting desistance in probation practice: A response to Maruna, Porter and Carvalho." *Probation Journal* 51(3): 341–352.

McNeill, F. (2006). "A desistance paradigm for offender management." *Criminology and Criminal Justice* 6(1): 39–62.

McNeill, F. (2009). Towards Effective Practice in Offender Supervision. Glasgow, Scottish Centre for Crime and Justice Research (available online at: http:http://www.sccjr@ac.uk/document/McNeill_Towards.pdf.

McNeill, F., et al. (2010). *Offender Supervision. New directions in theory, research and practice.* Cullompton, Willan.

McWilliams, W. (1983). "The mission to the English Police Courts 1876–1936." *The Howard Journal of Penology and Crime Prevention* XX11(3): 129–147.

McWilliams, W. (1985). "The mission transformed: Professionalisation of probation between the wars." *Howard Journal of Criminal Justice* 24(4): 257–274.

McWilliams, W. (1986). "The English probation system and the diagnostic ideal." *The Howard Journal of Criminal Justice* 25(4): 241–260.

Mearns, C. (1997). *Person-centred Counselling Training.* London, Sage.

Mearns, D. and B. Thorne (2008). *Person-Centred Counselling in Action.* London, Sage.

Mehrabian, A. (1972). *Nonverbal Communication.* Chicago, Aldine-Atherton.

Menzies, L. I. (1959). "A case-study in the functioning of social systems as a defence against anxiety: A report on a study of the nursing service of a general hospital." *Human Relations* 13: 95–121.

Messerschmidt, J. (1997). *Crime as Structured Action: Gender, Race, Class and Crime in the Making.* London, Sage.

Metropolitan Police (2013). "Community Engagement." 2013.

Miller, J. B. and I. P. Stiver (1997). *The Healing Connection: How Women Form Relationships in Therapy and in Life.* Boston, Beacon Press.

Miller, W. R. and S. Rollnick (2002). *Motivational Interviewing: Preparing People for Change.* London and New York, The Guilford Press.

Mills, K., Davies, K. and Brooks, S. (2007). "Experience of DTTO: The person in the process." *British Journal of Community Justice* 5(3): 5–22.

Ministry of Justice (2007). *Human Resources Workforce Profile Report*. London, Ministry of Justice.

Ministry of Justice (2010). Correctional Services Accreditation Panel Report. M. o. Justice. London, Ministry of Justice.

Ministry of Justice (2010). Green Paper: Breaking the Cycle: Effective Punishment, Rehabilitation and Sentencing of Offenders. Ministry of Justice. London.

Ministry of Justice (2010). Offender Engagement News. London, Ministry of Justice.

Ministry of Justice (2010). Offender Engagement Programme Research Bulletin. M. o. Justice. London, Ministry of Justice.

Ministry of Justice (2011). Criminal Statistics quarterly update January–March *Statistics publication schedule*. London, http://webarchive.nationalarchives.gov.uk/+/http://www.justice.gov.uk/publications/statistics-publication-schedule.htm.

Ministry of Justice (2011). National Standards for the Management of Offenders in England and Wales. London, Ministry of Justice National Offender Management Service.

Ministry of Justice (2013). Transforming Rehabilitation. A Revolution in the Way We Manage Offenders. Consultation Paper CP1/2013. M. o. Justice. London, The Stationery Office Ltd.

Monger, M. (1972). *Casework in Probation*. London, Butterworth.

Moriarty, N. et al. (2001). "Deficits in emotional intelligence underlying adolescent sex offending." *Journal of Adolescence* 24(6): 743–751.

Morran, D. et al. (2011). "Re-education or recovery? Re-thinking some aspects of domestic violence perpetrator programmes." *Probation Journal* 58(1): 22–36.

Morris, A. (1987). *Woman, Crime and Criminal Justice*. Oxford, Basil Blackwell.

Morrison, T. (2007). "Emotional intelligence, emotion and social work: Context, characteristics, complications and contribution." *British Journal of Social Work* 37: 245–263.

Moulden, H. M. and P. Firestone (2010). "Therapist awareness and responsibility in working with sex offenders." *Sex Abuse: A Journal of Research and Treatment* 22(4): 374–386.

Muller, R. J. (2000). When a patient has no story to tell: Alexythemia. *Psychiatric Times*.

Munro, E. (2011). The Munro Review of Child Protection: Final Report. A Child Centred System. D. o. Education. London, The Stationery Office Ltd.

Murdin, L. (2010). *Understanding Transference. The Power of Patterns in the Therapeutic Relationship*. Basingstoke, Palgrave Macmillan.

Nellis, M. (2007). Humanising justice: the English Probation Service up to 1972. *Handbook of Probation*. L. Gelsthorpe and R. Morgan. Cullompton, Willan.

Newburn, T. (2007). *Criminology*. Cullompton, Willan.

NOMS (2006). The NOMS Offender Management Model Version 2. Home Office. London, NOMs.

NOMS (2012). National Offender Management Service – Vision and Values. M. o. Justice. London, http://www.justice.gove.uk/about/noms/noms-vision-and-values.

Nordgren, L. F. and M.-H. M. McDonell (2010). "The scope–severity paradox: why doing more harm is judged to be less harmful." *Social Psychological and Personality Science Online* 000(00): 1–7.

NPIA (2010). INDOI (A5) Ethics and Values of the Police Service Student Notes Version 0.04. National Policing Improvement Agency (NPIA). London.

Oakley, A. (2005). *The Anne Oakley Reader. Gender, Women and Social Science*. Bristol, Policy Press.

Oatley, K. (2009). "Communications to Self and Others: Emotional Experience and its Skills." *Emotion Review* 1(3): 206–213.

Oatley, K. (2010). "Two Movements in Emotions: Communication and Reflection." *Emotion Review* 2(1): 29–35.

Oatley, K. et al. (2006). *Understanding Emotions*. Oxford, Blackwell.

Offender Engagement Team (2011). Engaging for Success: Enhancing Performance through Employee Engagement. *Offender Engagement Research Bulletin*. O. E. Team. London, Ministry of Justice. 5.

Office for National Statistics (2012). "UK National Statistics: Crime and Justice." http://www.statistics.gov.uk/hub/crime-justice/index/html. Retrieved 03/01/12, 2012.

Oldfield, M. (2007). Risk Society. *Dictionary of Probation and Offender Management*. R. Canton and D. Hancock. Cullompton, Willan.

Orbach, S. (2001). *Towards Emotional Literacy*, Virago.

Park, J. and M. Tew (2007). *Emotional Literacy Pocketbook. A Pocketful of Practical Strategies for Helping Pupils Use Emotional Understanding to Learn and Grow*, Management Pocketbooks Ltd.

Paton, R. and L. Dempster (2002). "Managing change from a gender perspective." *European Management Journal* 20(5): 539–548.

Payne, R. L. and C. L. Cooper (2001). *Emotions at Work. Theory, Research and Applications for Management*. Chichester, John Wiley and Sons.

Petrillo, M. (2007). "Power struggle: Gender issues for female probation officers in the supervision of high risk offenders." *Probation Journal* 54(4): 394–406.

Pizzaro, D., et al. (2011). "On disgust and moral judgment." *Emotion Review* 3(3): 267–268.

Plutchik, R. (1980). *Emotion: Theory, Research and Experience: Vol. 1 Theories of Emotion*. New York, Academic.

Prins, H. (1999). *Will They Do it Again? Risk Assessment and Management in Criminal Justice and Psychiatry*. London, Routledge.

Puglia, M. L., et al. (2005). "The emotional intelligence of adult sex offenders: Ability based EI assessment." *Journal of Sex Aggression* 11(3): 249–258.

Raine, J. W. (2007). Managerialism. *Dictionary of Probation and Offender Management*. R. Canton and D. Hancock. Cullompton, Willan.

Raynor, P., et al. (2010). Skills and Strategies in Probation Supervision: The Jersey Study. *Offender Supervision: New Directions in Theory, Research and Practice*. F. McNeill, P. Raynor and C. Trotter. Abingdon, Willan.

Reay, D. (2004). "Gendering Bourdieu's concepts of capitals? Emotional capital, women and social class." *Sociological Review*.

Renn, P. (2000). The Link Between Childhood Trauma and Later Violent Offending: A Case Study. *Violent Children and Adolescents. Asking the Question Why*. G. Boswell. London, Whurr.

Rex, S. (1999). "Desistance from offending: Experiences of probation." *The Howard Journal of Criminal Justice* 38: 366–383.

Rex, S. (2005). *Reforming Community Penalties*. Cullompton, Willan.

Rex, S. (2012). "The offender engagement programme – rationale and objectives." *Euro Vista* 2(1): 6–9.

Rich, P. (2006). *Attachment and Sex Offending*. Chichester, John Wiley & Sons.

Rivas, L. M. (2011). Invisible Care and the Illusion of Independence. *At the Heart of Work and Family. Engaging the Ideas of Arlie Hochschild*. A. I. Garey and K. V. Hansen. London, Rutgers University Press.

Roberts, B. and C. Baim (1999). "A community-based programme for sex offenders who deny their offending behaviour." *Probation Journal* 46(4): 225–233.

Rogers, C. (1943). *Counselling and Psychotherapy: Newer Concepts in Practice*. Boston, Houghton Mifflin.

Rogers, C. (2004). *On Becoming a Person: A Therapist's View of Psychotherapy*. London, Constable.

Romito, P. (2008). *A Deafening Silence: Hidden Violence Against Women and Children*. Bristol, The Policy Press.

Roy, A., et al. (2007). "Insiders or outsiders: Differing perspectives on the delivery of drug services in prison." *British Journal of Community Justice* 5(3): 23–39.

Rumgay, J. (2004). Dealing with Substance-Misusing Offenders in the Community. *Alternatives to Prison: Options for an Insecure Society*. A. Bottoms, S. Rex and G. Robinson. Cullompton, Willan.

Rutherford, A. (1993). *Criminal Justice and the Pursuit of Decency*. Oxford, Oxford University Press.

Ryam, M. K. and S. A. Haslam (2005). "The glass cliff: Evidence that women are over-represented in precarious leadership positions." *British Journal of Management* 16: 1–10.

Salovey, P. and J. D. Mayer (1990). "Emotional intelligence." *Imagination, Cognition and Personality* 9: 185–211.

Salovey, P. and D. J. Sluyter (1997). *Emotional Development and Emotional Intelligence: Implications for Educators*. New York, Basic Books.

Schaible, L. M. and V. Gecas (2010). "The impact of emotional labour and value dissonance on burnout among police officers." *Police Quarterly* 13(3): 316–341.

Schauben, L. J. and P. A. Frazier (1995). "Vicarious trauma: The effects on female counsellors of working with sex violence survivors." *Psychology of Women Quarterly* 19: 49–64.

Schaverien, J. (2006). *Gender, Countertransference and the Erotic Transference. Perspectives from Analytical Pyschology and Psychoanalysis*. Hove, Routledge.

Scheff, T. et al. (2002). "How emotions work." *Theoretical Criminology* 6(3): 361–380.

Schnall, S., et al. (2008). "With a clean conscience: Cleanliness reduces the severity of moral judgements." *Psychological Science* 19(12): 1219–1222.

Schon, D. (2003). *The Reflective Practitioner: How Professionals Think in Action*. Aldershot, Ashgate.

Seidler, V. J. (1998). Masculinity, violence and emotional life. *Emotions in Social Life*. G. Bendelow and S. J. Williams. London, Routledge.

Seidler, V. J. (2010). *Embodying Identities*. Bristol, The Policy Press.

Sharp, P. (2001). *Nurturing Emotional Literacy: A Practical Guide for Teachers, Parents and those in Caring Professions*. Abingdon, Oxon, David Fulton Publishers.

Silvestri, M. and C. Crowther-Dowey (2008). *Gender and Crime*. London, Sage.

Smart, C. (1977). *Women, Crime and Criminology: A Feminist Critique*. London, Routledge and Kegan Paul.

Smart, C. (1995). *Law, Crime and Sexity: Essays in Feminism*. London, Sage.

Smith, D. (2005). "Probation and social work." *British Journal of Social Work* 35: 621–637.

Smith, D. (2006). "Making sense of psychoanalysis in criminological theory and probation practice." *Probation Journal* 53(4): 361–376.

Smith, P. (1992). *The Emotional Labour of Nursing. How Nurses Care*. Basingstoke, Macmillan Education.

Spalek, B. (2002). *Islam, Crime and Criminal Justice*. Cullompton, Willan.

Sparrow, T. and A. Knight (2006). *Applied EI: The Importance of Attitudes in Developing Emotional Intelligence*, Jossey-Bass.

Spendlove, D. (2008). *Emotional Literacy. Ideas in Action*, Continuum International Publishing Group.

Steiner, C. (1997). *Achieving Emotional Literacy*. London, Bloomsbury.

Stevenson, A. (2010). *Oxford Dictionary of English*. Oxford, Oxford University Press.

Tait, S. (2011). "A typolology of prison officer approaches to care." *European Journal of Criminology* 8(6): 440–454.

Tamir, M. (2011). "The maturing field of emotion regulation." *Emotion Review* 3(1): 3–7.

Taylor, I., et al. (1973). *The New Criminology*. London, Routledge and Kegan Paul.

Teicher, M. H. (2000). "Wounds That Time Won't Heal: The Neurobiology of Child Abuse." *Cerebrum: The Dana Foundationi* http://www.dana.org/news/cerebrum.

Tewksbury, R. and G. E. Higgins (2006). "Examining the effect of emotional dissonance on work stress and satisfaction with supervisors among correctional staff." *Criminal Justice Policy Review* 17(3): 290–301.

Theodosius, C. (2008). *Emotional Labour in Health Care: The Unmanaged Heart of Nursing*. London, Routledge.

Thompson, N. (2006). *Anti-Discriminatory Practice*. Basingstoke, Palgrave Macmillan.

Thompson, N. (2009). *People Skills*. Basingstoke, Palgrave Macmillan.

Thompson, S. and N. Thompson (2008). *The Critically Reflective Practitioner*. Basingstoke, Palgrave Macmillan.

Travis, A. and R. Simon (2011). Revealed: the full picture of sentenes handed down to rioters. *Guardian, UK*. London.

Trotter, C. (1999). *Working with Involuntary Clients: A Guide to Practice*. London, Sage.

Truax, C. B. and R. R. Carkhuff (1967). *Toward Effective Counselling and Psychotherapy*. Chicago, Aldine.

Turner, J. H. (2009). "The sociology of emotions: Basic theoretical arguments." *Emotion Review* 1(4): 340–354.

Tyler, T. (2003). "Procedural justice, legitimacy and the effective rule of law." *Crime and Justice* 30: 283–284.

Van Stokkom, B. (2002) "Moral emotion in restorative justice conferences: Managing shame, designing empathy." *Theoretical Criminology* 6(3): 339–360.

Van Stokkom, B. (2011). Dealing with defiant citizens: building emotional intelligence into police work. *Emotions, Crime and Justice*. S. Karstedt, I. Loader and H. Strang. Oxford, Hart Publishing Ltd.

Vanstone, M. (2007). *Supervising Offenders in the Community: A History of Probation Theory and Practice*.

Vanstone, M. (2012). From a minority interest to accredited programmes. *Sex Offenders: Punish, Help, Change or Control? Theory, Policy and Practice Explored*. J. Brayford, F. Cowe and J. Deering. Abingdon, Routledge.

Ward, T., Polaschek, D.L.L. and Beech, A.R. (2006). *Theories of Sexual Offending*. Chichester, John Wiley and Sons.

Wellington, C. A. and J. Bryson (2001). "At face value? Image consultancy, emotional labour and professional work." *Sociology* 35(4): 933–946.

Whitehead, P. (2010). *Exploring Modern Probation: Social Theory and Organisational Complexity*. Bristol, The Policy Press.

Wierzbicka, A. (2010). "On emotions and on definitions: A response to Izard." *Emotion Review* 2(4): 379–380.

Wilkinson, R. and K. Pickett (2010). *The Spirit Level: Why Equality Is Better for Everyone.* London, Penguin Books.

Wood, J., Kemshall, H., Westwood, S., Fenton, A. and Logue, C. (2010). Investigating disclosures made by sex offenders: preliminary study for the evaluation of mandatory polygraph testing. London, Ministry of Justice.

Wykes, M. and K. Welsh (2009). *Violence, Gender & Justice.* London, Sage.

Zembylas, M. (2007). "Emotional capital and education: Theoretical insights from Bourdieu." *British Journal of Educational Studies* 55(4): 443–463.

Index

abuse, 7, 14, **35–6**, 47, 53, 81, 90, 128–39, 141, 144, 171, 194
   see also child abuse
acceptance, 32, 102, 113
accountability, 119
accredited programmes, 33, 131, 186
advise, assist and befriend, 71, 165
   see also probation service
age, 11, 26, 39–40, 56, 57, 77
   see also protected characteristics
agency, 11, 25, 27, 92
alcohol, 20, 36, 110
alexithymia, 26–7, 44, 132
   see also autism
ambivalence, 16, 51, 78, 80, 87, 119, 129, 140–42, 147
   see also conflict
amygdala, 22–3
anger, 4, 8, 13, 19, 21, 26, 28–9, 44–5, 49, 54, 59, 65, 69, 76, 80, 82, 84, 86–7, 93, 97, 101, 106, 112, 114–15, 118, 123, 135, 139, 141, 156, 159–60, 163, 171–72
anti-discrimination, 169
   see also, anti-oppressive, diversity, discrimination
anti-oppressive, 38
anxiety, 24, 37, 69, 86, 91, 98, 107, 112–13, 171, 194
appraisal,
   see emotion appraisal
approach goals, 144
Aristotle, 20
assessment, 32, 35, 37, 72, 111, 130, 136, 142, 168
   see also risk assessment, clinical assessment
attachment; theories of, 35–6, 41, 116–18, 186, 194, 198
   see also Bowlby, J.
authenticity, 121
   see also inauthenticity

autism, 27, 93
autonomy, 44, 48, 67, 92

basic emotions
   see emotions
beliefs, 3, 24, 39, 41, 52, 59–61, 65–6, 70, 118, 135–36, 144
benign emotional control, 4, 13, 61, **66–8**, 72, 82, 110, 152, 192
   see *also* emotional control, Layder, control
Better Lives Model (BLM), 34
   see also Strength-based Models, and Good Lives Model
black and minority ethnic, 38, 40, 56, 58, 80
blame, 59, 75, 112, 140
body language, 92–3, 99, 101, 121–22, 124
Bolton, S.C., 16, 113, 115, 151–52, 155, **157–60**, 165, 191, 195
Bowlby, J., 35, 116, 186, 198
brain, 12, 15, 21–3, 103, 104, 124
   see also neuroscience
bureaucracy, 157, 163
   see also managerialism
burnout, 4, 103, 150, 153

Canton, R., 38, 61–3, 66, 69, 70, 72, 77, 131–32, 162
catharsis, 22, 26
care, 14, 33, 62, 71, 72, 81, 82, 126, 149, 152–53, 155, 159, 165, 180, 187, 195
caring credo, 14, 51, 61, 66, **71–4**, 81, 83, 147, 150, 165
casework, 75, 174
challenging, offending behavior, 54–5, 76, 77, 79, 130, 133, 134, 138, 139–40, **144–48** , 192, 193
change, offending behavior, 1–3, 7–8, 12, 13, 15–17, 31–4, 42, 44, 53, 60, 62–3, 67, 71, 72–3, 76, 80, 93, 110,

Printed and bound in the United States of America